PAUL SELIGSON
LEANNE GRAY
LUIZ OTÁVIO BARROS
TOM ABRAHAM
CRIS GONTOW

Level
3

CB052389

English ID

Student's Book
& Workbook
Combo Edition
3A

Richmond

ID SB Language map

ID WB Language map

	Question syllabus	Vocabulary	Grammar	Speaking & Skills
1 1.1	Do you know all your classmates?		Questions with prepositions	Answer questions about yourself
1.2	How do couples meet?	Relationships Phrasal verbs		Compare well-known love stories
1.3	How many Facebook friends do you have?	Types of friend	Prepositions	Answer a quiz about someone you're attracted to
1.4	Do you have many social media profiles?	Personality adjectives	Emphatic forms	Give opinions about social media
1.5	How much time do you spend online?	Active listening phrases		Listen & order the story of Antony & Cleopatra
2 2.1	How green are you?	Going green		Answer questions about green habits
2.2	How long have you been studying here?	Time / frequency / degree phrases	Present perfect continuous	
2.3	How has the climate been changing?	The environment	Present perfect vs. Present perfect continuous	Ask & answer about personal habits
2.4	What's the best ad you've seen recently?		Simple past vs. Present perfect / continuous	Talk about your work experience
2.5	Do you support any charities?	Endangered species Expressions of percentage		Talk about endangered species
3 3.1	Which city would you most like to visit?	Cities	*a / the*	Describe your hometown
3.2	Was your last vacation as much fun as you'd hoped?	Social conventions	Past perfect	Write a review
3.3	Do you ever want to get away from it all?	Urban problems		Talk about the problems in your city
3.4	Have you ever missed any important dates?		Past perfect continuous vs. Past perfect	
3.5	Do you always follow the rules?	Sign phrases		Listen & make rules
4 4.1	Does your school system work well?	School subjects *do / get / make / take* collocations		Talk about school subjects
4.2	What's the ideal age to go to college?	School problems	*too / enough*	Talk about jokes in English
4.3	What do you regret not having done?		*Should have* + participle	Talk about regrets
4.4	What would you do if you won a million dollars?		First & second conditional	Use conditional sentences
4.5	What makes someone a genius?		*a / an / the* Third conditional	Sympathize & criticize
5 5.1	Are you a shopaholic?	Shopping & technology		Share shopping experiences
5.2	What shouldn't you have spent money on?	Loans		Talk about shopping habits
5.3	Have you ever borrowed money from a relative?		Modals of possibility / probability	Express surprise
5.4	Have you ever bought a useless product?	Word formation	Order of adjectives	
5.5	Do you often buy things on impulse?	Shopping		

Audioscript p. 54   Answer key p. 64   Phrase Bank p. 70   Word List p. 76

English ID

Welcome to English ID!

Finally, an English course you can understand!

Famous **song lines** illustrate language from lessons.

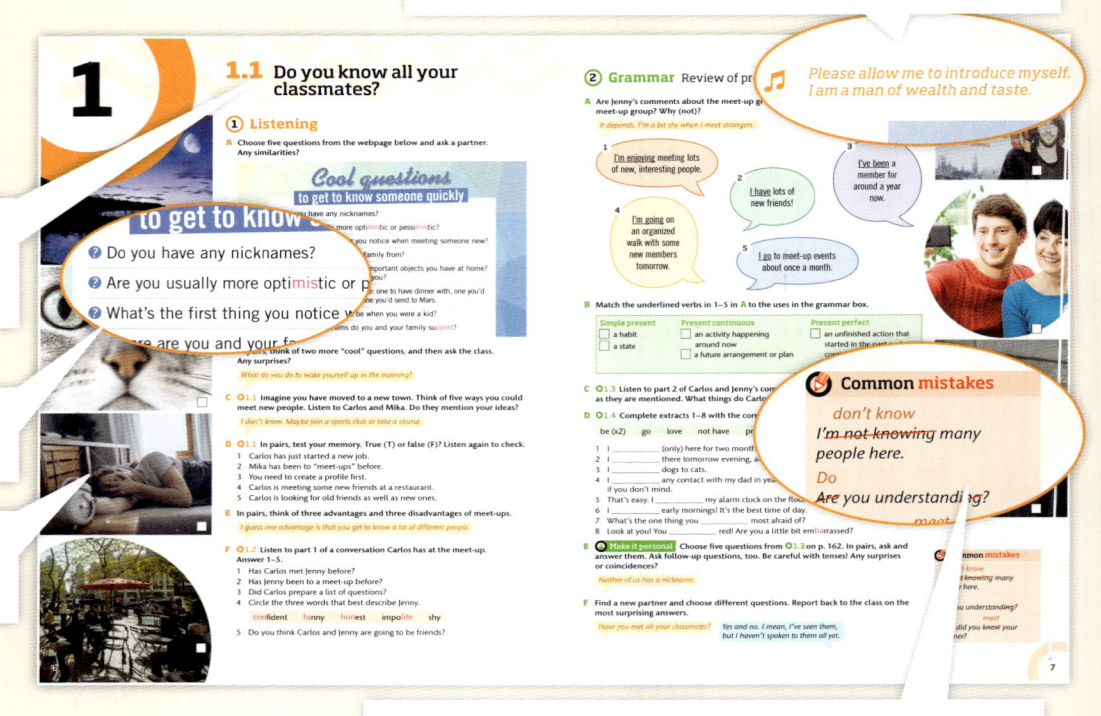

Lesson titles are questions to help you engage with the content.

Word stress in pink on new words.

Contextualized Picture Dictionary to present and review vocabulary.

Focus on **Common mistakes** accelerates accuracy.

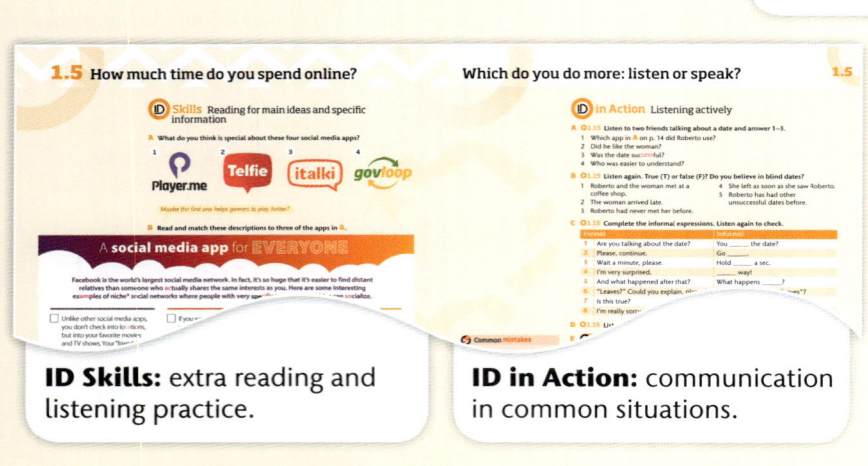

ID Skills: extra reading and listening practice.

ID in Action: communication in common situations.

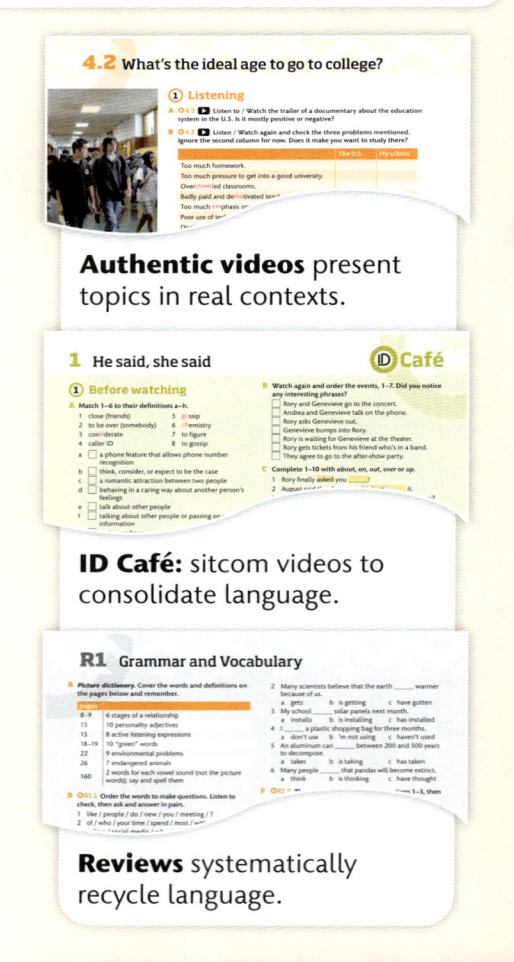

Authentic videos present topics in real contexts.

ID Café: sitcom videos to consolidate language.

Reviews systematically recycle language.

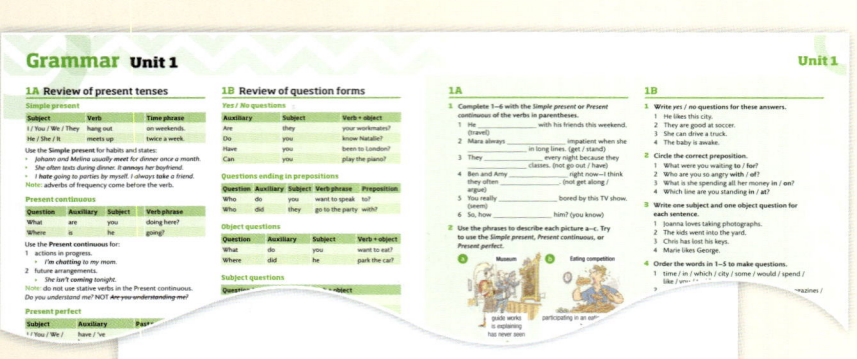

A complete **Grammar** reference with exercises.

Stimulating **Grammar** practice.

Speech bubbles: models for speaking.

Make it personal: personalized speaking tasks to help you express your identity in English.

Audioscript activities to consolidate pronunciation.

Pictures to present and practice **Pronunciation**.

Richmond *Learning* Platform

• Teachers and students can find all their resources in one place.

• **Richmond Test Manager** with interactive and printable tests.

• Activity types including pronunciation, common mistakes, and speaking.

Workbook to practice and consolidate lessons.

Phrase Bank to practice common expressions.

Learn to express your identity in English!

1

1.1 Do you know all your classmates?

① Listening

A Choose five questions from the webpage below and ask a partner. Any similarities?

Cool questions
to get to know someone quickly

- ❓ Do you have any nicknames?
- ❓ Are you usually more optimistic or pessimistic?
- ❓ What's the first thing you notice when meeting someone new?
- ❓ Where are you and your family from?
- ❓ What are the three most important objects you have at home? Why are they important to you?
- ❓ Choose three famous people: one to have dinner with, one you'd go on vacation with, and one you'd send to Mars.
- ❓ What did you want to be when you were a kid?
- ❓ Which sports teams do you and your family support?

B In pairs, think of two more "cool" questions, and then ask the class. Any surprises?

What do you do to wake yourself up in the morning?

C ▶1.1 Imagine you have moved to a new town. Think of five ways you could meet new people. Listen to Carlos and Mika. Do they mention your ideas?

I don't know. Maybe join a sports club or take a course.

D ▶1.1 In pairs, test your memory. True (T) or false (F)? Listen again to check.
1 Carlos has just started a new job.
2 Mika has been to "meet-ups" before.
3 You need to create a profile first.
4 Carlos is meeting some new friends at a restaurant.
5 Carlos is looking for old friends as well as new ones.

E In pairs, think of three advantages and three disadvantages of meet-ups.

I guess one advantage is that you get to know a lot of different people.

F ▶1.2 Listen to part 1 of a conversation Carlos has at the meet-up. Answer 1–5.
1 Has Carlos met Jenny before?
2 Has Jenny been to a meet-up before?
3 Did Carlos prepare a list of questions?
4 Circle the three words that best describe Jenny.

   confident   funny   honest   impolite   shy

5 Do you think Carlos and Jenny are going to be friends?

② **Grammar** Review of present tenses

A Are Jenny's comments about the meet-up group all positive? Would you enjoy a meet-up group? Why (not)?

It depends. I'm a bit shy when I meet strangers.

1
I'm enjoying meeting lots of new, interesting people.

3
I've been a member for around a year now.

2
I have lots of new friends!

4
I'm going on an organized walk with some new members tomorrow.

5
I go to meet-up events about once a month.

B Match the underlined verbs in 1–5 in **A** to the uses in the grammar box.

Simple present	Present continuous	Present perfect
☐ a habit	☐ an activity happening around now	☐ an unfinished action that started in the past and continues to the present
☐ a state	☐ a future arrangement or plan	

➜ **Grammar 1A** p.138

C ▶1.3 Listen to part 2 of Carlos and Jenny's conversation and number the photos 1–7 as they are mentioned. What things do Carlos and Jenny (not) have in common?

D ▶1.4 Complete extracts 1–8 with the correct form of these verbs. Listen to check.

be (x2)   go   love   not have   prefer   throw   turn   not want

1 I _____ (only) here for two months, so it's difficult to say.
2 I _____ there tomorrow evening, actually.
3 I _____ dogs to cats.
4 I _____ any contact with my dad in years. I _____ to talk about that if you don't mind.
5 That's easy. I _____ my alarm clock on the floor. I hate the noise it makes.
6 I _____ early mornings! It's the best time of day.
7 What's the one thing you _____ most afraid of?
8 Look at you! You _____ red! Are you a little bit embarrassed?

E 🔵 **Make it personal** Choose five questions from ▶1.3 on p. 162. In pairs, ask and answer them. Ask follow-up questions, too. Be careful with tenses! Any surprises or coincidences?

Neither of us has a nickname.

F Find a new partner and choose different questions. Report back to the class on the most surprising answers.

Have you met all your classmates?   *Yes and no. I mean, I've seen them, but I haven't spoken to them all yet.*

🚫 **Common mistakes**

don't know
I'm not knowing many people here.

Do
Are you understanding?

meet
How did you know your partner?

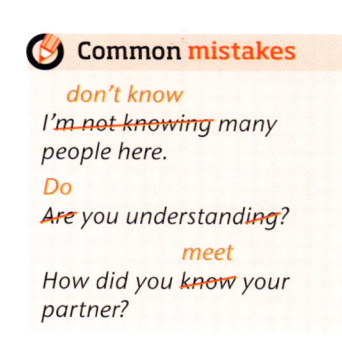

1.2 How do couples meet?

1 Vocabulary Relationships

A ▶1.5 **Match the phrases to pictures 1–6. Listen to the story to check.**

- ☐ be attracted to (someone)
- ☐ fall out (with someone)
- ☐ get along (well)
- ☐ get (back) together
- ☐ get to know someone
- ☐ break up

> ⊘ **Common mistakes**
> I instantly ~~felt~~ **fell** in love ~~to~~ **with** him!
> Jack isn't married ~~with~~ **to** Tina.

B **In pairs, retell the story in A. Do you know anyone who broke up and then got back together?**

> My sister broke up with her boyfriend last year, but they got back together after a week.

> Oh yeah? Are they still together?

C ▶1.6 **Read the celebrity gossip article. Can you identify couples 1–3? Match the photos to the texts. Do you enjoy celebrity gossip?**

FAMOUS 💔 EXES!

1 This couple **broke up** in 2017 after seven years of marriage. They originally **fell for** each other when they were working on the same movie.
☐
☐ Their divorce came as a shock to fans who believed they had the perfect marriage. However, she recently admitted that the image they showed on social media wasn't real.

2 They have known each other since they were very young. They met when they worked on the Mickey Mouse Club together and used to **hang out**.
☐
☐ They dated for a long time before they broke up. Some people say they **fell out** over her relationship with her choreographer.

3 This couple met when they both starred in the movie *Mr. & Mrs. Smith*. Their relationship became public after he broke up with his first wife.
☐ He **moved in** with her and her children soon after. They have six children.
☐ They say they began to **drift apart** and eventually got divorced in 2016.

D 🔒 Make it personal **Do you know of any other famous break-ups? Or anyone who has fallen out with a boss, a friend, a family member, etc.?**

> Taylor Swift and Calvin Harris broke up in 2016.

E Reread the article and match the highlighted phrasal verbs from **C** to definitions 1–6.

1 _fall out_ (with so / over sth) have an argument / fight
2 _____ (with so) spend time together
3 _____ (together / with so) start living in the same place

4 _____ (from so) become emotionally distant
5 _____ (so) fall in love with someone
6 _____ (with so) end a relationship

F Complete the sentences with phrasal verbs from **E**.

1 My best friend and I started to _____ when we went to different colleges.
2 Do you want to _____ this weekend? We could go to the movies.
3 After two years of dating, my parents decided to _____ together. That was 20 years ago!
4 My brother and I _____ with each other over a stupid argument about money.
5 I _____ with my boyfriend because he hated my dog. Love me, love my dog!

> **⚠ Common mistakes**
>
> *split up*
> My son ~~terminated~~ with his first girlfriend.
>
> *drifted apart*
> They ~~distanced themselves~~ after ~~a discussion~~.
> *an argument*

G 🔘 **Make it personal** Complete 1–5 however you like. Compare with a partner. How many similar ideas?

1 If you fall out with someone you love, you should …
2 I like to hang out with people who …
3 I'd never fall for someone who …

4 In my opinion, couples drift apart if they …
5 Before you move in with someone, I think it's really important to …

I'd never fall for someone who likes pop music – I can't stand it!

② Listening

A ▶1.7 ▶ Listen to / Watch three couples who have been together for over 40 years. Check the items they consider most important.

What's most important for a lasting relationship?		
☐ facing life's ups and downs	☐ communication	☐ shared interests
☐ being flexible	☐ physical attraction	☐ solving problems quickly

B Do you agree with their choices? Why (not)? What other advice can you think of?

C 🔘 **Make it personal** Think about a couple you know. How did they meet? How long were they / have they been together? In groups, share stories.

Justin Bieber met Selena Gomez in 2009 after his manager called her mom to arrange a meeting. They dated on and off for years, but they finally broke up in 2018.

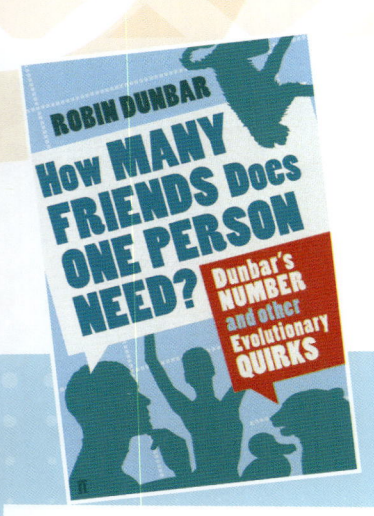

① Reading

A In pairs, how would you answer the question on the book cover? Define the differences between very close friends, good friends, friends and acquaintances.

B ▶1.8 Read and match the four paragraphs to the types of friendship in **A**. Can you guess the missing numbers (a–d)? Listen to check.

> I'd say everyone needs at least one really close friend to confide in. A good friend is someone who ...

1 _____

These are people you know slightly, but they aren't really friends. It might be someone you know through work or sometimes talk to on the train. You can memorize their names, faces, and traits, and remember them when necessary. Basically, if circumstances force you to talk to each other, you are this type of friendship; if you really want to talk to each other, you are friends. According to Dr. Dunbar, ᵃ_____ is the maximum number of such connections your brain can manage.

2 _____

You might have hundreds of them on Facebook or other social media, but are they real friends? These are the people you're usually in contact with, though not necessarily on a weekly or monthly basis. You might socialize now and then and enjoy each other's company, but if times get tough, they won't hang around to help you. Maximum number: ᵇ_____

3 _____

These are people you may hang out with and probably get along with. You have fun together and can tease each other. You know you can call on them if you need some help. However, if you have a serious problem, they're not necessarily people that you can count on. Maximum number: ᶜ_____

4 _____

These are the people you can rely on. You would trust them with your secrets, and your problems, and to take care of your children. They'll be there beside you in good times and in bad. These are the people you can borrow money from when you need it. Marlene Dietrich used to call them the friends you can call at four o'clock in the morning. They're like family in a way. Maximum number: ᵈ_____

C You are going to listen to a talk about Dunbar's theory of friendship. In pairs, guess what the significance of these seven items will be.

primates	brain	small villages	social media
Christmas cards		Facebook friends	Oxford University

> Dunbar probably went to Oxford University.

D ▶1.9 Listen to the talk and number the items 1–7 in the order you hear them. Were your ideas in **C** correct?

E 👤 Make it personal In pairs, use the infographic in **B** to explain Dunbar's theory. How well does it describe your relationships?

> I'm not convinced. I have a lot of very close friends.

Have I made it obvious? Haven't I made it clear? Want me to spell it out for you? F-R-I-E-N-D-S.

1.3

② Grammar Review of question forms

A. ▶1.10 Alison and her friend Jamie are looking at these photos on her phone. Listen and categorize the people according to Dunbar's theory.

B Match questions 1–7 to the four types of question in the grammar box. Then complete the rules with these words. There is one extra.

auxiliary (x2)   object   subject   verb (x2)   beginning   end

1 Are they your colleagues?
2 When did you take that one?
3 Who's that?
4 Does she play professionally?
5 Can she play any other instruments?
6 Who took this one?
7 Who are you closest to?

---

yes / no questions ☐ ☐ ☐
When there is an auxiliary or a modal verb, the word order is:

_____ + subject + _____ + ?

When there is no auxiliary, use *do* to form the question.
When the main verb is *be*, invert the subject and the verb.

Questions ending in prepositions ☐
The preposition comes at the _____ of the sentence.

Wh-questions
Object questions ☐
Ask for information about the object, so the word order is:

question word + _____ + _____ + verb + ?

Subject questions ☐ ☐
Ask for information about the subject, so the word order is:

question word + _____ + _____ + ?

➡ **Grammar 1B** p. 138

C Correct typical student question errors in 1–8. Which ones have you made?

I used to make that mistake a lot.

1 With who do you live?
2 To which country you would really like to go?
3 Did you went out the last Saturday?
4 Who does help you with your homework?
5 With which three people do you spend the most time?
6 How many languages you can speak well?
7 How arrived you to class today?
8 Have you a best friend?

⏱ **Common mistakes**

does
Where your best friend ~~lives~~?

said
Who ~~did say~~ that?

D In pairs, take turns asking the questions in **C**. Any coincidences?

E 🔵 **Make it personal** Write the names of a very close friend, a good friend, a friend, and an acquaintance.

1 For each person, think about these questions.

How long have you known her / him?	What's he / she up to these days as far as you know?
How well do you get along with him / her?	How often are you in touch?
How much do you have in common?	Are you doing anything together any time soon?

2 In pairs, take turns describing each person and your relationship. Work out where on the infographic each one belongs. Ask follow-up questions, too. Any surprising answers?

We've known each other since elementary school. We used to be really close.

What's she like?

1.4 Do you have many social media profiles?

Selfies

Nature photos

Couple photos

① Reading

A Read the introduction to the article and the paragraph headings on the photos. What do you think each photo type says about the person?

I think selfies show that someone cares a lot about what they look like.

B ▶1.11 Read the article and match the paragraph headings in **A** to 1–6. Listen to check.

Your INSTA PERSONALITY

Whether your social media posts are carefully planned or completely spontaneous, what you post reveals a lot more than you imagine. Psychological studies have found connections between personality, emotions, and the photos we post, showing Instagram can be a "window to your soul".

1 _____

Do you post a lot of these? If they are extreme images, e.g. taken while you are skydiving, it shows you have an adventure-seeking personality. If you enjoy posting funny ones, your followers can see that you are fun-loving and easygoing. But be aware that the need for "likes" reveals a desire for recognition and is often a sign that you are self-centered.

2 _____

If you often post images of yourself and your partner, it demonstrates a strong and stable relationship. We see two like-minded individuals who want to be together. Be careful about uploading too many of these. Ask yourself why you feel the need to prove yourself and your relationship to other people.

3 _____

If your profile has plenty of images of you with lots of people at parties, etc., sure, it sends the message that you're outgoing and sociable. However, it can also point to loneliness. Are you trying too hard to show everyone that you have plenty of friends?

4 _____

If you post photos of landscapes, it shows a thoughtful person who has the time to admire the beauty of his or her environment. On the other hand, it may also point to someone who is tired of the pace of life and needs some time off.

5 _____

Posting vacation images is a way of storing memories and emotions you felt while on your trip. A love of exploring the planet shows that you are open-minded and enjoy experiencing new places. Be aware that posting photos from a vacation is like posting an ad that you're not at home. Perhaps wait and post them when you're back home.

6 _____

If you post a lot of photos of your office, it shows your professional life is a priority for you. It can also mean that you want to portray yourself as a knowledgeable person with a high-status position. Or maybe you're just looking for promotion!

Work photos

Group photos

Travel photos

C True (T) or false (F)? Reread to check. Are you into Instagram?
1 Selfies show an adventurous, but sometimes fragile, personality.
2 Constantly posting couple photos is a sign of an insecure relationship.
3 Group photos can send both positive and negative messages.
4 Photos in a natural environment show someone who doesn't have much free time.
5 Posting travel photos can pose a security risk.
6 Workplace photos might mean you want to show people how important you are.

D 🔵 **Make it personal** The article gives some advice about social media security. What other advice can you think of?

Your friends may not always want you to tag them or show their locations.

② Vocabulary Personality adjectives

A Match the highlighted adjectives to definitions 1–10. Notice the hyphens.

1 _____ prepared to listen to new ideas
2 _____ considering things very carefully and thinking about others
3 _____ intelligent; knows a lot about something
4 _____ with similar ideas and interests
5 _____ enjoys having a good time
6 _____ likes doing dangerous or unusual activities
7 _____ friendly; extroverted
8 _____ relaxed
9 _____ thinking only about yourself and not other people
10 _____ enjoying being with other people

B 🗣 Make it personal In pairs, discuss the questions. Any discoveries?

1 Which of the adjectives in **A** best describe you?
2 Which kinds of images do you post?
3 Are the descriptions in the article true for you and your posts?
4 What about the images posted by your friends / people you follow? Are the opinions in the text true about them?

I post a lot of group photos, but I definitely don't feel lonely!

My brother is always posting selfies, and he's incredibly self-centered.

③ Grammar Emphatic forms

A ▶1.12 Anna wants to find new Instagram accounts to follow. Listen to her talking to her friend Betty. What different types of accounts does she mention?

B ▶1.13 Listen and repeat sentences a–e in the grammar box. Notice the stress and cross out the wrong option in the rule.

Emphatic forms with adverbs	With auxiliary *do*
a Wow! They sure look like they're having an amazing time.	d I do love this one.
b They certainly are worth following, I think.	e It does make perfect sense.
c That one's definitely for me.	

With emphatic forms, auxiliaries and adverbs are usually **stressed** / **unstressed**.

→ Grammar 1C p. 138

✋ Common mistakes

It does sounds interesting.
                  say
They did s̶a̶i̶d̶ they were going to Japan next.

C Complete Betty's comments with the words in parentheses and an appropriate verb.

1 **ANNA** Look at this one. What a view! Imagine being on that beach!
BETTY Yes, it _____ like an amazing place. (does)

2 **ANNA** "Life's a journey, not a race."
BETTY Yes, that _____ a good one to remember! (definitely)

3 **ANNA** I love this one of the man and the tiger together.
BETTY They _____ to have a strong bond. (sure)

4 **ANNA** Oh, goodness. What a cute little ball of fluff! I want one.
BETTY You _____ to get a kitten, don't you?! (do)

5 **ANNA** Look at them! Skydiving together.
BETTY Hmm … They _____ braver than me. (certainly)

D 🗣 Make it personal Which of these views on social media do you agree with? Compare with a partner. Any interesting conclusions?

"Social media apps make us less sociable."
"Instagram is the best social media app there is."
"How many friends or followers I have matters to me."
"You should be over 16 to have a social media account."
"Running a social media account is a special skill."
"You can have too many social media accounts."

I do believe that …   *I do agree that …*

People seem to …

I definitely think that …

1.5 How much time do you spend online?

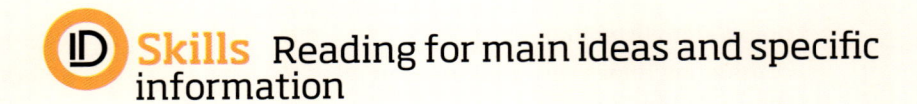

Skills Reading for main ideas and specific information

A What do you think is special about these four social media apps?

1  2  3  4

Maybe the first one helps gamers to play better?

B Read and match these descriptions to three of the apps in **A**.

A social media app for EVERYONE

Facebook is the world's largest social media network. In fact, it's so huge that it's easier to find distant relatives than someone who actually shares the same interests as you. Here are some interesting examples of niche* social networks where people with very specific tastes and hobbies can socialize.

☐ Unlike other social media apps, you don't check into locations, but into your favorite movies and TV shows. Your "friends" on this network see what you're watching right now, and it allows you to comment on and react to TV moments with other fans. You can also unlock digital stickers related to your favorite shows and bands.

☐ If you want something practical with your social networking app, then this app is perfect for you. It links people who are learning a particular language with others who are fluent. There are approximately 100 different languages available, including endangered ones. This is a brilliant way to learn a new language in a realistic setting and also learn about other cultures at the same time.

☐ This is a social media site for those who have a deep interest in gaming. With this app, you can connect and chat with other like-minded players and gaming friends. Create a gaming profile, then share your status updates, and photos, and stream live videos. There is also a group feature, so you can join and meet gamers who are into the same games as you. So, all you nerds out there, this is the place for you to network!

* niche exactly suitable for a small group of the same type

C ▶1.14 Cover the texts and listen to check. Which is harder, listening or reading? Why? Uncover, listen, and read. Any surprising pronunciation or spelling?

D Reread and match the apps to the descriptions.
1 It lets you chat about your favorite soap opera.
2 It helps you find members of your family.
3 It offers you the chance to hear a dying language.
4 It tells your friends what you're doing, but not where you are.
5 It combines social networking and learning a skill.
6 It introduces you to people who have a lot of computer knowledge.

Common mistake

It lets you / It allows you to
~~It's let you~~ tell your friends …

E ⏺ Make it personal In pairs, discuss 1—4. Which apps are most used by the class?
1 Which of the apps most appeals to you and why? And the least appealing?
2 Which app(s) would you recommend to the class?
3 Can you think of any other "niche" social media apps?
4 What kind of app do you think govloop might be?

I'm interested in indigenous languages, so I'd go for italki.

The apps I use most are ..

Which do you do more: listen or speak?

ⓘⒹ in Action Listening actively

A ▶1.15 **Listen to two friends talking about a date and answer 1–3.**
1 Which app in **A** on p. 14 did Roberto use?
2 Did he like the woman?
3 Was the date suc**cess**ful?
4 Who was easier to understand?

B ▶1.15 **Listen again. True (T) or false (F)? Do you believe in blind dates?**

1 Roberto and the woman met at a coffee shop.
2 The woman arrived late.
3 Roberto had never met her before.
4 She left as soon as she saw Roberto.
5 Roberto has had other unsuccessful dates before.

C ▶1.15 **Complete the informal expressions. Listen again to check.**

	Formal	Informal
1	Are you talking about the date?	You _____ the date?
2	Please, continue.	Go _____.
3	Wait a minute, please.	Hold _____ a sec.
4	I'm very surprised.	_____ way!
5	And what happened after that?	What happens _____?
6	"Leaves?" Could you explain, please?	What do you _____ "leaves"?
7	Is this true?	Are you _____?
8	I'm really sorry to hear that.	Oh, _____!

D ▶1.16 **Listen and practice the informal expressions in C, copying the intonation.**

E 👤 **Make it personal** **Tell an anecdote.**
1 In pairs, imagine what happened before, during, and after in cartoons 1–3.
2 In anecdotes, people often use the present tense so people and objects seem closer to the listener. In pairs, try telling the anecdotes from the pictures.

> *So, I finish work and I'm walking to my car. I'm tired and really looking forward to getting home. I open …*
> *Uh-huh. Yeah. And then …?*

3 **A:** Think of an anecdote of your own – a funny / embarrassing / scary situation like those in cartoons 1–3 – and tell your partner. Use informal language from **C**.
   B: Listen actively. Then change roles.

🗲 Common mistakes

see
I get into the car, and I ~~saw~~ this huge mouse!

crashed
I was running for the bus and ~~crash~~ into a street light.

♫ *What do you mean? When you nod your head yes,*
But you wanna say no. What do you mean?

Writing 1 A personal profile

Where have you been
All my life, all my life?
Where have you been all my life?

A Read the profile. Which kind of social media network is it for?

☐ professional ☐ dating ☐ social

GetConnected

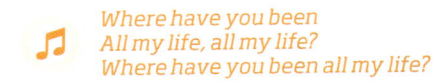

Pete Brill

1 _____
Hi, I'm Pete! I'm an adventure-seeking, outgoing, 22-year-old digital media studies graduate. Currently working in TV production and love it! Originally from Copenhagen and now living in London. I love the outdoors and socializing. Looking to meet like-minded, outgoing people for social and work-related connections. [a] PM me!

2 _____
OneStop Productions, London – Production Assistant
White Swan Clothing Co, London – Sales Assistant
Metropolitan University, London – 2015–2018
Copenhagen International School – 2007–2014

3 _____
Anything outdoors! I love skiing, surfing, running, and climbing. Anything adventurous! [b]
Taken part in four international triathlon events.
Eating out—Thai food is my absolute favorite. Know any good restaurants?

4 _____
Took a gap year and traveled through South America.
Highlights were teaching in a kindergarten in Bolivia, seeing Machu Picchu and being in Rio de Janeiro for Mardi Gras.
[c] Planning a tour in Norway next summer.

5 _____
Become a skydiving instructor!

6 _____
I mostly read non-fiction. [d]
Favorite book – *Sapiens* by Yuval Noah Harari.
[e]

7 _____
Anything by Spielberg—I love his imagination!
[f]

8 _____
Danish, German, English
[g]

9 _____
Friendship, running buddies, dinners out, movie trips, deep conversations, party partners, networking, [h]

B Complete 1–9 in the profile with these headings.

All about me   Ambitions   Books and music
Favorite movies   Interests   Languages
Looking for   Travel   Work and education

C Match the information about Pete to blanks a–h.

☐ Unfortunately, I broke my wrist on an Amazon canoeing trip.
☐ I enjoy live gigs and open mic nights.
☐ travel companions, travel tips, colleagues.
☐ I love science-fiction, too.
☐ Got any biography recommendations???
☐ I'd love to hear from you.
☐ Tried Mandarin!
☐ Just got my motorbike license!

D Read *Write it right!* and find examples of the features in Pete's profile.

✔ Write it right!

Social media profiles are usually divided into different sections with headings for you to fill in, e.g. *Favorite movies, All about me*.
To make them quick and easy to read, we often:
1 omit non-essential words such as pronouns and auxiliary verbs, e.g. *I'm looking forward to meeting you.*
2 use abbreviations, e.g. *PM (private message), Find me on FB (Facebook).*
3 use repeated punctuation marks, e.g. *Any good restaurant recommendations???*
4 ask questions to encourage reader interest, e.g. *Know any good local bands?*

E Rewrite 1–4 in social media profile style.
1 I am now living in California and looking for a job.
2 I can't stand romantic comedy movies.
3 At the moment, I'm working in public relations and I'm really enjoying it.
4 My dream is to visit New York City.

F *Your turn!* Write your own social media profile.

Before	Decide which headings you want to include. You don't have to complete all of them.
While	Make each entry short, friendly, and easy to read. Follow the tips in *Write it right!*
After	Show your profile to a classmate. Can they improve it in any way? Write a 'PM' back to each other in response, then email your profile to your teacher.

1 He said, she said

 Café

1 Before watching

A Match 1–6 to their definitions a–h.

1	close (friends)	5	gossip
2	to be over (somebody)	6	chemistry
3	considerate	7	to figure
4	caller ID	8	to gossip

a ☐ a phone feature that allows phone number recognition

b ☐ think, consider, or expect to be the case

c ☐ a romantic attraction between two people

d ☐ behaving in a caring way about another person's feelings

e ☐ talk about other people

f ☐ talking about other people or passing on untrue information

g ☐ no longer have romantic feelings for that person

h ☐ on affectionate terms

B In pairs, describe Rory and Genevieve. Who do you think calls who? Why? What are they saying?

Rory is about 25 and he's wearing ...

Maybe Genevieve calls Rory to gossip about a friend ...

2 While watching

A Watch to see if you were right, and check all you hear.

1 Genevieve's a musician. ☐

2 Genevieve hates the band Curious Fools. ☐

3 They're meeting at the Lexington Theater. ☐

4 August told Andrea that Rory likes Genevieve. ☐

5 Genevieve told Andrea that Rory was crazy about her. ☐

6 Genevieve said she found Rory attractive. ☐

7 Genevieve thought Rory would be over her by now. ☐

8 Genevieve and Rory don't have anything in common. ☐

9 Genevieve breaks up with boyfriends after one month. ☐

10 Andrea thinks Genevieve and Rory might have chemistry. ☐

B Watch again and order the events, 1–7. Did you notice any interesting phrases?

☐ Rory and Genevieve go to the concert.

☐ Andrea and Genevieve talk on the phone.

☐ Rory asks Genevieve out.

☐ Genevieve bumps into Rory.

☐ Rory is waiting for Genevieve at the theater.

☐ Rory gets tickets from his friend who's in a band.

☐ They agree to go to the after-show party.

C Complete 1–10 with *about, on, out, over* or *up*.

1 Rory finally asked you _____!

2 August said that Rory was thinking _____ it.

3 Why would your brother know _____ me and Rory?

4 They hang _____ all the time.

5 Rory told Auggie you'd probably never go _____ with him.

6 Rory likes you. He's crazy _____ you.

7 Really? I figured he'd be _____ me by now.

8 Do you and Auggie gossip _____ us?

9 When you date a musician, you end _____ breaking _____ with him.

10 All right. Let me sleep _____ it.

D Match seven phrasal verbs from **C** to their definitions.

☐ to wait a little before making a decision

☐ to spend time together

☐ to stop loving a person

☐ to date

☐ to end a romantic relationship

☐ to invite on a date

☐ to finally do or be something

3 After watching

A Complete 1–6 with the correct form of *have / have to*.

1 I was wondering if you _____ any plans.

2 I don't _____ anything in common with him.

3 You might _____ chemistry!

4 Rory _____ become close friends with August.

5 You _____ tell me how you met him.

6 And if you're interested, they _____ a party after their show.

B ○ Make it personal Do you think their date will be a success? Will they get along well? In groups of three, role-play their party conversation with Rory's friend, Max, from the band Curious Fools.

Hi Max. That was awesome! Thanks so much for the tickets!

2

2.1 How green are you?

① Vocabulary Going green

A How are photos 1–10 each connected with being "green"?

> Well, 1 is plastic bottles. I think it takes a lot of energy to produce them.

> Yes, and the oceans are full of plastic waste ...

B Match the **highlighted** words in the quiz to photos 1–10.

We all know what we should be doing.

The "going green" Quiz

But how green have you really gone?

1 Leaving appliances on stand-by mode isn't environment-friendly because it wastes energy. Do you always unplug your computer or cell charger when not in use? Y S N

2 Disposable plastic bags can take up to 1,000 years to decompose. Do you reuse plastic bags or take a reusable cloth bag when you go shopping? Y S N

3 Leaving the faucet running when you brush your teeth twice a day can waste almost 8 gallons of water. Do you turn the faucet off while brushing your teeth? Y S N

4 Energy-efficient light bulbs last from 6,000 to 15,000 hours. Do you use energy-efficient light bulbs in your house or office? Y S N

5 Solar heating is a renewable energy source, and it can help you save as much as one-third off your monthly power bill. Does your house or apartment building have a solar heating system? Y S N

6 It takes more than 30 million barrels of oil a year to make the plastic for the world's bottled water. Do you use refillable bottles for water at home? Y S N

7 A Styrofoam cup takes 500 years to decompose. Do you use Styrofoam cups at work or home? Y S N

8 A typical American family produces 30% more household waste than a typical Mexican family. Do you separate organic and non-organic household waste? Y S N

9 More than 1.5 million Americans over the age of 17 are now vegan. "Flexitarianism"* is now on the increase, with a 60% global rise in new vegetarian branded products between 2011 and 2015. Do you ever eat vegetarian meals? Y S N

10 A carbon footprint calculates all the greenhouse gases we produce in our activities as individuals and measures them in units of carbon dioxide. The world average is about 4½ tons of carbon dioxide per person. Do you ever feel concerned about your carbon footprint? Y S N

flexitarianism n following a vegetarian diet with the occasional inclusion of meat

Y = Yes **S** = Sometimes **N** = No

C ▶ 2.1 Listen, read, and answer the quiz. In pairs, compare answers. Who's greener?

> We're both similar, but ...

🖐 Common mistakes

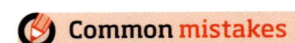

left
I ~~let~~ the lights on.

wastes
This fridge ~~spends~~ a lot of energy.

♫ Heal the world. Make it a better place for you and for me and the entire human race.

2.1

② Pronunciation /ɑ/ and /oʊ/

▶2.2 **Put these words in the correct column according to the <u>underlined</u> sounds. Listen to check.**

b<u>o</u>ttle   cl<u>o</u>th   cl<u>o</u>thes   disp<u>o</u>sable   ec<u>o</u>
pr<u>o</u>duct   pr<u>o</u>gram   s<u>o</u>lar   Styrof<u>oa</u>m

ɑ	oʊ
bottle	*clothes*

③ Vocabulary Adjectives from verbs and nouns

A We often form "green" adjectives by adding *-able*, *-efficient*, and *-friendly* to verbs and nouns. **Match the endings to their meanings.**

1 reus**able** cloth bag
2 energy-**efficient** light bulb
3 environment-**friendly** appliances

☐ that are safe for
☐ that use less
☐ that you can + verb

B ▶2.3 **Make seven "green" phrases using the suffixes in A. Listen to check. Then ask about a partner's home.**

1 water / fau**c**ets
2 environment / de**ter**gents
3 fuel / ve**h**icles
4 recharge / batteries
5 energy / ap**pli**ances
6 re**us**e / plastic containers
7 pet / in**sec**ticides

Do you have water-efficient faucets in your home?   *I have no idea!*

➡ **Grammar 2A** p. 140

C ⬤ **Make it personal** **What could you do to be greener?**

1 Look back at the quiz on p. 18. How could you be greener for each question? Make notes.
2 Compare your notes with a partner. Do you agree with each other?

I suppose I could try flexitarianism. I could be a vegetarian half the week.

That's a good idea. Vegetarianism is more animal-friendly and environment-friendly, too!

3 Then discuss how your school / class could be greener. Report back. Choose the top five ideas.

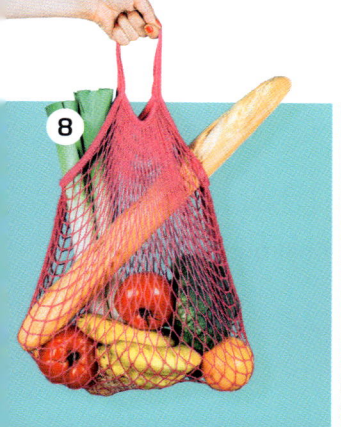

19

2.2 How long have you been studying here?

① Listening

A ▶2.4 ▶ In pairs, interpret the poster. Is it for a comedy or a documentary? What do you think "No Impact Man" is about? Listen to / Watch the video to check your guesses.

Do you think he's some kind of superhero?

B ▶2.4 ▶ Remember what Colin said about these items. Then listen / watch again to check.

> waste   travel and transportation
> food and drink   shopping   money
> health   relationships   happiness

I think he said he didn't buy tomatoes in January. Did you hear that?

C 🔘 Make it personal   In pairs, answer 1–3. Any big differences?
1 Why do you think he made these changes? What impact will they have on the environment?
2 What three things could you change to have less impact on the environment?
3 Would you consider going "no impact" for a year? A month? A week? Why (not)?

② Reading

A ▶2.5 Quickly read Al's blog. How green is his lifestyle these days? Circle 1, 2, or 3.

This morning I ran into an old friend on my way to work. He could hardly recognize me. "You look so … different," he said. "Have you been working out or something?" Well, yes, I've been working out like crazy every day, but I guess it's the "something" that has made the difference.

You see, I've been trying to copy the idea I saw in a documentary called *No Impact Man*. It's about a guy called Colin Beaven, who tries to have zero impact on the environment for a year. So instead of simply switching to energy-efficient light bulbs, buying eco-friendly cleaning products, avoiding disposable cups, and stuff like that, he takes the whole thing to the next level: no TV, no elevators, no public transportation, no household waste … The list goes on and on.

No Impact Man has had such an impact (!) on me that my family and I are trying to green up our lifestyles, too. For example, I've been walking to work at least twice a week, taking the stairs, using recycled paper, and so on. At home, we're beginning to recycle, trying to unplug all appliances, installing water-efficient faucets—you name it. And you know what? We've all been feeling great lately. But I think that's really as far as I can go. I'd never be able to give up TV, sell my precious car (which I've only been driving since Monday!), or buy used clothes.

So my question is: Can I make a difference, or am I wasting my time?

B Reread and find key points to justify your answer in **A**. Compare in pairs. Do you disagree at all? Is he wasting his time?

C What do the highlighted expressions mean?
1 ☐ eventually   2 ☐ more and more   3 ☐ etc.

D 🔘 Make it personal   In pairs, share your own answers to Al's final question. Any conclusions?

I do what I can, but it doesn't feel like it's changing anything.

Yeah, but we have to start somewhere. The real problem is education.

Lately I've been, I've been losing sleep, Dreaming about the things that we could be.

③ Grammar Present perfect continuous

A Sentences 1–3 are true. Find evidence in Al's blog in **2A**.

1 Al probably has a gym membership. 2 Al probably lives near his work. 3 Al has a new car.

B Follow the instructions in the grammar box.

> **1** Match examples a–c to the rules.
>
> a **Have you been working out** or something?
> b **I've been walking** to work at least twice a week.
> c **He's been driving** a brand new car since Monday.
>
> Sentences _____ and _____ emphasize the duration of an action or state.
> Sentence _____ has a general meaning of *lately*.
>
> **2** Cross out the group of words that CANNOT complete this sentence.
>
> I've been working out _____.
>
> a How often?   *regularly, every day, on and off, twice a week*
> b How much?   *a little, a lot, like crazy, more and more*
> c Since when?   *since April, for (five) years, lately, recently*
> d When?   *three weeks ago, in 2015, yesterday, last year*
>
> **3** Use *since* + a point in time (moment) and *for* + a period of time (duration). Complete with *for* or *since*.
>
> _____ 90 minutes   _____ yesterday   _____ four years   _____ 6:30 p.m.
> _____ my whole life   _____ the rest of the day _____ 2012   _____ June 4th
>
> **→ Grammar 2B** p. 140

⚠ Common mistakes

have been
I ~~am~~ walking to work once a week.

have been studying
I ~~study~~ English all weekend.

C Suzana has also watched *No Impact Man*. Use her notes to make sentences in the present perfect continuous. Which ones have you been doing recently?

		PAST	NEW HABITS	SINCE WHEN?
1	TV	watch a lot	watch far less	she saw the documentary
2	appliances	buy conventional	buy energy-efficient	lately
3	disposable products	use lots	try to avoid	past few months
4	car	use every day	walk to work	April
5	household waste	throw away	kids recycle	last two weeks
6	eco-friendly products	buy a few	husband buy lots	some time now

1 She used to watch a lot of TV, but she's been watching far less TV since she saw the documentary.

④ Pronunciation

A ▶2.6 Listen and copy the reduced form of *have / has*, the weak form of *been*, the stress, and the intonation.

/əv/ /bɪn/   /əz/ /bɪn/
1 How long have you been living in this city?   2 How long has she been trying to go green?

B ▶2.7 Listen to a friend giving you news. Pause after the "beep" and ask a *how long* question using the reduced form of *have* and *has*. Then listen to check.

Guess what! I go to the gym twice a week now.

C ⬤ Make it personal   In pairs, use these verbs to interview each other. Ask at least two questions for each verb. Any surprising answers?

Really? How long have you been going there?

collect   drive   go   live   play   read   study   swim   watch   work

Are you reading anything now?   *Yeah, I'm reading a graded reader.*   *How long have you been reading it?*

2.3 How has the climate been changing?

① Vocabulary The environment

A ▶2.8 Match photos 1–9 to the headlines. Listen to check. Which ones are good news?

ENVIRONMENTAL NEWS FROM AROUND THE WORLD

- [ ] **Droughts Seem to Be Getting More and More Severe**
- [ ] **Floods in All Parts of the World Have Been Getting Worse Year After Year**
- [ ] **Dumping of E-waste is on the Rise in Developing Countries**
- [ ] Countries Like India Are Becoming Less Dependent on Fossil Fuels
- [ ] Officials Say Amazon Deforestation Is Not As Bad As It Once Was
- [ ] The UN Has Labeled the World's Rising Sea Levels "Alarming"
- [ ] **Poaching in Latin America has Declined**
- [ ] **Experts Disagree on the Causes of Climate Change**
- [ ] Threatened Species List Is Getting Smaller

B 🔊 Do some research and compare your views.

1 Choose a topic in **A** to research online. Find out five facts about the topic. Report back to the class.
2 Which facts did you all find interesting? Which topics do you now feel optimistic / pessimistic about?

> I feel a bit more optimistic about threatened species because there are lots of conservation groups trying to stop extinction.

② Listening

A ▶2.9 You are going to listen to five scientists talking about points a–e. In pairs, guess what they will say. Then listen and match speakers 1–5 to a–e. How close were you?.

a	[ ]	Climate change is not just a problem for our future.
b	[ ]	Climate change affects threatened animals.
c	[ ]	The Earth is getting hotter, not the sun.
d	[ ]	Climate change has happened before, but this time it's our fault.
e	[ ]	Are we cooling down or heating up?

> I think the scientist who makes the first point will say climate change is also a problem right now.

B ▶2.9 Can you remember any of the missing words in extracts 1–8? Listen again and check. Who was the most convincing?

1 A number of independent measures of solar activity indicate that the sun _____ by a few degrees since 1960.
2 Over the last 35 years of climate change, sun and climate _____ in opposite directions.
3 Some people say, "Well, we _____ ice ages and warmer periods, so climate change is natural!"
4 This is like saying that forest fires _____ naturally in the past.
5 Climate researchers _____ papers for years.
6 Climate change deniers say the planet _____ since a peak in 1998.
7 However, experts _____ that in a climate being warmed by man-made carbon emissions …
8 A large number of ancient mass extinction events _____ to global climate change.

③ Grammar Present perfect simple vs. Present perfect continuous

A Read sentence pairs a–c and match them to uses 1–3 in the grammar box.

a The earth has gotten warmer before.
  The earth has been getting warmer since 1998.
b Tigers have lived in India for two million years.
  Tigers have been living in India for two million years.
c In the last century, sea levels have risen by 10–20 cm.
  Sea levels have been rising over the last century.

You can often use the *present perfect simple* or *present perfect continuous* interchangeably.
Generally use the *present perfect continuous* to emphasize duration.
Don't use the *present perfect continuous* with stative verbs.
The *present perfect simple* emphasizes completion.

	Present perfect	Present perfect continuous
1 ☐	No difference	No difference
2 ☐	Completed action	Process happening now
3 ☐	How much / many?	Emphasis on how long

→ **Grammar 2C** p. 140

⊘ Common mistakes

　　　　has been
The problem ~~is~~ getting worse since 2010.

　　　　known
We've ~~been knowing~~ about climate change for ages.

B Read the environmental news below and circle the correct verb tenses. Sometimes both options are possible.

New York's [1] **announced** / **been announcing** a plan to use human waste for renewable energy.

Scientists from Ohio University have [2] **found** / **been finding** a way to produce hydrogen from urine.

In the past few years, the auto industry has [3] **looked** / **been looking** into several different ways to produce vehicles that are less dependent on fossil fuels.

The European Union has [4] **tried** / **been trying** hard to meet the goal of at least a 27% improvement in energy efficiency by 2030.

Despite poaching and a recent drought, Kenya's elephant population has [5] **increased** / **been increasing** year after year. It has [6] **increased** / **been increasing** by nearly 10% in the past three years.

Although the world has [7] **lost** / **been losing** 18% of the Amazon Rainforest, the rate of deforestation seems to be slowing.

C ● Make it personal In pairs, look back at **1A**. For each photo, answer 1–3. Compare your ideas with other pairs. Do they agree / disagree with you?

1 Is this a major problem in your country / city?
2 Has this problem recently gotten better or worse? How?
3 Who's to blame for this, and why? What have they (not) done or (not) been doing?

Floods are a real problem in São Paulo.

And it's gotten worse recently.

D ● 2.10 ● Make it personal *Dictation*. Write the five questions you hear. In pairs, answer them. Any similarities?

I've known my best friend for 15 years. We met in kindergarten!

2.4 What's the best ad you've seen recently?

① Reading

A Do you believe most ads you see? Why (not)? Read the pop-ups quickly. Which promise(s) do you find hard to believe?

1

Thinking of upgrading your phone? _____? With the new, gorgeous green Sun 360, you get all the features you love: an ultrafast processor, powerful 12 MP camera, and an internal solar panel that allows up to eight hours of heavy, uninterrupted usage. Sun 360 produces the greenest cell phone on the market by using recycled materials. All of this, and it will still fit into your pocket! Introductory price—$259. _____

2

_____? Try Moringa Miracle Powder—the Moringa plant is a superfood believed to be one of the most nutritious foods on our planet. The leaves are packed with at least 92 different nutrients, vitamins, and minerals for good health. Just add our Miracle Powder to tea, soups, and smoothies, and start experiencing the benefits immediately.

3

Feeling stressed out? _____? Then *Mindful Me* is the place to be. Our meditation retreat located in the beautiful countryside will help you deal with life's ups and downs with more peace and serenity. We welcome people of all ages and cultures. Every day, you will have the opportunity to participate in yoga classes, meditation groups, and enjoy vegan meals prepared by our chefs. N.B. _____, so no modern interruptions.

B ▶2.11 Reread and complete the ads with 1–5. Listen to check. Practice the pink-stressed words.

1 Need some time out
2 Tired of batteries that won't last
3 Not looking your best
4 No cell phones or tablets allowed
5 Offer limited to one unit per customer

C Read the information in the box and find eight examples of grammatical omission in the completed ads in **A**.

> To be shorter, friendlier, and sound more exciting, ads often omit articles, auxiliary verbs, or subjects.
> - (The) offer (is) only available in (the) U.S.
> - (Our Hybrid car is) greener than you thought.

I'd never try the Moringa stuff. I don't believe in all these "superfoods"!

Hmm ... I'd most like to try the retreat. I need a rest.

D Order ads 1–3 from *I'd most* to *I'd least* like to try.

② Listening

A ▶2.12 Listen to the beginning of three conversations at a party. Which product in **1A** did each person buy?

B ▶2.13 Listen to the rest of the conversations. How many are satisfied customers?

I went to a retreat in India where you couldn't speak for 10 days!

C ▶2.14 True (T) or false (F)? Listen to check. Know any similar stories?

1 Beth has been on vacation.
2 Lorna doesn't believe in "superfoods".
3 Pedro's new cell phone battery dies after 90 minutes.
4 Pedro liked his old phone better.
5 Bruce left his old job because of the pay.
6 Bruce spent about a month away from New York City.

③ Grammar   Simple past vs. Present perfect simple / continuous

♫ *How long has this been going on?*
You've been acting so shady,
I've been feeling it lately.

A ▶2.15 Complete 1–6, and then listen to check. In pairs, remember all you can about each story.

1 I _____ (try) this new dietary supplement.
2 I _____ (really notice) the benefits.
3 I _____ (try) to call you back for about an hour, and I _____ (not be able) to get through.
4 I _____ (have) my old Samsung for three years … but the battery life was much better.
5 I _____ (work) there for over ten years, but … I just couldn't handle the stress.
6 I _____ (go) to a meditation retreat up in the mountains. I _____ (be) there for about a month.

→ **Grammar 2D** p.140

She's been trying a new superfood. It's made her feel much better.

B ▶2.16 **Form questions to ask the people in A. Listen to check. How do you think they would reply?**

1 you / got / a new phone / yet?
2 you / look for / a new job?
3 try / yoga / at the retreat?
4 how long / you / take / this supplement?
5 how / it / affect / your health?

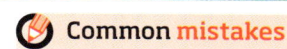

⚠ Common mistakes

James Dean's career ~~has lasted~~ *lasted* less than a decade.

I've ~~been having~~ *had* this new tablet since March. I love it!

~~For how~~ *How* long do you ~~have~~ *have you had* that smart watch?

C Read the pop-ups. Imagine you were tempted. In pairs, role-play a conversation about each one. Record the best one.

LEARN CHINESE IN 6 MONTHS!
Two hours a week, very little homework.
Learn in your sleep! First month free of charge.

Tired of dogs, cats, birds, and goldfish?
Maybe what you need is a pet alligator!
3000 happy owners can't be wrong. Come and choose yours today!
24-hour helpline: (555) 013-2689.

How much Chinese have you learned? When did you start?   *Have you bought a baby alligator?*

D 🔵 **Make it personal** In pairs, choose a topic and interview each other. Report back with anything interesting you found out.

a collection   an artist, band, or TV show you love
follow your favorite sport   a get-rich-quick plan
something you're trying to learn   a recent change in your life

I collect old vinyl pop records.

No way! How long have you been collecting them?

Well, it all started when …

2.5 Do you support any charities?

ID Skills Expressing numerical information

A 🔊 **Make it personal** In groups, answer 1–3. Share your answers with the class.

1 Find the animals' names in the chart. Which of them have you seen, either in the wild, in a zoo, or stuffed in a museum? What do you know about them?
2 Give three reasons why some species are more vulnerable to extinction than others.
3 Suggest two ways to help people care more about threatened species.

B ▶2.17 How many of these animals do you think might be left in the wild? Listen and fill in the middle column in the report. Anything shocking or surprising?

I can't believe there are only about 800 gorillas left!

Species we may never see again

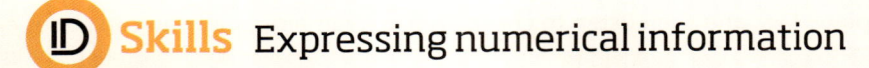

	Origin / Habitat	Number left in the wild	Other info
Giant panda		fewer than _____	
Monk seal	*Islands of Hawaii*	fewer than _____	
Golden lion tamarin		around _____	
Mountain gorilla		about _800_	*discovered 120 years ago*
North Atlantic right whale		fewer than _____	
Javanese rhino		approximately _____	
Ivory-billed woodpecker		maybe _____	

C ▶2.17 Can you remember any other information to complete the report? Listen again and fill in the other columns where possible.

D You are going to watch a video about threatened species. Before you watch, in pairs, circle the alternatives you think are correct.

We are living in the age of the [1] **fifth / sixth** mass global extinction. Experts warn that within the next [2] **30 / 50** years, we'll lose [3] **20% / 10%** of the entire species on the planet. And if trends continue, we'll lose [4] **a third / half** of our species in the next [5] **100 / 200** years. [6] **15% / 25%** of our mammal species are at risk of dying out in the wild.

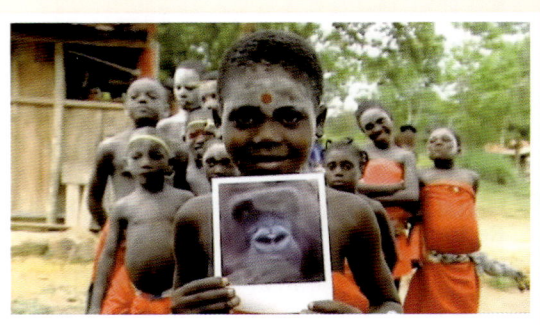

E ▶2.18 ▶ Listen / Watch to check. How does this extract make you feel? Why?

It makes me want to do something.

Me, too. I think it's actually worse. I heard recently we've lost more than half the world's wildlife since 1970!

Have you made any lifestyle changes recently?

(ID) in Action Encouraging and discouraging

There are almost no / There are hardly any
~~Almost no have~~ pandas.
I love ~~the~~ nature, ~~the~~ animals, and all ~~the~~ wildlife.

A Before watching the rest of the video, in pairs, brainstorm five ways to raise awareness of threatened species and change people's behavior.

We should all be taught more about it at school.

B ►2.19 ▶ Read five extracts from the video. Then listen / watch and number them 1–5 in the order you hear them.

- ☐ Showing the loss of animals in faraway places may pull a few heartstrings ...
- ☐ ... the single most important factor behind taking action is our childhood experience.
- ☐ It's not the depressing accounts of the wildlife we are losing that moves us. It's awe and wonder ...
- ☐ Have we forgotten what first inspired our love of nature?
- ☐ In all parts of the world, we're beginning to see that public awareness does lead to change.

I disagree. Remembering what we've lost makes us more determined to ...

C Choose the best summary of the video, 1–3. Do you agree with them all? Why (not)?

1 Developing a love of nature is more important than thinking about what we have already lost.
2 Children need to be encouraged to spend more time in nature.
3 Showing images of species we have lost increases donations to animal charities.

D ►2.20 Listen to five people explaining how they're going to help threatened species. Match each speaker 1–5 to these actions. There's one extra.

- ☐ Collect for charity
- ☐ Raise awareness online
- ☐ Reduce waste
- ☐ Sponsor an animal
- ☐ Use an environment-friendly product
- ☐ Volunteer at an animal shelter

E ►2.20 Listen again. Are the speakers' friends encouraging ☺ or discouraging ☹?
1 _____   2 _____   3 _____   4 _____   5 _____

F ►2.20 Listen again and complete the expressions for expressing encouragement and discouragement. Write three words in each blank.

☹ Why ¹_____ to (adopt a whale)?
☹ What is ²_____ (spending money on) ...?
☺ Keep up ³_____.

☺ Wow, you are determined! ⁴_____.
☹ What's ⁵_____ (buying that)?
☺ Every time? ⁶_____!

G ⭕ **Make it personal** Are you improving your lifestyle?

1 List three things (real or imaginary) that you have or haven't been doing, to improve your lifestyle.
2 In groups, take turns telling each other what you have or haven't been doing. Ask extra questions and use the expressions in **F** to encourage or discourage.
3 Share the most imaginative changes from your groups with the class. Which group is / has been making the most changes?

I haven't been studying much outside class recently.

Don't give up. What's the point of paying for classes if you don't do homework?

♫ *I got the eye of the tiger, a fighter*
Dancing through the fire, 'Cause I am a champion

Writing 2 A report

A Read Nina's report and mark ➕ for the most popular and ➖ for the least popular practices.

☐ using solar energy
☐ separating waste
☐ reusing plastic bags
☐ recycling containers

To:	Ms. Lang, Geography Teacher	Going
From:	Nina Diaz	Green
Subject:	Going Green in the Neighborhood	

1 **Introduction:** The aim of this report is to describe the most and the least popular practices in this neighborhood to help save the environment. It also makes recommendations about what we can do to become greener. The findings are reported below.

2 **The survey:** This survey involved interviewing 30 people from the ages of 18 to 35 by asking them ten questions about popular practices to save the planet. Respondents had to say how often they did these things: always, sometimes, rarely, or never.

3 **Most popular practices:** The survey showed that the two most popular practices to protect the environment in our neighborhood are to recycle bottles, cans, and plastic containers, in addition to separating organic and non-organic household waste.

4 **Least popular practices:** The two least popular practices, according to the questionnaire, were reusing plastic bags, or using cloth bags for shopping, and installing solar heating systems in houses.

5 **Conclusion:** As we can see from this report, people in this neighborhood try to adopt some environmentally friendly practices. However, some simple things could also be done to make a difference to the planet. Therefore, I recommend we organize a campaign to stimulate the use of cloth bags and cardboard boxes for shopping.

B The report is divided into five headings. Which heading, 1–5:

☐ describes the survey?
☐ summarizes and makes suggestions?
☐ says why the report is being written?
☐ discusses the first point?
☐ discusses the second point?

C Read *Write it right!* Then mark 1–6 appropriate (A) or inappropriate (I) to include in a report.

1 I think this is a very important topic.
2 This report will present the results of a survey about protecting the environment.
3 In my opinion, respondents enjoyed the survey.
4 That's just great for the environment!
5 To summarize, the main ideas are easy to implement.
6 I also have some bad news!

✅ Write it right!

- Begin reports with the names of the recipient and the author, and then the subject.
- Keep to the facts. Use personal opinions only in the conclusion.
- Use paragraphs with headings for each subtopic.
- Use formal language and fixed phrases to organize ideas and add clarity.
- Don't contract and be careful with punctuation.

D Mark 1–6 introduction (I), reporting an observation (R), generalizing (G), making a recommendation (M), or summarizing (S).

1 The objective of this report is to present / review ...
2 The most / least common answer was ...
3 It was found that ...
4 In general ...
5 This report describes ...
6 In conclusion ...

E Identify and correct four spelling, one punctuation, and two style mistakes in this draft.

This report's based on recent interviews about tourists' expectations in our city. Acording to the people interviewed, our main problem is adequate accomodation. Tourists complained they can't find enough family rooms or rooms with air-conditioning! They also reccomended establishing more tourist information points to provide better information and sugestions for tourists.

F 🔘 Make it personal In pairs, choose one of the topics and prepare a five-question survey. Conduct it in class and record the results.

Use of technology for learning English.

Most popular free time activities.

G *Your turn!* Write a report in 100–180 words.

Before	Look at the results from **F**. What are your conclusions?
While	Follow the five tips in *Write it right!*
After	Ask a classmate to read it and check formality, spelling, and punctuation, then email it to your teacher.

2 Down to earth

1 Before watching

A Match the words to the photos. Which have you seen in real life?

- ☐ jaguar
- ☐ tamarin monkey
- ☐ logging
- ☐ toucan
- ☐ forest canopy

None of them except logging, sadly!

B ⊘ **Make it personal** In pairs, think of three ways we can help endangered species.

I guess we could build more zoos.

C In pairs, describe Daniel. What do you think he might be doing / saying?

He might be doing an interview about endangered species.

2 While watching

A Watch up to 1:30 to check your guesses, and then circle the correct alternative.

1 Daniel's in a **zoo / studio**.
2 He's been researching **wildlife / global warming**.
3 Daniel **has / hasn't** had a lot of pets.
4 He's been taking classes in **environmental science / climate change**.
5 He plans to be a **weatherman / reporter**.
6 Polar bears have been **dying of hunger / drowning in the sea**.
7 Lucy knows little about **endangered species / Antarctica**.
8 Daniel's talking about very **contemporary / controversial** issues.

B Watch from 1:30 to 2:40 and number these items as you hear them, 1–10. What else can you remember him saying?

- ☐ cover
- ☐ difference
- ☐ impact
- ☐ lights
- ☐ logging
- ☐ mankind
- ☐ recycling
- ☐ species
- ☐ walk
- ☐ victims

C Watch the second part again to check. Then, in pairs, answer 1–4.

1 Where has logging been going on?
2 Who have been victims of logging?
3 Which actions / things impact negatively on the earth?
4 Which actions make a difference?

D Watch from 2:40 to the end. Who said these words: Daniel, Lucy, or August? Can you remember the complete phrase?

1 coming
2 impressive
3 knowledgeable
4 heartbreaking
5 lunch place
6 dying to try
7 on me

3 After watching

A Complete 1–6 with the present perfect or present perfect continuous of the verbs.

1 He _____ always _____ a fanatic about weather and the environment. (be)
2 I _____ never _____ such an animal lover. (know)
3 _____ he _____ to be a weatherman? (study)
4 Daniel _____ environmental science classes. (take)
5 The effects of global warming _____ serious harm to wildlife. (cause)
6 This _____ for the past several years and the results _____ devastating. (go on / be)

B ⊘ **Make it personal** Which items that Daniel talks about concern you most? In your opinion, what changes do we need to make to have the biggest positive impact on planet Earth?

I think using hybrid cars will make a big difference.

R1 Grammar and Vocabulary

A *Picture dictionary.* Cover the words and definitions on the pages below and remember.

pages	
8–9	6 stages of a relationship
13	10 personality adjectives
15	8 active listening expressions
18–19	10 "green" words
22	9 environmental problems
26	7 endangered animals
160	2 words for each vowel sound (not the picture words); say and spell them

B ▶R1.1 **Order the words to make questions. Listen to check, then ask and answer in pairs.**

1 like / people / do / new / you / meeting / ?
2 of / who / your time / spend / most / with / you / do / ?
3 follow / social media / who / do / on / you / ?
4 are / what / friend / qualities / in a / most important / ?
5 can / which / of / always / on / your friends / you / depend / ?
6 you / who / you / up / feel / when / cheers / down / ?

C 🔊 Make it personal **Match the sentence halves, then modify the underlined phrases to make them true. Compare in pairs.**

1 I sometimes fall
2 I often go to the mall to hang
3 I'm usually attracted
4 I don't get
5 When you want to get
6 If someone wants to get
7 The family member I can count

a ☐ to know someone better, you should go camping with them.
b ☐ to people who have a good sense of humor.
c ☐ out with my friends after work.
d ☐ back together with an ex-partner, they'd have to be really romantic.
e ☐ along well with people who are too arrogant.
f ☐ out with my parents over using the car.
g ☐ on the most is my older sister.

D **Choose three phrases from 1E on p. 9. Write a short story, leaving gaps for the phrases for your partner to guess.**

E **Circle the correct alternative.**

1 My family always _____ all our plastic bottles and food packaging.
   a recycles   b is recycling   c has recycled

2 Many scientists believe that the earth _____ warmer because of us.
   a gets   b is getting   c have gotten
3 My school _____ solar panels next month.
   a installs   b is installing   c has installed
4 I _____ a plastic shopping bag for three months.
   a don't use   b 'm not using   c haven't used
5 An aluminum can _____ between 200 and 500 years to decompose.
   a takes   b is taking   c has taken
6 Many people _____ that pandas will become extinct.
   a think   b is thinking   c have thought

F ▶R1.2 *The animal in you* **Follow instructions 1–3, then listen to find out what the combinations mean.**

1 Think of and write three names of animals.
2 Think of and write three personality adjectives.
3 Combine them.

G **Complete 1–8 with the verbs in the *present perfect simple* or *continuous*.**

1 The population of the earth _____ by over one billion this century. (grow)
2 Greenpeace is an international environmental organization. It _____ since 1971. (campaign)
3 It _____ for hours now! When is it going to stop? (rain)
4 I _____ a wild monkey before. (never see)
5 The mammoth _____ extinct for over 10,000 years. (be)
6 André _____ 5000m today. (run)
7 Sorry about the mess. We _____ all afternoon and _____ yet. (cook, not tidy up)
8 How many times _____ you _____ exercises like this? (do)

H **Correct the mistakes in each sentence. Check your answers in units 1 and 2.**

🖊 **Common mistakes**

1 *When you went in New York? (2 mistakes)*
2 *When did you feel in love to her? (2 mistakes)*
3 *Jed was engaged with Clara during six years. (2 mistakes)*
4 *With who are you usually hang out? (3 mistakes)*
5 *Sofía is thinking BlacKkKlansman is a sad movie, but Paulo isn't agree. (2 mistakes)*
6 *She don't often eats meat, but she did liked my barbecue. (3 mistakes)*
7 *Don't let your laptop in stand-by mode for too long. (1 mistake)*
8 *Leo is living in Boston since two years. (2 mistakes)*
9 *We has been knowing each other from 2008. (2 mistakes)*
10 *The tree in my garden been grown two meters I've planted it. (2 mistakes)*

Skills practice

♪ *I've been running through the jungle,*
I've been running with the wolves, To get to you, to get to you,
I've been down the darkest alleys, Saw the dark side of the moon to get to you

R1

A Listen to Al's blog ▶2.3 on p. 20 and pause after each paragraph. In pairs, summarize, then continue. Finally, read to check. Did you miss anything because:

a it was too fast to understand?
b you didn't think it was important?
c you didn't remember the words?
d of another reason?

B ▶R1.3 *Dictation.* Listen and write the numbers. In pairs, try to retell each fact. Listen again to check.

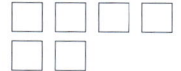

C ▶R1.4 Use the prompts to make questions 1–4. Listen to check and add the emphatic words.

1 nicknames? *Do you have any nicknames?*

Not really, no. Although my brother calls me "big ears." Oh, it _____ annoy me!

Aw! That's mean! They used to call me "potato" at school, but I've _____ no idea why.

2 first / notice / meeting / new?

Oh, I'm _____ a shoe person. I always notice if people have dirty shoes.

Me, I don't notice clothes, but I _____ notice teeth. If they have something in their teeth ... yuk!

3 more often optimistic / pessimistic?

Oh, I don't know. I guess I'm about fifty-fifty.

No, you always seem _____ laid-back and happy. I think you're a _____ positive person.

4 only three electrical appliances?

Hmm, difficult. Only three? Well, the first is my laptop. I _____ use it almost every day.

Lights? Do they count as an appliance? They _____ are important.

D ▶R1.4 In pairs, imitate dialogues 1–4 in **C**. Listen again to compare with the audio.

E Read the title of the magazine article and first paragraph only. Guess what *Boston500* involves.

Maybe it's a plan to make 500 companies do more to be greener.

F Read the rest of the article and find:

1 two economic benefits of the scheme.
2 a reason for thicker walls.
3 a problem with current solar panels.
4 a use for windows.
5 a problem with using biodegradable waste.

Save the world, save your money!

The city of Boston, capital of Massachusetts, and the most populous city in New England, is already one of the greenest cities in the U.S. Public transportation is eco-friendly, all the taxis are hybrids, and, with Grow Boston Greener, the city is trying to plant 100,000 trees by 2020. Now, with *Boston 500*, it has set its citizens a challenge: to go even greener. City officials claim that if just 500 families join the *Boston500* scheme they can each save $100 a year on their energy bills, cut 25% of dangerous gases, and create lots of new "green" jobs for the community.

So what is the *Boston500* scheme?
The idea is to encourage people to live in more efficient homes. Construction workers have already started building houses with thicker walls to protect against both high and low temperatures. Many homeowners have installed more energy-efficient appliances and use solar panels to power them, but they still need to buy some electricity, as solar panels don't usually generate enough. The ultimate goal, say developers, is to create houses that generate enough electricity to provide power for others as well.

Scientists and engineers have been working hard on this problem and there are some very innovative ideas out there. One plan is to turn windows into solar panels to increase the total area of panels—and they already have a prototype that works. Another is to use biodegradable waste—a smelly but efficient solution.

If the *Boston500* scheme is a success, we could all be paying less for electricity in the near future!

G In pairs, brainstorm ways to save energy at home. How many can you think of in two minutes?

Some people put aluminum foil on the roof to reflect the sun.

H ▶R1.5 🔵 **Make it personal** *Question time!*

1 Listen to and answer the 12 lesson titles in units 1 and 2.
2 In pairs, practice asking and answering. Use the map on p. 2–3. Ask at least two follow-up questions, too. Which was the most interesting conversation?

So, do you know all your classmates?

No, there are a few new students I don't know.

3

① **Vocabulary** Cities

A Look at photos a–g. Do you recognize any of the cities? Find the ==highlighted== words in texts 1–4 in the photos. What else can you see?

These two look like fashionable neighborhoods …

There's a bridge in this one.

B Read the texts. Can you guess which cities the people are describing?

1

OK, my turn now. "You're <u>at the heart of</u> the city, in the middle of the world's largest city ==square== and the country's most important <u>land</u>mark. This square separates the country's capital from the "Forbidden City". Which Asian city is it?"

Hmm, I don't know. Is it _____?

Yeah, well done. At last you got one right!

2

Marta: Hey! I thought you'd be busy sightseeing. What are you doing online?

Ed: It's raining. Just having coffee and waiting for the rain to stop.

Marta: So … how do you like _____?

Ed: Well, if you like avenues full of ==skyscrapers==, **chaotic** traffic, dangerous neighborhoods, and the ugliest ==harbor== I've ever seen, <u>it's the place to go</u>.

Marta: Well, OK … Anything you do like, Mr. Grumpy?

Ed: Hmm … Well, streets and avenues are numbered, so it's easy to <u>find my way around</u> … I guess. And the city is mostly flat, so it's very easy to walk. It's very lively, I suppose. Lots going on, some good shopping. Oh, and then there's the huge park. And the statue. Yep, I think that's about it.

3

Second day in _____, this marvelous city. I'm at a beautiful beach right now, people exercising and sunbathing everywhere. Some of them even sunbathe standing up so they can be seen! Looking up to my right, I can see a magnificent statue, but to my left, up on the hill, is one of the most ==rundown areas== of the city. It's really strange that only a few blocks away there's an **upscale**, fashionable ==neighborhood==. You gotta love this place—so many great <u>tourist spots</u>, such a lot to do.

4

"… such fabulous colonial architecture. If you have time, be sure to go all the way up to the 44th floor. There's an observation deck where you'll get an exceptional view of _____'s ==skyline==. On a clear day, you can see the soccer stadium, lots of beautiful old churches, volcanoes, and even the pyramids. Problem is, this city is sometimes **smoggy** so we don't get too many really clear days, I'm afraid."

f

 Concrete jungle where dreams are made of,
There's nothing you can't do,
Now you're in New York.

3.1

g

C ▶3.1 **Match each text to its type. There is one extra type. Listen to check.**

☐ Friends talking on WhatsApp.
☐ A guide talking to tourists.
☐ A vacation blog post.

☐ Friends playing a guessing game.
☐ Introduction to a guidebook.

D **Write the underlined words and phrases in the texts next to their definitions.**
Describe examples of these features in your area.

1	_____ *noun [C]*	a well-known building or site
2	_____ *noun [C]*	places / attractions popular with visitors
3	_____ *phrase*	know where you're going
4	_____ *phrase*	I recommend it
5	_____ *phrase*	in the most important place

> *We have a beautiful square in the heart of our town. It's a real tourist spot because it has such great cafés and restaurants.*

E **Match the bold adjectives in the texts to their synonyms. Which adjectives would**
you use to describe your town, city, or another place you know? Why?

conf**used** and dis**org**anized   ener**get**ic and active   expensive and chic
neg**lec**ted and poor   poll**u**ted   popular

> *I'd say our city is chaotic. There's lots of traffic and millions of people.*

② Pronunciation /eɪ/

A ▶3.2 **Cross out the words that do *not* have /eɪ/. Listen to check. Make a tongue**
twister with three or four of the words.

 eɪ   ancient   Asian   chaotic   dangerous   ~~fashionable~~
flat   skyscraper   stadium   statue   sunbathe
traffic   upscale   volcanoes

> *A dangerous, ancient, Asian skyscraper!*

B 🔴 **Make it personal**   **Think of a city you'd love to visit.**

1   Spend a few minutes thinking about why you'd like to visit it and make some notes.
2   Describe the city, without naming it, for your partner to guess.

> *The city I'd like to visit has beautiful beaches, great music, and some of the best colonial architecture in South America. It's well-known for its mix of European, African, and indigenous cultures. Famous landmarks include …*

3   Share your ideas with the class. Is there one place everybody would like to visit?

3.2 Was your last vacation as much fun as you'd hoped?

① Reading

A ▶3.3 ▶ Match the underlined words to photos a–h, and then circle the correct alternative in 1–9. Listen to / watch the video to check.

VISITING HONG KONG FOR THE FIRST TIME?

Here's what you need to know:

1. It's **usual / rare** for people to <u>shake hands and bow</u> slightly.
2. When you greet people, you **should / shouldn't** <u>hug</u> them and <u>kiss them on the cheek</u>.
3. When you're walking through a crowd, you should gently <u>push your way through</u> and **say nothing / apologize**.
4. When you receive a gift, it's good manners to open it **later / immediately**.
5. Clocks make **good / bad** gifts.
6. When drinking tea, you should <u>pour</u> your **own / friends'** cup first.
7. In Hong Kong, it's OK to **<u>blow on your soup</u> / chew loudly**.
8. Leaving your <u>chopsticks</u> straight up means **good / bad** luck.
9. After eating, you **should / shouldn't** <u>leave a tip</u> on the table.

B If you were going to Hong Kong, which social conventions would be hard to adapt to?

It would be difficult not to open a gift right away.

C 🔒 **Make it personal** What are the rules where you live? In small groups, write six tips for a foreign visitor and share them with the class.

You shouldn't really talk on your phone on the train. People get annoyed and don't like it.

② Grammar Past perfect

A ▶3.4 Rita is in Hong Kong for the first time to meet her in-laws. Match these phrases with 1–5 in her travel blog. There's one extra. Listen to check.

☐ she'd made   ☐ He hadn't told me   ☐ I'd never seen anyone do that
☐ I'd left on the table   ☐ I hadn't had it before.   ☐ I'd said sorry

First few days in HK! I got mad at Hue. ¹_____ about the shaking hands thing here! Guess how surprised his dad was when I kissed him! Slightly embarrassing! Hue's mom gave me a gift ²_____. Fortunately, I remembered not to open it in front of her. Went out for lunch, and I saw a man blowing on his soup. ³_____ before. Then I forgot to tip the waitress directly. Luckily, Hue went back and took the money ⁴_____ and gave it to her. I was walking through crowded streets this afternoon when this man suddenly looked at me strangely. I realized ⁵_____ to him. Typical tourist! To be honest, it's so unnatural for me not to apologize! But loving being here.

*For some reason I can't explain,
Once you'd gone there was never,
Never an honest word,
And that was when I ruled the world.*

B **Reread the blog in A and complete the grammar box.**

1 What happened first?
   Hue's mom <u>gave</u> me a gift that <u>she'd made</u>.
   ☐ She gave the gift. ☐ She made the gift.

   The past perfect has only one form for all persons: *had / hadn't* + past participle. The past perfect shows a relationship with another past event. Use the past perfect for the earlier event and the simple past for the later event.

2 Match pictures a and b to the phrases below.
   ☐ When I arrived, everybody started leaving.
   ☐ When I arrived, everybody had left.

   → **Grammar 3A** p. 142

a

b

C **Complete Rita's tweets with the *past perfect* of these verbs. There's one extra verb.**

be   commit   finish   make   read   not told   visit

> In HK to meet the in-laws! I ¹_____ (never) on a long-haul flight before, so I was exhausted when we landed! #jetlag #experiencechina #exploreHK
>
> ← Reply ⇄ Retweet ★ Favourite

> When Hue's parents began their meal, I ⁴_____ (nearly) mine! I didn't know I was supposed to wait for the hosts! #HongKong #dinnerout
>
> ← Reply ⇄ Retweet ★ Favourite

> I ²_____ once that some of Hong Kong's skyscrapers had no 13th floor. Guess what? It's true! #superstitions
>
> ← Reply ⇄ Retweet ★ Favourite

> Blew my nose in public yesterday, and everybody looked at me as if I ⁵_____ a crime. What did I do? #cultureshock #HongKongculture
>
> ← Reply ⇄ Retweet ★ Favourite

> Made the mistake of wearing white yesterday. @Hue2008 ³_____ me that it's the color of death. #embarrassing
>
> ← Reply ⇄ Retweet ★ Favourite

> On way to HK airport. Hue said I ⁶_____ a good first impression. His parents actually liked me. #relieved
>
> ← Reply ⇄ Retweet ★ Favourite

D **Bruno was an exchange student in London last year. Choose the correct alternative.**

1 I loved most of the landmarks. I **thought / 'd thought** Big Ben was amazing.
2 At first I hated the food, but by the time I left, I **got / 'd gotten** used to it.
3 I was shocked to find out how fast Londoners **spoke / 'd spoken**.
4 It was nice to hear all the words I **learned / 'd learned** in class over the years.
5 By the time my stay was over, I **visited / 'd visited** most of the tourist spots.
6 My first car ride wasn't too bad. I **never drove / 'd never driven** on the left side of the road.

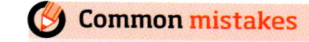

🔥 **Common mistakes**

been
I'd never ~~gone~~ to L.A. before.

gone
He'd already ~~went~~ when I arrived.

E 🎙 **Make it personal** *Mystery Monologue!* **A:** Use questions 1–7 to plan a one-minute monologue about a place you've been to. Don't name the place. **B:** Wait until **A** finishes, and then guess the place or ask more questions. Then change roles. How many of you have been to the same place?

1 When did you go? How long did you stay?
2 Had you been there before? If so, how many times?
3 Had you heard a lot about this place / seen it on TV?
4 What were you surprised to discover?
5 Did you do / see / eat anything you'd never done / seen / eaten before?
6 What were the people like? Any different from what you'd imagined?
7 Was anything else special? Would you recommend it?

Last year I went to this amazing place. I'd never been there before, and to my surprise, it was completely empty. I'd expected it to be full!

3.3 Do you ever want to get away from it all?

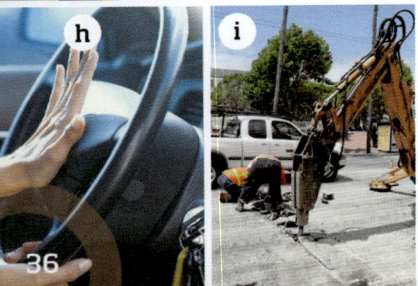

① **Vocabulary** Urban problems

A Read the magazine and match the **highlighted** words to the photos.

The stresses of *CITY LIVING*

❝ The traffic is a nightmare. There's construction everywhere, and you get stuck in traffic jams every day. Drivers sometimes go through red lights and it's impossible to find a parking spot. ❞

❝ The crime rate is high. There is a lot of vandalism, car theft, and pickpocketing. I don't feel safe in my neighborhood. ❞

❝ There is so much pollution! The air is smoggy, there's trash everywhere, and there's noise pollution from the cars. People are always honking! ❞

❝ It's difficult to find a work-life balance, and there just isn't enough "me-time," We are all in debt and constantly connected to the Internet, but not to each other, so a lot of people suffer from loneliness and anxiety. ❞

B ▶3.5 Reread and listen to check the pronunciation of the highlighted words. Do you agree with all four opinions of city living?

> *That sounds just like where I live!*

C 🔊 Make it personal In pairs, from the photos, choose the five most serious problems in your city. Can you agree on the order?

> *I think the worst problem by far is the traffic.*

> *No way! I'd say vandalism is a much more serious issue.*

> ⚠ **Common mistake**
>
> *In my neighborhood, there is trash ~~in every place~~.*
> *everywhere*

② **Reading**

A In pairs, list five ways you could escape the problems mentioned in **1B**.

B ▶3.6 Read the article on p. 37. Are any of your ideas mentioned? Complete the article with a–f. Then listen to check echoing the pink-stressed words.

a Overcome this by volunteering at an animal shelter.
b Finding a quiet place to switch off and enjoy peace is so important.
c Use lavender for relaxation and peppermint to invigorate.
d Try by your window or on your balcony.
e Try going to events to inspire your creative self.
f It's not easy to find these things in the city, though.

♫ It's like a jungle, sometimes it makes me wonder how I keep from going under. A-huh-huh huh-huh.

3.3

How to *get away* from it all

Living in a lively city is amazing, but the stresses and strains of urban life can affect our mental and physical health. Read the following tips to help you find a more balanced, peaceful city life.

Nature

Natural light and fresh air will instantly make you feel better. 1_____ Try to find a park and go for a walk there, or just sit and read a book. You'll be amazed how these simple activities can improve your mood.

Indulge your sense of smell

Clearly, the city does not smell pleasant. You can really transform your home environment and mental health with smell. 2_____

Get some pet therapy

If you've lived in the countryside, you'll notice how disconnected city dwellers are from nature and animals. 3_____ Bonding with an animal naturally reduces anxiety, and loneliness can never be a problem while walking a dog!

Grow something

Nowadays we're disconnected from where our food comes from. Even though you might not have a garden, you can grow food anywhere. 4_____ Producing your own vegetables makes you appreciate food more, waste less, and feel closer to nature.

Find some silence

We live among permanent noise—roadworks, traffic jams, phone calls, advertising, even our own minds are noisy. 5_____ Just a few minutes every day will make you feel more positive.

Do what you love

Everyone has a talent: painting, playing an instrument, or gardening, but we rarely spend time nurturing these gifts. When we take the time to do what we love, we feel more grounded. 6_____ Life isn't all about work, money, and success!

C 🔊 **Make it personal** In groups, discuss these questions.

1 Which of the activities in the article have you tried to "get away from it all"? Which would you like to do?
2 What other things do you / people you know do to reduce the stress of modern life?

③ Listening

A ▶3.7 **Listen to three city dwellers describe changes they made in their lives. Complete the chart.**

	Problem	Change
Raul		
Tomiko		
André		

B ▶3.8 **Complete 1–6 with these words. There is one extra. Then listen to check.**

bother   driving   find   'm   mind   stand   takes

1 … and my nonstop lifestyle was _____ me crazy.
2 I'm still just as busy, but it doesn't really _____ me as much.
3 Now, I _____ it annoying if I don't have time to eat properly.
4 It takes more time, but I don't _____ that.
5 I couldn't _____ coming home to an empty apartment every day.
6 I still find the city a bit lonely sometimes, but I _____ OK with it.

C **Read Common mistakes. Then circle the correct alternatives in 1–4.**

1 The noise **drive** / **drives** me crazy! Absolutely insane!
2 I love my city, but the huge lines really **annoy** / **annoys** me.
3 I can't stand people who **go** / **goes** through red lights.
4 There are massive traffic jams in my city, but that **don't** / **doesn't** bother me at all. I'm a cyclist!

D 🔊 **Make it personal** *City Stress Survey.* **Choose a topic from the article. Write three questions and interview your classmates. Report your findings.**

How often do you go for a walk in a park or the countryside?

My brother turns off his phone for an hour every day. He says he enjoys the peace and quiet.

I do the opposite. I listen to music or play video games.

✍ Common mistakes

drive
All the traffic jams ~~drives~~ me crazy.
(traffic jams = they)

bothers
Littering ~~bother~~ me a lot.
(littering = it)

doesn't
The traffic ~~don't~~ bother me.
(traffic = it)

3.4 Have you ever missed any important dates?

① Listening

A ▶3.9 **From the pictures, imagine Juan and Sandra's stories. Listen to check. Were you close?**

OK, so it looks like Juan's going to work.

Juan Alvarez from Bogotá

Sandra Machado from São Paulo

B ▶3.9 **Listen again. True (T) or false (F)? How much more did you understand the second time? Who do you feel most sorry for? Why?**

1 Juan had high hopes for the job interview.
2 Juan gave himself one hour to get there.
3 Sandra bought the tickets two weeks before the show.
4 Sandra and her friend managed to watch 30 minutes of the show.

I feel most sorry for … because …

C Read ▶3.9 **on p. 165 and write the underlined expressions in the chart.**

Listening actively	
1	I'm not sure I understand.	*What do you mean?*
2	I'm sorry this happened to you.	
3	I'm not surprised to hear that.	
4	What happened in the end?	
5	I'm very surprised.	

⚠ **Common mistake**

missed
I ~~lost~~ my flight.
You *lose* objects, but you *miss* transportation, events, and opportunities.
I missed the chance to see U2 because I was sick.

D ⬤ **Make it personal** Have you ever been stuck in traffic for a long time? In pairs, take turns sharing your stories. Remember to listen actively. Who has the funniest story?

I was going to visit my grandparents once, and we got stuck on the highway for four hours.

Oh, no. You poor thing. What happened?

② Grammar Past perfect continuous

A Read the example sentence and answer 1–3 in the grammar box.

> When we finally **got** to the stadium, **she had been singing** for well over an hour.
> 1 When they arrived:
>   a) was Taylor Swift already singing?   b) did the music stop?
> 2 Do we use the past perfect continuous for an action that:
>   a) had finished?   b) was in progress before another past action?
> 3 Is the form *had(n't)* +   a) *being*?   b) *been* + verb + *-ing*?
>
> → **Grammar 3B** p. 142

B Complete 1–8 with the *past perfect* or *past perfect continuous* of these verbs. Use contractions.

arrange   dream of   drive   get up   go through   try   rain   wait for

1 Juan _____ to find a job as an architect for months.
2 He wasn't worried about the traffic as he _____ at 6.
3 He heard on the radio that a bus _____ a red light.
4 He didn't get the job he _____ since he graduated.
5 Sandra bought tickets for the show she _____ since she was 16.
6 Sandra's friend _____ to pick her up in her car.
7 They _____ for a little while when the car broke down.
8 They were stuck in traffic because it _____ nonstop.

C Complete the grammar box with the tenses below. Then, in pairs, role-play Juan and Sandra telling their stories. Retell the stories in your own words.

Past perfect   Past perfect continuous   Past continuous

> **Narrative tenses**
> The simple past is the most common past tense. In general, use the others like this:
> ¹_____: an action in progress at a point in the past.
> *I **was chatting** online when you called. Sorry!*
>
> ²_____: one action that happened before another in the past.
> *By 8 p.m. Jo **had done** all her work, so she went home.*
>
> ³_____: action in progress or repeated before a point in the past.
> *But she**'d been working** so hard she fell asleep in the car.*
>
> → **Grammar 3C** p. 142

D ⬤ **Make it personal** Have you ever missed or forgotten anything important? In groups, share stories and choose the saddest and funniest ones. Use these questions to plan what to say first.

1 What was the important date or event?
2 Had you been looking forward to it?
3 Why did you miss or forget it?
4 What happened?
5 How do you feel about it now?

Common mistakes

had been   for
They ~~were~~ driving ~~during~~ 48 hours so they'd ~~been~~ very tired.
                        were

So, I was going for a job interview. I'd been looking for a job as an architect for ages, so I was really nervous.

Well, it was my cousin's birthday, and I'd been planning …

Had you spent many birthdays together in the past?

3.5 Do you always follow the rules?

ID Skills Understanding rules and regulations

A ▶3.10 **Match the signs to photos a–i. Listen to check. In pairs, think of two places where you might find each one. Which four are intended to be funny?**

That one could be at a public beach.

 a
 b
 c
 d
 e
 f
 g
 h
 i

DOGS MUST BE ON LEASH.

TRESPASSERS WILL BE PROSECUTED
(IF THE DOGS DON'T GET YOU FIRST.)

SPEED LIMIT 10 MPH

ATTENTION, DOG GUARDIANS!
PLEASE PICK UP AFTER YOUR DOG.
THANK YOU.
ATTENTION, DOGS!
GRRRR, WOOF. GOOD DOG.

DON'T EVEN THINK OF PARKING HERE! UNAUTHORIZED VEHICLES WILL BE TOWED AWAY AT OWNER'S EXPENSE.

PLEASE FASTEN SEAT BELT WHILE SEATED. LIFE VEST UNDER YOUR SEAT.

SMILE! This building is under 24 hr surveillance.

SWIM AT YOUR OWN RISK – THE SHARKS WILL BE DELIGHTED! BY THE WAY, NO LIFEGUARDS ON DUTY HERE.

IN ORDER TO MAINTAIN A RELAXING ENVIRONMENT, PLEASE REFRAIN FROM **CELL PHONE USE.**

B ▶3.11 **Match 1–10 to their meanings. Listen to a teacher to check.**

	Verbs	Meanings
1	refrain from	remove someone's car using another vehicle
2	pick up after	avoid
3	tow away	close securely
4	fasten	clean up someone's mess
	People	
5	a lifeguard	someone who enters private property without permission
6	a trespasser	someone who helps swimmers in difficulty
	Expressions	
7	under surveillance	whoever owns it will pay all costs
8	on duty	although you know it's dangerous
9	at owner's expense	working
10	at your own risk	monitored

C In groups, create and share signs for places 1–6. Any funny ones?

1 an airport
2 a hospital
3 your favorite beach
4 your English school
5 a theater
6 a zoo

D ⬤ **Make it personal** Have you, or people you know, ever broken any of these (or similar) rules? Would you ever break any of them?

My parents never used to pick up after their dog, but now they always do.

When did you last break a rule?

1

2

3

4

ID in Action Explaining and questioning rules

A ▶3.12 Listen to three dialogues and circle the correct signs on p. 40. Which speakers 1–3 don't accept the regulations easily?

B ▶3.13 Complete 1–7. Listen, check, and copy the stress and intonation.

Stating a rule	1	I'm a_____ you c_____ park here.
Apologizing	2	I'm sorry. I didn't r_____ that.
Questioning a rule	3	What do you m_____ I can't park here? S_____ who?
	4	Oh, c_____ on! Be reasonable!
Reinforcing	5	I'm afraid s_____.
	6	I'm afraid n_____.

✎ Common mistakes

so	*not*	*don't so*
I'm afraid ~~yes~~.	I'm afraid ~~no~~.	I ˇthink ~~no~~.

C ▶3.14 Match these confessions to photos 1–4. What rule(s) had they broken?

☐ Well, a few years ago I was on a work trip to Poland. I was crossing the street when these police officers suddenly stopped me and tried to give me a fine for crossing in the wrong place! I had no idea it was illegal! I didn't speak any Polish and pretended not to understand. In the end, they let me go with just a warning. Weird!

☐ Once, my brother was taking photos in the countryside in Egypt. Suddenly, two soldiers appeared and confiscated his camera. Apparently, without knowing it, he'd taken photos of a military installation. And he'd thought it was just a nice bridge over a river!

☐ My wife and I were visiting Rome and the Vatican. I'd been wearing shorts all day, around the museums and stuff, no problem, but then they wouldn't let me in to St. Peter's. I had to wait outside while my wife got to see it all. Anyway, lucky for me, it's a beautiful square.

☐ My wife used to get into trouble all the time at school for not wearing the right uniform. The wrong shoes, the wrong shirt, she never wore a tie, dyed her hair purple … She was a real punk and it all seemed so stupid to her. Actually, she's still a bit of a rebel today. That's why I love her!

D In pairs, role-play a sign from p. 40. Act it out for the class to guess which sign you chose.

Excuse me, ma'am. Haven't you read the sign?   *No, I'm sorry, I haven't. Is there a problem?*   *Well …*

E 👤 **Make it personal** *Confessions!* Have you / your friends ever gotten in trouble for breaking a rule? Share stories in groups. Who has been the most disobedient?

Hmm … well, the police stopped my uncle for using his phone in the car.   *Did he get a fine, or did they let him go with a warning?*

♫ *I don't want to go to school, I just wanna to break the rules.*

Writing 3 A narrative

A *Innovation* magazine has held a "best vacation narrative" competition. Read the winning entry and circle the correct photo for the story.

A vacation to remember

By Stef Stiller

1 ☐ My best friend Karen hadn't had a vacation for a long, long time. ☐ She was desperate to go somewhere new and do something she had never done before. ☐ So, last winter, after looking into many options, she decided to go skiing in Courchevel, a resort in the French Alps.

2 When Karen arrived, she was so excited about the comfortable hotel, delicious food, and such incredible views. ☐ The following day, she joined a ski-school. The other skiers seemed like fun-loving, sociable people, so she knew she'd have a great time. Karen had never skied before, but the instructor Alain, was great and reassured her.

3 However, she found skiing so hard she almost gave up. She kept trying, but then a horrible thing happened. While she was going down a hill, she fell badly and broke her leg. Her special trip had turned into a nightmare. Unable to move, she was stuck in a hospital in Courchevel.

4 But she had a wonderful surprise. ☐ They visited every day and brought gifts. Karen began to fall in love with the French Alps and decided to stay and get a job. She worked in a ski-chalet, learned to ski, and guess what? Now she's an instructor herself!

B Which paragraph, 1–4, answers these questions?
- ☐ What was the hotel like?
- ☐ Why did she go there?
- ☐ Where did she decide to go?
- ☐ Who is the main character?
- ☐ What happened while she was there?
- ☐ What happened in the end?
- ☐ Who did she meet?
- ☐ When did she go?

C Reread and underline examples of *simple past* (SP), *past continuous* (PC) and *past perfect* (PP).

D Read *Write it right!* and notice the nine **time expressions** in the story. Can you think of any others?

✔ Write it right!

- To enrich a narrative, use a variety of past tenses.
- Sequence it with a mix of **time expressions** to start, end, and connect sentences.
- Use plenty of adjectives and adverbs to add color to your story and *so* and *such* to emphasize them.

E Complete 1–5 with a time expression and the correct form of the verbs in parentheses.

after	ago	finally	occasionally	while

1 _____ leaving all her bags in the hotel, she _____ for a walk. (go)
2 _____ Karen _____ on her own. (travel)
3 This story _____ a few months _____. (happen)
4 _____, she _____ to go skiing. (decide)
5 Her new ski-friends and Alain _____ her the whole time _____ she _____ in bed. (help / recover)

F Match 1–5 from **E** to the boxes in Stef's story.

G Circle the correct word in each pair.
1 Courchevel was **so / such beautiful / beautifully** that she didn't want to leave.
2 The days passed **so / such slow / slowly**.
3 It was **so / such a special / specially** trip that she'll always remember it.
4 That trip **complete / completely** changed her life!
5 Alain was **so / such a friend / friendly** guy.

H *Your turn!* Choose one of this year's topics for *Innovation* magazine's competition and write an entry in 100–180 words.

That was really embarrassing!

What a frightening experience!

Before	Note down the main events in your story. Use the questions in **B** to help. Number the events in the order you want to tell them.
While	Write four paragraphs. Follow the tips in *Write it right!*
After	Ask your partner to check spelling and punctuation and give suggestions before emailing it to your teacher.

3 Global swarming

1 Before watching

A Are the photos city (C), coast (Co), landmark (L), or scenery (S)? In pairs, describe them in detail and include these adjectives.

amazing awesome beautiful buzzing
chaotic congested crowded historic

Photo 4 looks like somewhere in Asia.

B ⬤ Make it personal In pairs, describe your favorite place or historical landmark.

I saw the pyramids in Egypt five years ago. I'd never seen anything so old before!

2 While watching

A Do you think 1–9 will be true or false? Watch and check (✓) your guesses. How many right?

1 ☐ August and Andrea had lived in many places before they moved back to the U.S.
2 ☐ Rory wants to go somewhere he has been before.
3 ☐ Silicon Valley is home of the computer nerds.
4 ☐ Rory has never been to Quebec City before.
5 ☐ August doesn't think New York is so chaotic.
6 ☐ Andrea and August lived in Buenos Aires.
7 ☐ Mexico City and New York are very crowded.
8 ☐ Rush hour in Mexico City is similar to New York.
9 ☐ Quebec City has lots of little cafés.

B Watch again and check the features of each place.

	Buenos Aires	Mexico City	New York	Quebec City
architecture				
cafés				
chaotic				
good public transportation				
historic landmarks				
scenery				
traffic				
unpredictable weather				

3 After watching

A Circle the correct alternative(s).
1 The siblings had a lot of passport stamps because their **father** / **mother** was a photojournalist.
2 Rory goes to Dublin every year to **play soccer** / **visit his grandparents**.
3 August said they'd lived in **more than ten cities** / **more cities than he could name**.
4 Andrea and August mention "swarming like bees" to describe cities buzzing with **people** / **the noise of the traffic**.
5 Genevieve's gigs at the café draw **big** / **small** crowds.

B Complete 1–5 with the simple past or past perfect.
1 Rory _____ about visiting the West Coast. (think)
2 Rory didn't know they _____ in Argentina. (live)
3 Before Genevieve arrived for her gig, she _____ the others several times. (text)
4 August and Andrea _____ Rory pictures of Buenos Aires. (show)
5 Rory _____ in Dublin before he moved to the U.S. (live)

C ⬤ Make it personal Compare cities you know with those mentioned in the video. What would be your dream vacation destination?

I've never been abroad, so I don't know any of these places.

Me neither. My home town, Trujillo, is a much smaller city, but it has some great colonial architecture.

4

4.1 Does your school system work well?

① Reading

A In groups, compare your thoughts when looking at photos 1–8.

All the books remind me of my school bag. It was really heavy!

B Say the subjects on the school schedule together. Pay attention to the pink-stressed syllables. In pairs, compare how you feel / felt about each one. Any good stories?

2

	Monday	Tuesday	Wednesday	Thursday	Friday
7:10	Literature	Geography	Biology	Math	Chemistry
8:05	Math	Art	Information and Communication Technology	Math	Physics
9:00	Biology	Chemistry	History	Languages	Math
9:50	Break	–	–	–	–
10:05	Music	Math	Geography	Chemistry	Art
11:00	Physical education	Math	Languages	Physical education	Music
11:55	Lunch	–	–	–	–
12:30	History	Physics	Art	Literature	Literature
1:25	Languages	Philosophy	Music	Economics	Geography
2:20	Physics	Literature	Politics	Biology	Physical education

I used to hate math because the teacher couldn't explain it to us.

C ▶4.1 Guess which countries have the world's best education systems, and why. Listen, read, and complete the first part of an article to check.

> ⚑ **Common mistake**
>
> subject
> My worst ~~material~~ was math.

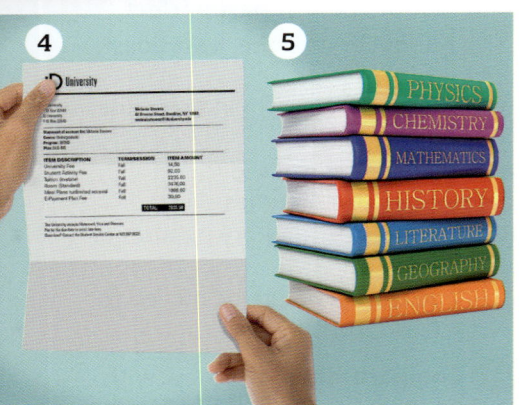

▶ HEY, TEACHER, THOSE KIDS ARE DOING GREAT!

A certain education minister once joked that his country's education goal was a modest one: to be one of the best in the world. Well, looks like he's been successful. His country—which also has one of the largest per capita cell phone use on the planet—has the world's best school system, and 66% of its five and a half million population are university graduates. Here are some reasons why _____'s school system works so incredibly well and is considered the best in the world.

D Why might this country's system be so good? Make a prediction about 1–8.

1	class size	4	number of tests	7	popularity of arts subjects
2	discipline	5	public vs. private education	8	uniforms
3	homework	6	teachers' qualifications		

♫ *Hey, Teacher, leave them kids alone! All in all you're just another brick in the wall.*

Maybe they have lots of expensive private schools.

E ▶ 4.2 Read the rest of the article to check your predictions. How many were correct? Match the **highlighted** phrases to photos 1–8.

Yes, I guess the teachers are well qualified, too.

▶ **Tuition fees**? Forget it. Education is free and there are very few private schools.

▶ Classes are small, with rarely more than twenty students. The atmosphere is relaxed (lots of students don't wear uniforms or even shoes, only socks!), but students rarely **behave badly**. They hardly ever get kicked out of class or **cheat on exams**.

▶ Students in grades one through nine spend a lot of time each week taking classes in **subjects** such as art, music, and cooking. This helps to generate interest and motivate students.

▶ In Finland, kids have a lighter **schedule** than American students and do less **homework**, too— half an hour per day, tops. Having too much homework, they believe, can interfere with a child's passion for learning.

▶ During the first few years of school, students don't take tests. Instead, they get continuous feedback and a **report card** twice a year so their parents know if they're doing well. Students are actively encouraged to make mistakes and learn by doing.

▶ If students get low grades and **fail* a test**, they have extra support and **one-on-one tutoring**, if necessary. And it works really well. Every classroom has a teaching assistant to help students who are experiencing difficulties and everyone makes progress.

▶ What really makes the difference, though, is the status teaching enjoys in Finland. Education is the most competitive professional field in Finland— more so than medicine and law—and you must have a master's degree if you want to become a teacher.

* the opposite of *pass*

② **Vocabulary** School life

A Check the correct *verb + noun* collocations. Then scan the article in **1E** and *Common mistakes* to check.

	do	get	make	take	
1					a class / tests
2					a low / high grade
3					homework
4					kicked out of class
5					mistakes
6					well (in school)

🖊 **Common mistakes**

doing
My wife is ~~making~~ an MBA.

take
She'll have to ~~make~~ an exam at the end.

passes
If she ~~gets~~ the exam, she'll get a promotion at work.

make
She hopes she doesn't ~~do~~ too many mistakes.

B 🔘 **Make it personal** Follow the instructions.

1 In pairs, use the **highlighted** phrases and collocations in the article to compare the Finnish system with yours. How many differences can you find? Which would you introduce in your country?

They have one-on-one tutoring sometimes. We don't get that if we fail a test.

2 Describe your ideal school, its policies, and schedule. Who came up with the best ideas? Any disagreements?

It'd be a nice modern building. We would only do a little homework every day and not take a lot of tests. And I think uniforms are a good idea.

No way! I love wearing my own clothes.

4.2 What's the ideal age to go to college?

① Listening

A ▶4.3 ▶ Listen to / Watch the trailer of a documentary about the education system in the U.S. Is it mostly positive or negative?

B ▶4.3 ▶ Listen / Watch again and check the three problems mentioned. Ignore the second column for now. Does it make you want to study there?

	The U.S.	My school
Too much homework.		
Too much pressure to get into a good university.		
Overcrowded classrooms.		
Badly paid and demotivated teachers.		
Too much emphasis on tests and grades.		
Poor use of technology.		
Discipline problems.		
Not enough career counseling.		

② Grammar *too / enough*

A Read the phrases in **1B** and the rules in the grammar box. Then correct the mistakes in the typical student errors 1–9 below.

1	*too* = more than necessary	*Our classes start too early.* *The classrooms get much too hot.*
2	*enough* = the necessary amount	*There was enough time to check my work.* *Do you work hard enough?*
3	*not enough* = less than necessary	*There aren't enough chairs for everyone.* *I wasn't sitting close enough to see.*

too goes before an adjective or adverb
(not) enough goes after an adjective but before a noun

→ **Grammar 4A** p.144

                   a lot of

1 My school was ~~too~~ fun. I really enjoyed it.

2 Are there windows enough in your classroom?

3 It was a too hard class. I didn't understand anything.

4 There was not money enough to buy new projectors.

5 I have too many friends at school. I feel lucky!

6 My teacher is too helpful. She's really friendly as well.

7 This is too difficult homework. I can't do it.

8 This exercise was very easy. It wasn't enough challenging for me.

9 I gave up Chinese because it was a too difficult language.

B 🔵 **Make it personal** Complete the *My school* column in **1B**. In pairs, share your experiences. Overall, are your feelings positive or negative? Any big differences?

> *At my school, students have too much homework. It takes me four or five hours a day.*

> *Well, when I was in high school, I had a lot of homework, too.*

C ⭕ **Make it personal** **Read the Education Debate statements.**
1 How much do you agree with them? (1 = strongly agree, 5 = completely disagree)
2 🔊 Research online to support your ideas.
3 In pairs, share your opinions and evidence. Do you have similar ideas?
4 Share your thoughts with the class. Any disagreements?

🎵 *Baby, we don't stand a chance,*
It's sad but it's true,
I'm way too good at goodbyes.

Education Debate

(1) Pressure and competitiveness are positive for students.
(2) Technology helps students learn better.
(3) Training good teachers is the best investment a country can make.
(4) There are too many problems with my country's education system.

I think too much pressure can be very stressful for students.

You're absolutely right, but without enough competition, students can get lazy.

③ Vocabulary College life

A **Match the highlighted words in the website article below to their definitions.**

1 _____ to specialize in a subject in college
2 _____ to begin again
3 _____ money to pay for your education
4 _____ to enter
5 _____ your main subject of study
6 _____ to stop going to

B ▶ **4.4 Reread and match classic mistakes 1–6 to the typical examples. Listen to check.**
Have you, or anyone you know, made these mistakes?

A backup plan might be a good idea, in case 'being a celebrity' doesn't work out.....

CAREERS ADVISOR

WAYS TO PICK THE **WRONG CAREER**

Are you going to be a graduate soon? Choosing a career is one of the most important decisions you'll ever make, so you'd better do it right. Here are six mistakes to avoid.

BY GABI WATSON

Classic mistakes

1 Living someone else's dream.
2 Doing what everybody else is doing.
3 Following your head, not your heart.
4 Being afraid to make big changes.
5 Being afraid of failing.
6 Not planning for the future.

Typical examples

☐ "I can't throw away $40,000, drop out of college, forget about my business major, and start over."

☐ "I'd love to get a scholarship to go to Harvard, but it's so hard I won't even try."

☐ "All my friends will major in business, so that's what I'll do."

☐ "My parents have always wanted me to get into medical school. I can't disappoint them, and they are desperate for me to succeed."

☐ "I'd love to get a degree in music. I've already got my intermediate piano certificate, but what will I do when I graduate? How will I get a decent job?"

☐ "I have all the education I need. I'm not illiterate! It's time for fun, fun, fun!"

C ⭕ **Make it personal** **Complete 1–5 with words from A. In pairs, ask and answer. Any disagreements?**
1 If you could get a _scholarship_ to study anywhere in the world, where would you go?
2 How difficult is it to _____ a good college in your country?
3 What did you / would you like to _____ at college? Why?
4 Do you know anyone who _____ college? How did things go for him / her?
5 If you could _____ at high school, what would you change?

I'd study gastronomy at the Sorbonne in Paris!

⭕ **Common mistake**

I am graduated from law school. =
I majored in law. /
I have a law degree.

4.3 What do you regret not having done?

① Listening

A In pairs, discuss the questions.

1 What kinds of regrets do people sometimes have about school?
2 Guess what these three people studied / are studying? What might they regret now?

B ▶ 4.5 Listen to three interviews about career choices and complete 1–3.

1 Justin says he should have studied _____ instead of _____.

2 Zoe studies _____, but she says she _____ writing.

3 George dropped out of _____ and became a _____.

C In pairs, do you know anybody who had trouble choosing a career? Are they happy now?

> Yes, me! I tried three completely different jobs until I found the right one for me.

> Really? What did you do?

② Grammar *should have*

A ▶ 4.6 Match the sentence halves. Listen to check. Any resonate with you?

1 Dad wanted me to follow in his footsteps, but	☐ I should have <u>chosen</u> another major.
2 I'm way too old now.	☐ I should have <u>gone</u> to music school years ago.
3 Basically, journalism's not my thing.	☐ I shouldn't have <u>listened</u> to him.
4 I know it was a stupid decision, and	☐ Should I have <u>persevered</u> a little more?
5 Every day I wake up and ask myself:	☐ I should have <u>thought</u> about it more carefully.

B Reread 1–5 in **A** and the grammar box. Then answer 1–2.

1 What form are the underlined verbs in? Complete the form below.
   subject + *should (not)* + *have* + _____
2 How do you form questions?

Common mistakes

have
I should ˅ studied English when I was a kid.

learning
I regret ~~to~~ not ~~learn~~ English before.

> Use **should have** to express regret about something in the past.
>
> *I should have thought about it more carefully.* (= I didn't think about it carefully, and I'm sorry.)
> *I shouldn't have listened to him.* (= I did listen to him, and I regret that.)
>
> Also use **should have** to ask for or give advice about a past event.
>
> *What should I have studied instead?*
> *You should have been more open.*
> *You shouldn't have kept it secret.*
>
> → **Grammar 4B** p.144

C ▶4.7 *Should've* is common in informal speech and writing. Listen and write down regrets 1–5. Notice the weak sound in the contractions /ʃʊdəv/ and /ʃʊdntəv/. In pairs, practice saying the sentences dramatically!

1   *We should've gone by train.*

♫ *Too young, too dumb to realize that I should have bought you flowers and held your hand.*

D Think of four regrets about your school days. Share them with your partner and then the class. What is the most common / unusual regret?

I shouldn't have missed so many classes.   *Me, too. I should have participated more.*

E In pairs, write two *should have / shouldn't have* captions for each photo. Compare with other pairs. Choose the best caption for each photo.

I should have stayed home with Mom!

Exam **F**

F 🔘 **Make it personal** *Oops, I did it again!* We've all done things we regretted later. What's your story?

1   Choose a topic below and prepare your story. Include a lie.
2   In groups, share your stories. Can you spot the lie?

Your hair / looks	Dis**as**trous vacations	Eating / drinking	Things you bought
Things you said	Relationships	Missed opportunities	Studies Career

I shouldn't have told my sister I didn't like her new dress.

Why would you say such a thing? I think you're lying about that!

4.4 What would you do if you won a million dollars?

① Listening

A Match the two halves of the quotes. Which ones do you like the most? Why?

1	If I had my life to live over,	☐ you'll probably end up somewhere else.
2	If you never try,	☐ live as if you'll die today.
3	If you don't know where you're going,	☐ you'd never think a negative thought.
4	If you realized how powerful your thoughts were,	☐ you'll always get what you've always got.
5	Dream as if you will live forever;	☐ I'd dare to make more mistakes next time.
6	If you always do what you've always done,	☐ you'll never learn.

I like number 4. Positive thinking is very powerful.

B Look at photos 1–6. What are the people's aspirations? Match them to these categories.

Career	Education / skills	Family life	Health and fitness	Travel

C How can these people achieve their goals? Do you have any similar goals?

This couple want to own their own property.

They'll have to save a lot. Buying an apartment is so expensive. I'll never be able to get my own place.

D ▶ 4.8 Listen to three people talking about their goals and aspirations. Match them to the photos in **B** and complete what they say.

Speaker 1: My big dream is …
Speaker 2: My main wish is …
Speaker 3: My **ul**timate aim is …

E ▶ 4.8 Listen again and complete 1–6 with the verb forms. There's one extra. Who do you think will achieve their goal?

'll go **back**packing	'll prove	didn't train	were
work hard	wouldn't be able	'll have	

1 If I didn't live at home, I _____ to save anything.
2 If I _____ and save my money, I'll see the benefits later.
3 If there _____ nine or ten continents, I would still want to visit each one!
4 If I save enough this year, I _____ around Southeast Asia.
5 If I pass this level, I _____ to myself that I can do anything I want.
6 If I _____ in martial arts, I wouldn't be the person I am now.

F 🔘 **Make it personal** In groups. Do you know anyone who has achieved their dream? What are your current aspirations? Share your best stories.

My ultimate aim is to be a DJ.

If I could turn back time, If I could find the way, I'd take back all those words that hurt you, And you'd stay.

② Grammar First and second conditional

A Study the examples in the grammar box and complete the rules with these words.

"unreal" or impossible   real and possible   past   present (x2)   future

---

First conditional

if + simple present, *will* + infinitive

If I have time, I'll come and visit you.

Use the first conditional to talk about something that is [1]_____ .
The *if* clause uses a [2]_____ tense and talks about a [3]_____ situation.

Second conditional

if + simple past, *would* + infinitive

If you had to spend a year with just one person, who would it be?

Use the second conditional to talk about something that is [4]_____ .
The *if* clause uses a [5]_____ tense and talks about a [6]_____ situation.

*Remember: use the zero conditional (*if* + present simple, present simple) for facts or things that are generally true.*
If you heat ice, it melts.
Don't tell me you need me if you don't believe it. (Ed Sheeran)

➡ **Grammar 4C** p.144

B Look back at the quotations in **1A**. Is each one in the first or second conditional?

C ▶4.9 Circle the correct alternative to make either first or second conditional sentences. Listen to check, and then repeat.

1 If I **have / did have / had** more time, I **'d practice / did practice / practice** the piano more.
2 If you **'ll save / would save / save** money now, you **'d have / 'll have / had** a good pension when you retire.
3 If we **knew / 'd known / know** the answer, we **told / 'd tell / tell** you.
4 You **are / 'll be / were** late if you **didn't take / won't take / don't take** the bus.
5 I **bought / 'd buy / 'll buy** an apartment if I **have / 'll have / 'd have** enough money.

Common mistakes

If you ~~will~~ study hard, you will pass your test.

    had
If I ~~would have~~ more space, I'd get a dog.

I'll be at school tomorrow unless I~~'d~~ still feel ill.
    I

D In teams of two, race around the game. Write an ending for each segment before you go again. Which team can get to the end first?

START: If I don't go out this weekend … | I'll get up early tomorrow … | If I found a wallet … | If I don't pass my exams … | I'd be really excited …
Toss a coin … | Heads move 1 space | Tails move 2 spaces
FINISH: If I knew the future … | I won't complain … | If I didn't have a smart phone … | If my team wins … | If I could learn something new …

E 🔵 **Make it personal** Think of a goal you have. Use the categories in **1B** to help you.

1 What is your goal and why? Prepare your answers to these questions.

What is your goal? What are you going to do to get there?
Why do you want to achieve this? What will the challenges / difficulties be?
How will you feel if you achieve your dream? And if you don't?

2 In pairs, share your goals. Ask and answer follow-up questions. Any similar ones? Who has the most unusual goals?

If I get my driver's license soon, I'll be able to get a better job.

What kind of job would you get if you passed your test?

4.5 What makes someone a genius?

ID Skills   Predicting and checking predictions

A Look at the photo and headline. Guess what the items below refer to.

5,000	IQ (intelligence quotient)	autism	trouble sleeping
learning disability	researcher	Stephen Hawking	huge equations

Maybe he earns $5,000 a day?

B Read in pairs to check. A: Read paragraph 1, B: Paragraph 2. Share what you remember. Then repeat. A: Read paragraph 3, B: Paragraphs 4 and 5.

SMARTER THAN EINSTEIN?
Meet the 19-year-old who might change the way we see the world

1 Jacob Barnett is what we might call a genius. He has an IQ of 170 and, in his free time, is developing an expanded version of the theory of relativity. Not bad for a 19-year-old, especially one who was diagnosed with Asperger's syndrome (a mild form of autism) and has trouble sleeping because he constantly sees numbers in his head! Not bad at all!

2 At the age of two, Jacob—or Jake, as most people call him—still hadn't learned how to talk, so his parents suspected he might have a learning disability. As he grew up, however, they realized their son was actually incredibly gifted. By the age of three, Jacob could easily solve 5,000-piece jigsaw puzzles, calculate the volume of the cereal box while having breakfast, and learn by heart every single highway on the Indiana state road map. Just a few years later, while other kids were playing soccer or watching TV, Jake was having fun drawing complex geometrical shapes and writing huge equations on the living room windows.

3 By the time he had reached fifth grade, aged eight, it was clear that his mathematical ability was unusually high (at the level of a doctorate degree, actually!), so he dropped out of elementary school, taught himself all the math he needed to know in only one week, skipped high school, and enrolled at Purdue University, where he was allowed to attend advanced astrophysics classes. Five years later, Jake moved beyond the level of what his professors could teach him, so he eventually became a paid researcher—at only 13!

4 After college, Jake moved to Perimeter Institute, a place where the world's top thinkers, including Stephen Hawking, have taught. Jake was Perimeter's youngest ever student and submitted his master's thesis at 15. Today, he's still at Perimeter and the University of Waterloo.

5 For now, though, Jake's long-term plans are probably similar to the average teenager: to be happy doing something he finds challenging and rewarding. I wonder if he blames his autism for his early difficulties. If he wasn't autistic, however, he wouldn't be at the place he is right now. Autism is his way of viewing the world and it's because of that that he's able to do what he does so well.

C ▶4.10 True (T), false (F), or not mentioned (NM)? Listen and reread to check.
1 Jacob's speech developed when he was two.
2 Jacob enjoys playing soccer.
3 Jacob didn't attend high school.
4 Jacob has a "normal" social life.
5 Jake's very happy with his life.

D ▶4.11 In pairs, try to pronounce these words. Then listen to check. Any difficult ones?

3 syllables	theory	actually	constantly	easily
4 syllables	ability	incredibly	unusually	eventually
5 syllables	relativity	elementary	disability	

E ▶4.12 Play *Guess the word!* Listen to the first part of the sentence, then say the missing word from **D** after the beep.

Guess the word!
1 point = the right word
2 points = the right word and stress

F ○ Make it personal   In pairs, answer 1–3. Any similar views?
1 Do you know anybody with a very high IQ?
2 Would you like to be like Jacob or have kids like him?

Apparently, anyone with over 160 on an IQ test is 'profoundly gifted'. My dad scored 161!

How do you deal with criticism?

(ID) in Action Sympathizing and criticizing

A ▶4.13 Listen to four dialogues and match them to the situations in the photos.

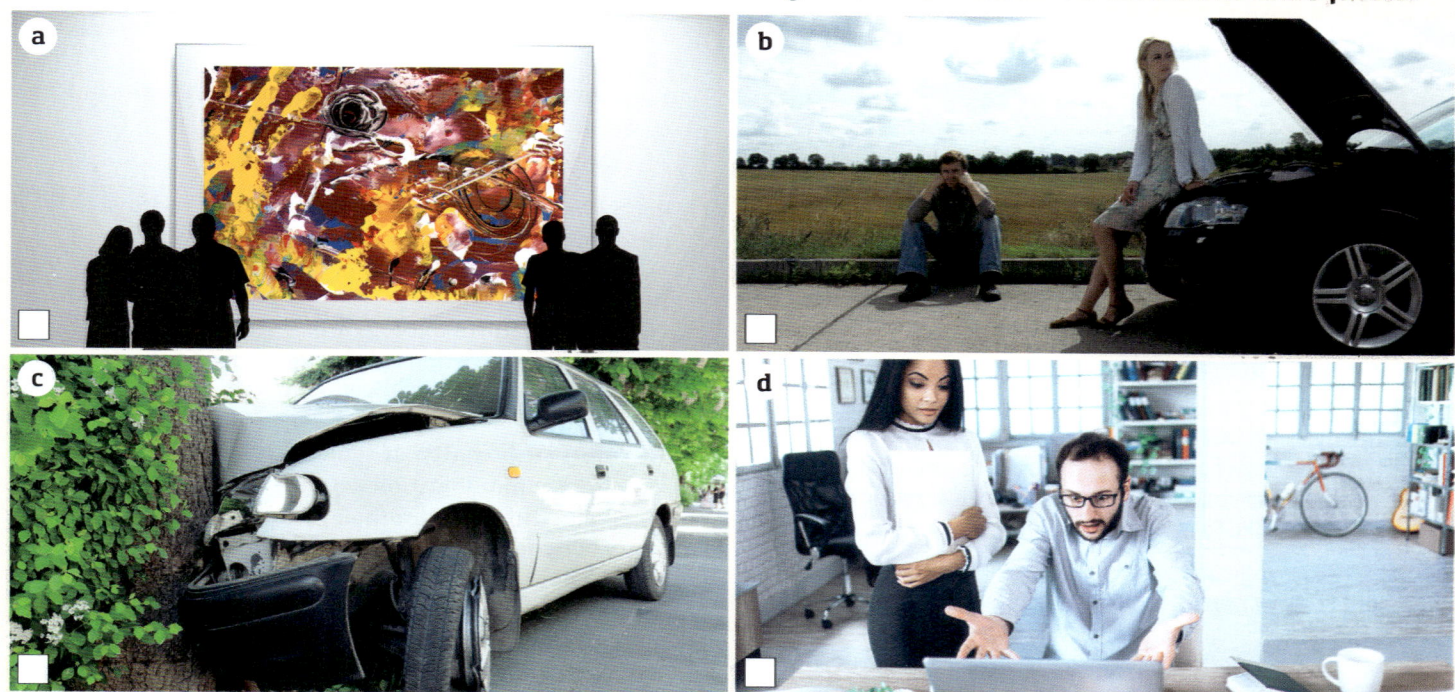

B ▶4.14 Listen again. After each beep, predict the next line from those in the chart. How many correct guesses?

Dialogue	Sympathy	Criticism
1	It could have been worse.	Will you ever learn?
2	Don't let it get you down.	You should have known better.
3	What's done is done.	How could you do such a thing?
4	It's not the end of the world.	What were you thinking?

C ▶4.15 Listen and repeat the expressions in **B**. Copy the intonation for each. In pairs, practice the expressions.

Common mistake

have
He shouldn't ~~had~~ bought that car.

D In pairs, answer questions 1–3 for each situation.
1 What should / shouldn't each person have done? *The first person should have …*
2 Who do you feel most sorry for?
3 Have you or people you know ever had any problems like these?

E ⏺ **Make it personal** In pairs, tell a new story. Then change roles. Who was the most sympathetic listener? Whose story was funniest?
A: Choose a context (a–f) and plan what to say.
B: Ask follow-up questions and react to A's story using sentences from **B**.

a an accident that could have been a lot worse
b an image or message you sent by mistake
c something you bought on impulse
d something important you forgot / missed
e an unpleasant meeting
f a disastrous meal / vacation

 I should've known better than to cheat a friend, And waste a chance that I've been given. So I'm never gonna dance again, The way I danced with you.

Writing 4 A blog

A Use the title and photo to guess what the blog post will be about.

> *It might be about contractions or funny expressions.*

B Read the post. Did you guess correctly? Do you think it is too late for the writer?

"Shoulda, Coulda, Woulda"

"I shouldn't have done this." "I should've done that." (a) _____ Regret is something we all experience in life. I know, I have tons, but what's my biggest regret? My biggest regret is my choice of career. Yep, my career! Pretty big thing to get wrong, huh? Well, I did. (b) _____ Let's go back …

When I was eight years old, I started to learn to play the piano. I did it because my big bro was having lessons, too. Turns out I was way better at it than he was! (c) _____ Really, good, in fact. By the time I was 14, I had passed my grade 8 test. I loved it and played whenever and wherever I could. I started to compose my own stuff, and even had a gig playing in a local restaurant when I was 16. The tips were great! (d) _____

At 18, I had to make tough decisions. What did I want to do with the rest of my life? At that age, I was pretty focused on money. I wanted to do something I knew would give me a good income and stable future. (e) _____ playing piano in a restaurant wasn't that. So, I took a finance degree and I became a financial advisor, but I really regret that now. I had the dough, the stable future, but ten years down the line, what's missing?

I miss the music! I work long, hard hours and my piano is gathering dust. I hardly have time to play. (f) _____ I shouldn't have looked for the money. I should've stuck with something that gave me joy and fulfillment, but I guess it's too late now.

What do you think? Have you any shoulda, coulda, wouldas of your own? (g) _____

C Match 1–7 to a–g in the blog.

1 You guessed it,
2 Please share your regrets, and if you've managed to moved on from them!
3 Ever find yourself using these words?
4 How could I have let go of something so important to me?
5 Thank you to the generous patrons of Mama's Italian.
6 So, where did I take a wrong turn?
7 (Sorry, Mitch!)

D Read *Write it right!* Then match 1–7 in **C** to the different features commonly found in blogs.

✓ Write it right!

Common features of blogs are:
- rhetorical questions (a question asked to make a point rather than elicit an answer)
- humor
- informal / "chatty" language
- direct communication with the reader
- asking the reader for their ideas / opinions / experiences

E Find informal words and phrases in the blog to match the more formal ones below. Why are blogs written using this kind of informal language?

1	should have, could have, would have	5	brother
2	many	6	considerably
3	That's correct	7	job
4	Isn't it?	8	money

F Study the highlighted phrases in the blog. Then complete these sentences with the correct form of the verbs.

> take go out not listen send

1 I regret _____ to my heart.
2 I shouldn't have _____ last night
3 I would've _____ my dad's advice if I'd known.
4 I regret _____ that email.

G *Your turn!* Write a blog post in 120–180 words.

Before	Choose a regret to write about.
While	Use informal language and the *Write it right!* tips.
After	Ask a partner to read your blog post, check spelling and punctuation, and leave a comment. Then send it to your teacher.

4 AIQ: Artificial Intelligence Quotient!  Café

1 Before watching

A Match 1–6 to their definitions a–f.

1 disciplinary action   4 outcome
2 calculated   5 procrastination
3 input   6 sophomore

a ☐ the result of something
b ☐ delaying things, not managing time
c ☐ punishment for breaking a rule
d ☐ planned
e ☐ a second year college student (U.S.)
f ☐ enter data into a computer

B ◉ Make it personal Check the bills you pay monthly. Any paper bills or is it all online?

☐ cell phone   ☐ insurance   ☐ water
☐ electricity   ☐ Internet   ☐ other
☐ gas   ☐ mortgage

The only mail I still get are fliers advertising services!

C Guess which four bills August gets, and what's in the large envelope.

2 While watching

A Watch to 3:19 and check your ideas, and then check the three synonyms you hear for *intelligent / intelligence*.

☐ brilliant   ☐ crazy   ☐ Einstein
☐ genius   ☐ IQ   ☐ insane
☐ socially gifted

B Watch again and complete 1–5.

1 If you hadn't _____ the phone, I would've totally _____ insane.
2 Whatever happens, you _____ have done things any differently.
3 If only I hadn't been _____ of class ... for _____.
4 Look, if I'd _____ more confidence, I would have _____ it immediately.
5 He _____ 've made me get up.

C How does his AIQ machine work? Order these steps, 1–5, then watch from 3:19 to the end to check. Do you think the letter will contain good news or bad?

☐ He inputs the presence or absence of people.
☐ The robot / machine calculates the outcome.
☐ It sends him a message.
☐ August types in his situation.
☐ He enters data about the scholarship.

3 After watching

A True (T) or false (F)? Correct the false statements.

1 August tried to contact several people.
2 Rory gives August good advice.
3 August was punished for a disciplinary action.
4 Daniel woke August up early.
5 August's program doesn't have a name yet.
6 August was in a higher physics class than Rory.
7 August lacks self-confidence.
8 His project results were great.
9 August won a scholarship for $25,000.

B Check all the correct answers. Do you ever procrastinate like this?

Yes, quite often. It took me a long time to decide to ...

1 Why doesn't August want to open the letter?
a ☐ He's not confident.
b ☐ He's worried about the outcome.
c ☐ He already knows the result.

2 Why is August the "king of procrastination"?
a ☐ He keeps changing the subject.
b ☐ His project is incomplete.
c ☐ He won't open the letter.

C Why do we say it? Write C (change a subject), E (express regret), G (get a subject back on track), R (reassure) or S (speculate about the past).

1 ☐ If you hadn't ..., I would've ...
2 ☐ If only I hadn't ...
3 ☐ You couldn't have done things any differently ...
4 ☐ Hey, remember that time ...
5 ☐ Stop changing the subject and get on with it.
6 ☐ If I'd had more confidence, I would've ...

D ◉ Make it personal In pairs, use the expressions in C to share past regrets or experiences. Any coincidences?

If I'd had more confidence, I would have sung at the karaoke competition.

You never know. The winner wasn't that good.

Do you think you'd have won?

R2 Grammar and Vocabulary

A *Picture dictionary.* **Cover the words on the pages below and remember.**

pages	
30–31	6 features of a city
34	8 social rules in Hong Kong
36	10 urban problems
38	5 more active listening phrases
40	10 verbs from regulations
44	8 school words & 16 school subjects
55	5 types of shopper
160	2 words for each diphthong (not the picture words); say and spell them

B ▶R2.1 **Complete 1–6 with the correct form of the verbs in parentheses. Listen to check.**

1 If you _____ as I tell you, you _____ into trouble. (do / get)
2 I can't understand what he's saying. If he _____ more slowly, I _____ more. (speak, understand)
3 When we _____ out of the restaurant, my car _____ there. Someone _____ it. (come / not be / take)
4 The authorities _____ that the athlete _____ drugs for months so they _____ him. (discover / use / disqualify)
5 I _____ to visit you if I _____ enough money, but I'm broke. (come / have)
6 I was really excited when I _____ in Barcelona. I _____ to it for ages. (arrive / look forward)

C ▶R2.2 **In groups, imagine the rest of the story in pictures 1–3. Use a variety of tenses. Listen to compare stories and write the six past verb forms you hear. Have you had an experience like this?**

The three of them had spent the day packing all their camping stuff, and then they took the bus to the festival.

D 🔘 Make it personal **In pairs, circle *a*, *b* or *c* for 1–5 and explain your reasons.**

1 Homework from this class:
   a too much b the right amount c not enough
2 Tuition fees in your country:
   a too low b a fair price c not low enough
3 Green spaces in your city:
   a too small b perfect size c not big enough
4 Buses or trains in your town / city:
   a too many b a good number c not enough
5 Tourists in your capital city:
   a too many b the amount c not enough

I'm happy with the homework. And you?

Hmm. I don't think we do enough.

E ▶R2.3 **Match 1–5 to a–e to make short exchanges. Imagine who is speaking in each one. Listen to check.**

1 Are we lost?
2 That was a dirty game.
3 I'm sorry. I shouldn't have said that.
4 I can't believe I crashed my car.
5 What! Vic's going out with Jill?

a ☐ You didn't know? Forget I said anything. I shouldn't have mentioned it.
b ☐ You really should have known better than to drive that fast.
c ☐ Yes! There should have been three red cards.
d ☐ Maybe. I think we should have turned left.
e ☐ I agree. But we all say stupid things sometimes.

F **Correct the mistakes in each sentence. Check your answers in units 3 and 4.**

✏️ Common mistakes

1 *I'm graduated of math.* (2 mistakes)
2 *If you would got up earlier, you wouldn't lose the bus every morning!* (2 mistakes)
3 *"Did you do many mistakes?" "I think no."* (2 mistakes)
4 *He loves traveling. He's gone in every place in Europe.* (2 mistakes)
5 *L.A. is so big city and the people are such nice!* (3 mistakes)
6 *Studying hard don't mean you will get the test, but it helps.* (2 mistakes)
7 *I feel bad. I shouldn't to have ate all that pizza.* (2 mistakes)
8 *You should went at the party last night.* (2 mistakes)
9 *He was angry because he was waiting during 40 minutes before the police arrived.* (2 mistakes)
10 *People who goes to Miami are often surprised because they haven't expected Spanish speakers.* (2 mistakes)

Skills practice

A Read and listen to the four stories ▶3.14 on p. 41 and underline any words that are difficult to hear / understand. Listen again. Are they difficult because:
a these words link to the following word?
b they're unstressed and virtually disappear?
c their pronunciation changes in context?

B ▶R2.4 Listen and complete extracts 1–6 from videos in units 3 and 4.
1 Kissing _____ cheek _____ hugging _____ not practiced.
2 Gifts _____ never opened _____ person _____ gave them.
3 Fill _____ tea cups _____ others before pouring _____ own cup, _____ their cups _____ not empty.
4 In America, _____ you don't earn _____ money, something _____ wrong.
5 Everyone expects _____ superheroes.
6 You have _____ smart and you have _____ involved _____ arts.

C ▶R2.5 Listen to and imitate each phrase.

D Look at the photo and title. Guess what these words refer to. Read the text to check your predictions.

Netflix   12 years old   Spain   Calvin Klein
Drake and Maroon 5   youngest person ever

Maybe she's the daughter of the owner of Netflix?

E Reread. True (T) or false (F)?
1 Millie Bobbie Brown had won nine awards before *Stranger Things*.
2 She's half English, half Spanish.
3 She has lived in at least three different countries.
4 Her family moved to L.A. a week after she was spotted by a talent agent.
5 She's also also worked as a pop singer and a model.
6 She had appeared in two movies when this article was written.

F ▶R2.6 Cross out the word with the different underlined sound. Listen to check, then in pairs create a funny sentence with the remaining words. Say them slowly, then quickly.
1 afr**ai**d ~~apples~~ **A**sia th**ey** volc**a**no
In Asia they are afraid of an eruption from the volcano.
2 cr**a**zy f**a**shionable st**a**tue t**a**xi tr**a**ffic
3 aw**ay** **eigh**t p**ai**r st**ay** str**aigh**t

G *Role-play.* Social rules
1 In pairs, list three more "social etiquette" rules. Then exchange with another pair.
2 A: You're a tourist. Mime breaking each rule.
B: Explain the rules to A.

H ▶R2.7 ⬤ Make it personal *Question time!*
1 Listen to and answer the 12 lesson titles in units 3 and 4.
2 In pairs, practice asking and answering. Use the map on p. 2–3 and choose the two most interesting questions from units 3 and 4. Which one produces the most interesting conversation?

Which city would you most like to visit? *There are lots of cities I'd love to see, but number one has to be …*

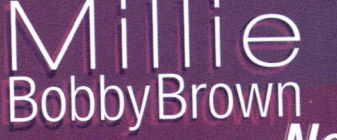

Millie Bobby Brown
Next big thing?

Name: Millie Bobby Brown
Born: 19 February 2004
Occupation: actor and model

Many people say that Millie Bobby Brown is the next big thing in Hollywood. What do they mean? She is already there!

Brown caught the attention of the world in 2016 with her role in the hit Netflix series *Stranger Things*, which she won approximately nine awards for! She achieved that when she was only twelve years old, but she had already acted in five different TV series. Pretty incredible, huh? Well, it's even more amazing when you realize that she was actually born in Spain to English parents, moved to England when she was four, and then to the U.S. when she was

eight. In 2011, she was spotted by a talent agent at a drama class. Her family later moved to L.A. and after only a week, Millie was meeting talent agencies. After only three months in Hollywood, she was given her first TV role.

What a career so far! Millie is extremely hardworking. The adults she works with praise her for her maturity and talent. Although she is so young, she has already played some very challenging roles. Apart from film and TV, she has also starred in music videos with Maroon 5 and Drake and modeled for Calvin Klein. In 2018, she was the youngest person ever included on *Time* magazine's list of the "World's most influential people". In 2019, she'll be in her first movie, *Godzilla: King of the Monsters*.

Watch out for this girl in the future!

5

5.1 Are you a shopaholic?

① Reading

A In pairs, list five things you expect from a store when shopping. Are your shopping habits and expectations similar to your parents'?

I expect good customer service.

Yes, and I like it to be well organized, so I can find things easily.

B Look at the cartoons. Who or what do you think Generation Z is? Read the introduction to the article to check.

GenZ TRANSFORMING THE **SHOPPING EXPERIENCE**

Generation Z, born between 1996 and 2012, came into a digital world with technology at the center of everything. This generation is expected to have a huge impact on the future of shopping. Let's examine how:

WE LEARNED TO SPEAK YOUR LANGUAGE SO YOUR GENERATION WILL PAY ATTENTION TO OUR ADS.

© marketoonist.com

WHAT DO WE KNOW ABOUT GENERATION Z, SO THAT WE CAN GET THEM TO BUY STUFF?

SO FAR, ALL WE KNOW IS THAT THEY HATE BRANDS THAT TRY TO GET THEM TO BUY STUFF.

© marketoonist.com

TECHNOLOGY. Members of Gen Z have a device they interact with constantly so, while shopping, they compare prices, read reviews, and even buy online. They still want to do in-store shopping, but they want an experience, and technology has to be at the center of this experience. Stores need smart phone self-checkouts, interactive screens, and virtual try-ons. A discount code and loyalty programs are an incentive and should be accessible online. Gen Z expects free Wi-Fi in stores. In fact, it is wise for stores to provide charging stations, so shoppers can keep their batteries full.

HIGH EXPECTATIONS. Gen Z is demanding. If the in-store experience doesn't meet their expectations, they move on. They want a store that embraces technology and makes products easy to test, but they still want human interaction. They have less patience and will instantly share a poor experience on social media. Attractive prices are still essential, or they'll just have Amazon deliver it to their door, again!

INFLUENCERS. Gen Z is influencing the decisions of the whole family. Apparently 70 percent of parents ask their kids for advice before they shop. Gen Z trusts friends rather than advertising and has a strong social media presence. Gen Zers post their thoughts and images of products on Snapchat, Instagram, and YouTube and want to connect directly with the brand. There is even a rising trend in videos, which are posted online, of shoppers displaying items they have recently bought and talking about them. Brands should use this user-generated content if they want to encourage brand loyalty with Generation Z.

C In groups, brainstorm how you think Generation Z is changing shopping. Then each read a different paragraph and report back. Were your ideas mentioned?

Well, they probably all shop online and don't go to real stores anymore.

D ▶ 5.1 Listen, reread, and give the author's answers to 1—5. Do you agree with them all?

1 What should stores provide Gen Z shoppers with for in-store shopping?
2 What does Gen Z expect from a store in addition to technology?
3 What happens when Gen Z has a negative shopping experience?
4 How does Gen Z influence their parents?
5 How can stores encourage brand loyalty?

E 🔘 Make it personal How might shopping evolve in the next 30 years? Will there still be any small stores?

Maybe we'll have chip implants so we won't need cash or credit cards.

⟳ Common mistakes

expect everything to be
My parents ~~wait that all is~~ really cheap.

most successful brand
Apple is the ~~mark of most success~~.

② Vocabulary Shopping

 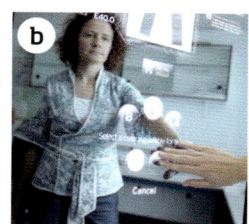   

A Match the highlighted words in the article to the photos.

B Complete 1–8 with the words in **A**. Which ones do you hear / say often?

1 There's no need to stand in that long line. They have _____ here.
2 My battery is running out. Are there _____ in here?
3 Smart brands use customers' _____, such as YouTube videos and blog posts, to advertise their products.
4 I would rather do _____ than shop online. At least you can try things on.
5 I've got a _____ for that store—you get 10% off everything today.
6 I can't get online to check the reviews. They don't even have _____ in here!
7 These glasses looked good on me with _____, but they don't look good in real life.
8 I don't have much _____ except for my cell phone—I'd never consider getting any other make.

C 🗣 **Make it personal** In pairs, answer 1–3.

1 Are you a member of Generation Z?
2 Which points in the article do you agree / disagree with, and why?
3 How many of the people in the class shop like a Gen Z?

I agree with a lot of it, but I still prefer to buy things online. It's so much easier!

③ Listening

A Do you ever post images or videos of things you buy on social media? Why (not)? Have you seen (YouTube) vloggers describe things they have bought?

No way, what for? Who would care about my shopping?

B ▶5.2 You're going to listen to a radio program about "shopping haul" and "anti-shopping haul" videos on YouTube. Guess what these videos are.

C Listen again and complete 1–5.

1 A "shopping haul" video shows a vlogger _____ they've bought.
2 People watch these videos because it's satisfying to see how _____.
3 In an "anti-haul" video, vloggers talk about products they don't plan to buy because they think they are _____.
4 Kimberly Clark's first "anti-haul" video has had _____ views. Now there are over _____ "anti-haul" videos online.
5 Research shows that Millennials would much rather _____.

D 🗣 **Make it personal** In pairs, make a "shopping haul" or "anti-shopping haul" video. Follow these instructions.

1 🔊 Decide which type of video to make. Search online for examples of these videos to give you ideas.

- **Shopping haul:** Make notes about products you have bought recently (where, how much, why, how happy you are with them, etc.)
- **Anti-shopping haul:** Make notes about products you don't think people should buy, explaining your reasons why.

2 Practice what you want to say. Then record yourselves using a cell phone or act out your video for the class. Who made the best one? Any future YouTube stars?

 **Common mistake**

Buying
~~Buy~~ things online is much ~~more easy~~.
easier

Today, we're gonna be showing you things that we're not actually gonna buy, then explain why.

5.2 What shouldn't you have spent money on?

① Listening

A How do people get into debt? List five things they can do to get out of debt.

B ▶5.3 Listen to a college graduate giving a talk to some freshmen about debt. Answer the question in **A** for her. Did she mention any of your ideas?

> *She was 18 when she started getting into debt.*

C ▶5.3 Listen again. What is the significance of the following numbers?

| 18 | 25 | 30 | 50 | 2,000 | 12,000 | 20,000 |

D Match the verb and noun collocations. Check your answers in ▶5.3 on p. 167.

Money collocations		
1 take out / pay back / pay off	☐	debt
2 go on	☐	money
3 run out	☐	of money
4 waste	☐	a shopping spree
5 be in / get into / get out of	☐	a loan / a credit card / an overdraft

E 🔘 **Make it personal** Is there a lot of debt in your country?

> *Absolutely, and not only students. Most of us spend our lives owing money to someone.*

② Pronunciation Silent consonants

A ▶5.4 Pronounce these words. Listen to check. Know any others?

| de~~b~~t | lis~~t~~en | cas~~t~~le | thum~~b~~ | su~~b~~tle | hig~~h~~ | boug~~h~~t |

> **Common mistake**
>
> ~~had~~
> If the word hadn't
> silent letters, I would
> have pronounced it
> correctly.

B ▶5.5 Listen and cross out the two silent consonants in 1–5. In pairs, say the sentences simultaneously, as fast as you can.
1 I have no doubt you'll be able to pay off your debt.
2 The traffic cop whistled and told me to fasten my seatbelt.
3 It's difficult to understand signs in a foreign language.
4 My neighbors' daughter has moved out.
5 The police will climb the mountain to look for the bomb.

③ Grammar Third conditional

A Look at the example and answer 1–5 in the grammar box.

> *If I'd **listened** to some advice, I wouldn't have **gotten** into financial mess.*
>
> 1 Is she imagining changing the past or the present? Is that possible?
> 2 Did she take advice? Did she get into a financial mess? Can she change what happened?
> 3 What form are the bold verbs: simple past or past participle?
> 4 What is the full form of *I'd listened*: *I had listened* or *I would listened*?
> 5 Complete the form:
>   *If + subject + had (not) +* _____ *, subject +* _____ *+ past participle + phrase*
>
>   If you are not sure about the result, you can use *might / could have*:
>   *If I'd listened to advice, I might not have gotten into financial mess / could have avoided it.*
>
> → **Grammar 5A** p. 146

♫ *It's a bittersweet symphony, this life.*
Trying to make ends meet.
You're a slave to the money, then you die.

B ▶5.6 **Complete the third conditionals 1–5 with the verbs. Use contractions. Listen, check, and repeat.**

1 If you _____ (tell) me you were in debt, I _____ (lend) you some money.
2 If he _____ (be) more sensible, he _____ (save) more money.
3 I _____ (not buy) a new car even if I _____ (earn) enough money last year.
4 If we _____ (pay) the bill on time, they _____ (not cut off) the electricity.
5 The bank _____ (might give) you a credit card if you _____ (ask) for one.

⊘ **Common mistake**

had
If I ~~would have~~ paid to
park my car, I wouldn't ~~get~~
a parking fine. *have gotten*

C **Make sentences about the speaker in** ▶5.3 **using the third conditional.**

If she hadn't gone to college, she might not have gotten into debt.

D ⬤ **Make it personal** **Think about a mistake you made or something you wish you'd done differently. In pairs, share your stories. Ask follow-up questions. Whose was the biggest mistake?**

If I hadn't played so many video games, I'd have been better at sport!

Which sports would you have played?

④ Reading

A **Look at the photos and read the first three lines of the website. What do you think Volunteer2Zero is?**

B **Read on to check. A: Read the main text, B: Read *How it works*. Then share. Were you right?**

C ▶5.7 **Cover the text and remember the five benefits of Volunteer2Zero. Listen and reread to check. Any surprises?**

Volunteer2Zero

Do you have a student loan?
Wondering how you're going to pay it back?
That's where Volunteer2Zero comes in …

Volunteer2Zero is a crowdfunding idea with a difference. We all know that crowdfunding is getting lots of people to give small amounts of money in order to fund a project. But, with **Volunteer2Zero**, instead of just fund-raising to pay back your debts, you can give a little more in return and help make the world a better place.

With **Volunteer2Zero**, you can reduce your student debt by volunteering. In exchange for your time and skills, you will:

→ receive donations from your community
→ improve your professional skills
→ develop professional contacts
→ improve your community
→ increase your chance of graduating debt-free

HOW IT WORKS

→ You register with us as a volunteer or donor
→ You say where and how much time you can volunteer
→ Our donors decide what help they need and how much to sponsor you
→ You do work in your community and receive donations for every hour you volunteer
→ You pay off your debt and pay back your community. It's simple!
Volunteer2Zero

D ⬤ **Make it personal** **Discuss.**

1 Would Volunteer2Zero work in your country? Is crowdfunding common? Would you register with an organization like this?
2 List three things you could volunteer to do in your community.
3 In pairs, role-play a conversation with someone who got out of debt by joining Volunteer2Zero.

I'd volunteer to help with reading at my local elementary school. I think some parents would donate to V2Z.

If I hadn't joined V2Z, I wouldn't have escaped from debt.

5.3 Have you ever borrowed money from a relative?

① Listening

the website Kickstarter

the Statue of Liberty

Mozart

British rock group Marillion

the Pebble smart watch

Could Kickstarter be something to do with old motorbikes?

A In pairs, share what the photos make you think of. Then guess what they have in common.

B ▶5.8 Listen to a lecture and check your ideas for **A**. Have you ever donated to a crowdfunding project?

My cousin ran a marathon last year to raise money for cancer research. I donated to that.

C ▶5.8 True (T) or false (F)? Listen again to check.
1. Crowdfunding has existed much longer than the Internet.
2. Only wealthy people funded the Statue of Liberty.
3. Crowdfunding has changed a lot over the years.
4. Marillion fans paid for the band's tour and albums.
5. Pebble Technology holds the record for the most money ever raised through crowdfunding.

Let's raise money to clean our polluted river.

D 👤 **Make it personal** In groups, think of a project you could start with crowdfunding and why.
1. Make notes on your ideas. Use these questions to help you.

How will you organize it?	Why should people donate to it?
How much do you want to raise?	What will donors get in return?

2. Present your project to the class. How many people want to "donate" to it? Which one gets the most "donations" from the class?

② Grammar Modals of possibility / probability

A ▶5.9 Try to complete excerpts 1–4. Listen to check.

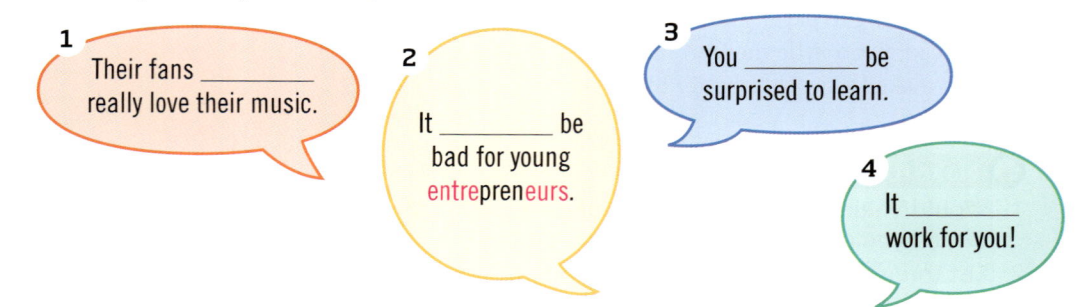

1. Their fans _____ really love their music.
2. It _____ be bad for young entrepreneurs.
3. You _____ be surprised to learn.
4. It _____ work for you!

B Study 1–4 in **A** and check the correct definitions in the grammar box.
Then read the information. Do you find any of these difficult?

	must	can't	might	could
I'm 100% sure this is true.				
I'm 100% sure this isn't true.				
Maybe this is true.				

The opposite of **must** is **can't**. (NOT ~~mustn't~~)
You must be ready for the exam. You've studied a lot.
You can't be ready for the exam. You haven't studied at all.

You can use **may** instead of **might** or **could** in affirmative sentences.
The business may / might / could close because it isn't doing very well.
But **couldn't** does not mean the same as **may not** or **might not**.
The business is doing better so it may not / might not close. (NOT ~~couldn't close~~)

→ **Grammar 5B** p.146

⚡ **Common mistake**

was able to
I ran and ~~could~~ catch the last bus.

Use *was / were* able to to express success in the past.

C Complete these comments about crowdfunding projects with *must* or *can't*.

1 Surely you _____ be serious. You want me to donate $1,000?! You're joking.

2 You _____ be so excited about the project. It's almost fully funded!

3 That _____ be right. It's not possible to fund a business for that little money.

4 You _____ seriously expect people to buy this product! It's a pile of junk.

5 You _____ be really determined. This is the third time you've tried crowdfunding.

D ▶5.10 **Listen to five different extracts. In pairs, guess and note your answers.**

1 Who's Alberto talking to?
2 Where's Laura?
3 What's Ernie talking about?
4 Why's Tony breathing in and out like that?
5 What kind of problem does Susie have?

I think he must be talking to his son.

Hmm ... Not sure. I think he might be talking to a friend.

E ▶5.11 **Listen to the complete conversations and check your guesses. Who's in the most difficult situation?**

F *Fact or fiction?* In pairs, say whether 1–5 may be true.

1 Chewing gum is good for your teeth.
2 An ant can lift fifty times its own weight.
3 The brain is approximately 80% water.
4 Humans are the only living beings that can cry as the result of emotions.
5 You're more likely to have a heart attack on a Monday than on any other day.

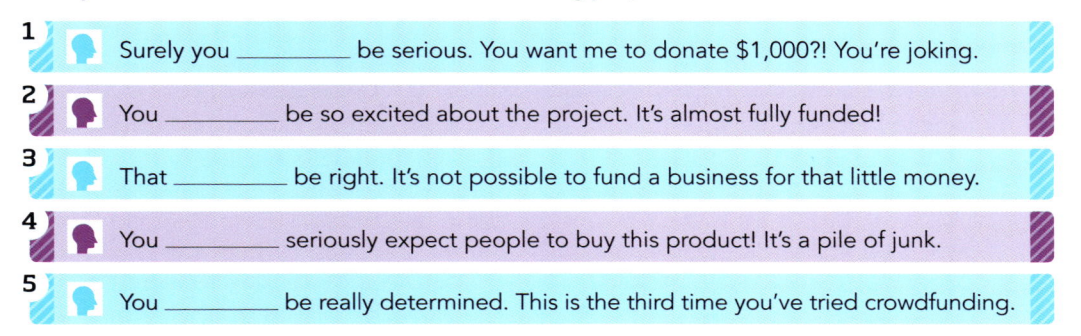

I think the first one might be true, but I'm not really sure.

Really? I actually think it could be bad for your teeth.

G 🔵 **Make it personal** In groups, speculate about each other's lives. Who's the best guesser?

Favorite free time activities?
Favorite stores / restaurants?
Musical taste?
Reasons for learning English?
Soccer fan? If so, what team?
Use of cell phone / the Internet?
How green they are?

You must be quite green. You always bring a reusable bottle of water.

Yeah, and you never use plastic bags.

Yep—you're both right. I'm actually a member of Greenpeace!

5.4 Have you ever bought a useless product?

① Reading

A Listen and read the introduction of an article about infomercials (= information + commercial). The writer:

☐ wants a refund on items she / he bought. ☐ is often entertained by infomercials.

☐ is often disappointed with the products. ☐ is angry about infomercials.

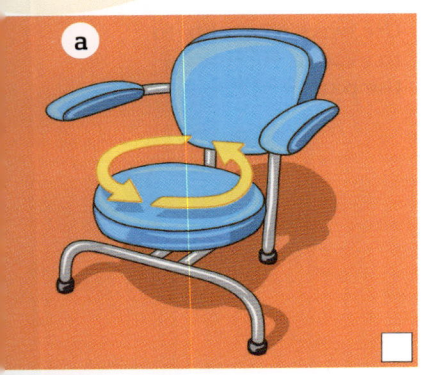

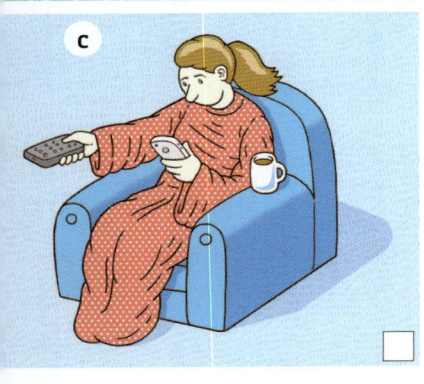

TWO USELESS PRODUCTS I'VE BOUGHT

As far as I'm concerned, infomercials are an unappreciated art form. I mean, they are pure comedy, and who doesn't love to laugh? The truth is, though, that staying up and watching them can seriously interfere with my common sense. You see, I bought apparently useful products that promised to give me the physique of a good-looking fashion model, make me a math genius, and help me pass my exams. Yet, shockingly, guess what: I'm actually heavier now, I still have trouble understanding my credit card statement, and I'm currently taking all my exams again. Now, I don't want to generalize, but here, for your enjoyment, are two of the most useless gadgets I've ever bought.

1 **"READY TO SNUGGLE UP ON THE SOFA?**

But, you can't reach the remote or hold your cup of cocoa! Hug Rug, the blanket with sleeves, is the solution! Hug Rug is a blanket with sleeves, which means you can change channels, have a drink, or check your phone without getting cold. Hug Rug is super-soft to the touch and comes in eight gorgeous bright colors. Enjoy the convenience of free movement while also experiencing the comfort of a warm blanket. Read, watch TV, text your friends, even get takeout with Hug Rug, the blanket with sleeves."

OK, it is really cozy, but it looks ridiculous. And "free movement"?! Once I got into it, I couldn't figure out how to get out. Stick to a blanket.

2 **"FEELING THE EFFECTS OF SITTING AT YOUR DESK ALL DAY?**

It's time to tighten that tummy and get the flexibility you've been dreaming of with the Wonder Chair! Wonder Chair helps you flatten your abdominal muscles, massage your lower back, and improve your fitness. By doing our recommended exercises, you can fully train your upper, lower, and side abs. Help tone your lazy, aching muscles and get rid of your stiff appearance! This remarkable device also offers comfortable support for your spine, thighs, and arms. Don't waste another second! Sit at your desk with the Wonder Chair and wave good-bye to aches, pains and lethargy."

You'd better hope your office mates have a sense of humor. Sadly, mine didn't, so the chair stayed at home, and I got a gym membership.

B ▶5.12 In pairs, each read about one product and match it to a picture. Then tell your partner about it. Listen to check each other's answers.

C Match the underlined words to their definitions.

1	_____ adj.	very beautiful or pleasant
2	_____ adj.	very special, amazing
3	_____ adv.	in fact
4	_____ verb	make flat / level
5	_____ verb	tone / make tighter

6	_____ adv.	now
7	_____ noun	cooked food from a restaurant that you buy to eat somewhere else
8	_____ noun [U]	pleasure
9	_____ adj.	good for nothing

D ▶5.13 Listen to two friends talking about the product that isn't mentioned in the article. Why wasn't she happy with it? Which was the worst purchase?

E 🔒 **Make it personal** Think of an item you bought because of an infomercial / ad. Describe the product and ad to your partner. Why did you buy it? Did it work? Would you recommend it? Why (not)?

> I bought a hairdryer. It didn't work and I wasn't able to send it back.

② Vocabulary Word formation

A Complete the chart with the <mark>highlighted</mark> words from the article. Underline the suffixes.

Nouns	Verbs	Adjectives	Adverbs
enjoyment			

B ▶5.14 Complete 1–8 with forms of the words in parentheses. Listen to check.

1 I bought it on impulse. It was pure ___*madness*___ ! (mad)
2 It can't work the way they _____ it would. (advert)
3 I felt really _____ afterward. (guilt)
4 It seemed like a _____ product ... (wonder)
5 ... but it was such a _____. (disappoint)
6 This stuff is _____ quite _____. (actual / danger)
7 They go on and on in the infomercial about how _____ it is. (nature)
8 I guess it's just so _____ these days. (fashion)

C 🔘 **Make it personal** Think about 1–8 in **B**. When was the last time you felt like that? In pairs, each choose and share an experience. Whose was worse?

I bought some very expensive sunglasses and left them in a taxi. I felt really guilty afterward—and stupid, too.

③ Grammar Adjective order

A Study the examples and circle the correct alternative in the grammar box. Then read the information below and underline the fact adjectives in **1A**.

> *You'll get the physique of a [handsome] fashion model.*   *Help tone your [lazy], aching muscles.*
> *They can buy them in [gorgeous] bright colors.*   *Tom's a [nice] little kid.*
>
> If we use two or more adjectives before a noun, [opinions] usually come **before** / **after** facts.
>
> *I'm wearing the most expensive, round, contemporary, black, Korean, titanium, multi-function smart watch.*
>
> If you have more than one fact adjective in a sentence, they tend to go in a particular order:
> number – size – shape – age – color – nationality – material – purpose + noun
> But don't worry, it isn't usual to use more than three adjectives together!
>
> **➜ Grammar 5C** p. 146

B Read infomercials 1–7 and correct five adjective order mistakes.

1 *A spray that promises more attractive dark hair—instantly!*

2 Glamorize your look with these star-shaped fashionable earrings.

3 A Japanese camping miraculous knife that can cut through anything!

4 A bizarre green plastic blanket with sleeves to keep you warm while watching TV.

5 Jeans that look fashionable, but feel like cotton comfortable pajamas.

6 A SMALL METAL INCREDIBLE ACCESSORY THAT CREATES GORGEOUS HAIRSTYLES INSTANTLY!

7 Throw out your leather brown ugly shoes and buy our fantastic waterproof boots today!

C 🔘 **Make it personal** 🔊 In small groups, search online for a funny or interesting infomercial. Act it out or describe the product to the class. Can your classmates guess what the product is? Who found the best / worst / funniest products?

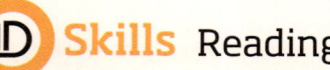

ID **Skills** Reading for confirmation

A In pairs, match the areas to photos a–c. Then list six more items in the photos. Which aspects of grocery store shopping do / don't you enjoy?

the bakery   a checkout   fresh fruit and vegetables

B Guess what "supermarket psychology" refers to? Read the introduction to the article to check. Who are "they"?

I'd say it's probably about consumer behavior.

C In pairs, brainstorm how grocery stores "assault our five senses." Give an example for sight, hearing, touch, taste, and smell. Then quickly read and match each sense to a paragraph. Were your ideas mentioned?

D ▶5.15 Listen and reread carefully. A: read 1–4, B: read 5–8. How else do grocery stores make us spend more and how can we avoid it? Share your information.

Supermarket PSYCHOLOGY

Ever noticed that whichever grocery store you go to, you'll inevitably find the same basic arrangement of products? It's a trick they play on us so we buy more and more things, even stuff we don't really need. Virtually all the products are carefully displayed to affect our shopping experience. Psychological tactics, you know. Clever devils! Read on to find out how grocery stores assault our five senses.

1 You can rarely leave the grocery store through the same door you walked in. This means you'll have to go around the whole place and maybe buy more stuff on your way out. They even let you try tasty food and drink items to tempt you further, so you feel like you're eating for free while you explore this "wonderful world."

2 Fresh fruits and vegetables are always right near the entrance. You think this is just by chance? No way. It's so you will feel fresh and happy at the start of your shopping adventure. They're nice to touch, too, and you feel you can choose the best ones for yourself. Plus, it's best to have these items near the entrance because of the sunlight. Smart, huh?

3 Everyday items like dairy, meat, or rice are always at the back of the store. They know you want to get to the checkout as fast as possible, so they make you go all the way to the back, past the clothes, watches, and gadgets—the most lucrative items. You know, just in case.

4 Ever feel hungry when you're doing your weekly shopping? Grocery stores know that food aromas make us hungry, so they have an in-store bakery and sometimes a restaurant, and the smell of food inspires us to buy more. They even use a manufactured bread-smell to catch customers on the street.

5 Want to buy shampoo? Well, don't look straight ahead: the products at eye level are always the more expensive ones. The cheaper ones are either placed at the very bottom or really high up, on the top shelves. Yeah, right there.

6 And why those long, endless aisles filled with unrelated products? Like cereals for breakfast next to a treat like candy. Well, parents usually buy boxes of cereal for their children, and when they make the mistake of taking them to the store, the magic happens: "I want to buy candy, Mommy. Pleeeaaaase."

7 Ever find yourself singing as you shop? There's a reason you're more likely to hear The Eagles or Celine Dion than Foo Fighters or Iron Maiden. Slower music creates slower traffic, which means people shop for longer. Genius, huh?

8 So, if this all sounds familiar, wise up! If you don't want to be a victim of these strategies, here's my advice: make a shopping list and stick to it!

E 🔵 Make it personal In pairs, ask and answer 1–4. Do you regularly succumb to 'shopping psychology'? If so, what's your best example?

1 Which grocery stores do / don't you usually shop at? Why?
2 Do you visit every aisle? Do you stick to your list, or do you ever buy more?
3 Which tactics from the article have you noticed? Any others?
4 What psychology do you find in other stores? (travel agency, technology, clothes, cosmetics …)

Supermarket psychology doesn't work on me. I only buy what I need.

When did you last complain in a store?

ID in Action Shopping problems

A ▶5.16 Listen to three dialogues. What are the three problems? Which were successful shopping experiences? Which one is most familiar to you?

B ▶5.16 Match the phrases and mark them C (customer) or SC (store clerk). Listen again to check. Have you ever worked in a store?

<table>
<tr><td colspan="2">Choosing</td><td></td></tr>
<tr><td>1</td><td>I like these shoes. Can I</td><td>□ charge?</td></tr>
<tr><td>2</td><td>What size do you</td><td>□ refund.</td></tr>
<tr><td>3</td><td>Do you have a size 10</td><td>□ take?</td></tr>
<tr><td>4</td><td>I'm sorry ma'am,</td><td>□ card, please.</td></tr>
<tr><td colspan="2">Paying</td><td>□ declined.</td></tr>
<tr><td>5</td><td>Cash or</td><td>□ we're sold out.</td></tr>
<tr><td>6</td><td>Insert / Tap / Swipe your</td><td>□ in stock?</td></tr>
<tr><td>7</td><td>I'm afraid your card has been</td><td>□ receipt.</td></tr>
<tr><td colspan="2">Complaining</td><td>□ try them on?</td></tr>
<tr><td>8</td><td>Unfortunately, we can't give you a</td><td>□ exchange it for another one.</td></tr>
<tr><td>9</td><td>But we'd be happy to</td><td></td></tr>
<tr><td>10</td><td>I just need to see your</td><td></td></tr>
</table>

C In pairs, cover the endings in **B** and test each other.

D ▶5.17 Can you remember the missing words? Listen to check.

1 It _____ impossible to _____ larger sizes. Can you _____ me when you _____ some in stock?

2 _____! I don't _____. It's a new card, and I _____ I'm not over my limit. There _____ be a problem with your card machine.

3 I'd _____ to _____ this phone. I _____ it here the other day, and it's _____.

E In pairs, choose a situation from **B** and read ▶5.16 on p. 168 for one minute. Then role-play the situation. Who complained successfully?

F ◉ **Make it personal** In pairs, role-play a situation, 1–3, below. Use sentences from **B** and **D**. Who complained successfully?

Hi. Are those shoes in the sale?

I'm afraid I'm unhappy with this phone.

1 You bought a smart phone last week, but you don't like it anymore. You want to get a refund or exchange it for a new one. There's a slight scratch on the screen, though.

2 You bought two pairs of jeans last month, but couldn't try them on because the store was too crowded. They don't fit. You want to exchange them or get a refund.

3 You bought some strawberries at the grocery store, but when you got home, you noticed that some of the fruit was rotten. You want a refund.

♫ *There's a lady who's sure all that glitters is gold, And she's buying a stairway to heaven.*

Writing 5 An advert

♪ *Come on, vogue,*
Let your body move to the music,
Hey, hey, hey
Come on, vogue,
Let your body go with the flow.

A Read the ad and circle the correct alternative.

1. Shape U Shoe is mainly for people who **do / don't** go to the gym.
2. Shape U Shoe shoes come in **"one size fits all"** / **various sizes and colors**.
3. They are good for **your arms and legs** / **your legs and body position**.
4. To get the benefits you need to walk with Shape U Shoes 20 **times per week / minutes a day**.

Are you [1]constantly *trying to get* [2]fitter?

[3]Always needing to tone up those muscles?

[4]Joined a gym several times *but kept giving up* [5]'cos *you* [6]can't *find the time–or* will*power–to go?*

YES

If your answer is
to any or all of these, then we have [7]the perfect solution *for you:*

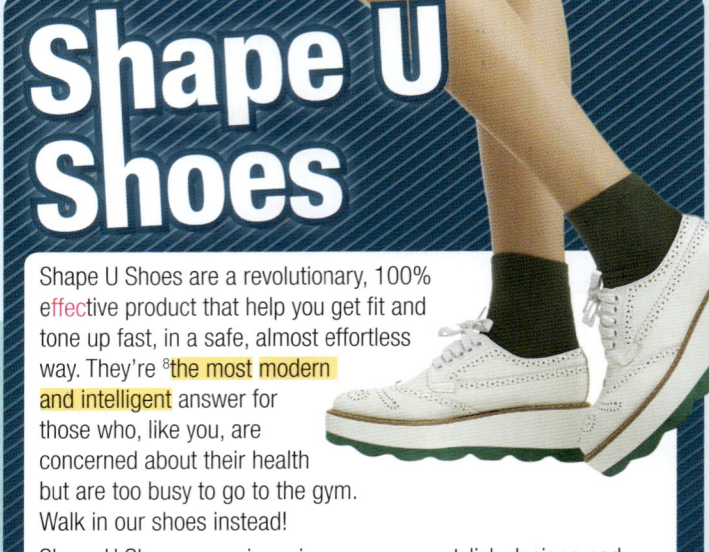

Shape U Shoes

Shape U Shoes are a revolutionary, 100% effective product that help you get fit and tone up fast, in a safe, almost effortless way. They're [8]the most modern and intelligent answer for those who, like you, are concerned about their health but are too busy to go to the gym. Walk in our shoes instead!

Shape U Shoes come in various gorgeous, stylish designs and colors. They strengthen legs and thighs, by boosting your muscle activity by up to 35% simply by walking. Imagine that! Shape U Shoes can also improve your posture. You will soon look and feel fitter, [9]less tired, and get that shape you've been dreaming of. [10]All these benefits without any risks!

Shape U Shoes are [11]the scientific solution that was missing in your life. Walking for just 20 minutes a day is [12]the secret to [13]a better and happier life! Remember, [14]it's no miracle. It's Shape U Shoes!

Available online for next-day delivery. Satisfaction guaranteed!

B Read *Write it right!*, then match highlighted items 1–14 to rules a–d.

✓ Write it right!

To write a good ad,

a. use comparatives and superlatives. ☐☐☐☐☐
b. use emotive, exaggerated language to make opinions sound like facts. ☐☐☐☐☐☐
c. remove articles, auxiliaries, or subjects to make it short and exciting. ☐☐
   (Our new car is) faster than you thought.
   (The) offer (is) limited to the United States.
d. use informal language, such as contractions and abbreviations. ☐☐☐
   Don't wait any longer!
   You're gonna love this!

C Complete 1–6 with the adjective or adverb forms of the words in parentheses.

1. You'll be _____ _____ by the fast results. (total / surprise)
2. This product is 100% _____. (safety)
3. The most _____ solution to your problems. (efficiency)
4. Use it _____ to see _____ results. (regularity / wonder)
5. Achieve _____ results. (success)
6. Feel _____ _____ all the time. (complete / energy)

D Circle the correct alternative in 1–7.

1. Get **long beautiful / beautiful long** hair.
2. Looking for a **perfect new / new perfect** solution?
3. Feel like **an attractive young / a young attractive** model!
4. Take only one **gentle short / short gentle** walk a day.
5. A **strong new / new strong** body!
6. It's the **better / best** and **modernest / most modern** solution.
7. Learn English using the **faster / fastest** method with the **less / least** effort.

E *Your turn!* Write an ad in 130–150 words.

Before	Choose a product (e.g. from **3C** in Lesson 5.4 on p. 65) and note down five adjectives to describe it. Think who it's for and how you can "sell" it.
While	1 Begin your ad with a question or a catchy sentence. 2 Use tips a–d in *Write it right!* 3 End with a powerful statement.
After	Show your ad to three different classmates. Would they buy your product? Then email it to your teacher.

5 Shop around

① Before watching

A Match 1–7 to five of the definitions a–e.

1 A clothes hoarder
2 A discount shopper
3 A loyal shopper
4 An online shopper
5 A reluctant shopper
6 An upcycler
7 A shopaholic

a ☐ loves shopping sprees
b ☐ reuses materials (e.g. clothes, furniture) to create something new
c ☐ shops around to buy things when they're cheaper
d ☐ always buys clothes at the same store
e ☐ keeps all their clothes, never throwing any out

B ⬤ Make it personal Which of 1–7 in **A** best describes you and your friends?

> I guess I'm 4 for most things except clothes. I like to try things on before buying.

② While watching

A Watch the first two minutes and check: Andrea (A), Genevieve (G), or Lucy (L)?

	A	G	L
1 Has beautiful, sophisticated clothes.			
2 Needs beautiful, new clothes.			
3 Likes to wear dark clothes.			
4 Works with demanding actors.			
5 Used to be a mad shopper.			

B Watch again and check all you hear.

1 What is Lucy doing?
☐ Demanding things.   ☐ Working with actors.
☐ Starring in a film.   ☐ Shooting a film.

2 How does Andrea describe her past behavior?
☐ Anxious.   ☐ Creative genius.
☐ Kidding.   ☐ Tired.

3 What does Andrea want to do?
☐ Make her own clothes.   ☐ Have better taste.
☐ Stop shopping.   ☐ Sew curtains.

Café

C Study Andrea's clothing rental website. In pairs, explain how it will work. Who might use it? What are the benefits? Would you use it?

> Shop Around ♡
>
> Are you a:
> ◉ COMPULSIVE SHOPPER?
> ◉ CLOTHES HOARDER?
> ◉ TIME WASTER?
>
> Don't Fret!
> ◉ CLOTHING RENTALS
> ◉ FAST PICK-UP
> ◉ ECONOMICAL RETURNS

> It could be good for clothes hoarders.

> Yeah, they could sell clothes they haven't worn.

D Watch the rest and number 1–9 the order these are mentioned.

a performance	☐	Genevieve	☐
all the girls on campus	1	Lucy's actors	☐
dark clothing	☐	make curtains	☐
design clothing	☐	make money	☐
		save money	☐

③ After watching

A Match the noun and adjective used to describe it.

1 best
2 crazy
3 creative
4 mad
5 different
6 shopping
7 sophisticated

a ☐ clothes
b ☐ friend
c ☐ genius
d ☐ sizes
e ☐ shopper
f ☐ shopping
g ☐ spree

B Complete 1–4 with the correct adverb.

actually   definitely   probably   seriously

1 I _____ went a little crazy on spending.
2 No, _____ I believe it.
3 _____, I have an idea.
4 You are _____ the best friend anyone could ask for!

C ⬤ Make it personal In pairs, compare your usual taste in clothes and colors. Any surprises?

> I like to wear dark colors, especially at night.

> Not me. I'm into bright shirts or T-shirts.

Mid-term review — Game: 55 seconds

UNIT 1 — TOPIC TALK

Relationships
Friendship
Personality

DESCRIBE ▶ DISCOVER

COUNT THE QUESTIONS

ROLE-PLAY

UNIT 2 — TOPIC TALK

Going green
The environment
Endangered species

DESCRIBE ▶ DISCOVER

COUNT THE QUESTIONS

ROLE-PLAY

UNIT 3 — TOPIC TALK

Cities
Stress and relaxation
Rules

DESCRIBE ▶ DISCOVER

COUNT THE QUESTIONS

ROLE-PLAY

INSTRUCTIONS

TOPIC TALK

The opposing team chooses a topic and counts the mistakes.
Talk about the topic together. Give opinions on the ➕ and ➖ points.
Score: Start with 10 points. Lose:

- 1 point for each mistake the opposing team notices.
- 1 point each time you pause for five seconds or more.

Calculate the points at the end. Use each topic only once.

DESCRIBE ▶ DISCOVER

The opposing team chooses one noun, one adjective, and one verb from that unit, writes them on a piece of paper, and gives it to player A.
A: Define and describe three words without using the word itself.
B: Discover the word.
Score: 5 points for a correct discovery.

COUNT THE QUESTIONS

The opposing team chooses a photo and counts the correct questions.
A: Ask your partner questions to find "the story behind the photo." The more questions you ask, the more points you score!
B: Answer A's questions however you like. Use your imagination!
Score: 1 point per correct question. Use each photo only once.

ROLE-PLAY

Act out the situation in the cartoon. Be creative! You have 30 seconds to prepare.
Score: Start with 10 points. Lose:

- 1 point for each mistake the opposing team notices.
- 1 point each time you pause for five seconds or more.

Calculate the points at the end.

UNIT 4

TOPIC TALK

Education
Career choices
Regrets

DESCRIBE ▶ DISCOVER

COUNT THE QUESTIONS

ROLE-PLAY

UNIT 5

TOPIC TALK

Shopping
Spending habits
Useless products

DESCRIBE ▶ DISCOVER

COUNT THE QUESTIONS

ROLE-PLAY

Grammar Unit 1

1A Review of present tenses

Simple present

Subject	Verb	Time phrase
I / You / We / They	hang out	on weekends.
He / She / It	meets up	twice a week.

Use the **Simple present** for habits and states:
- *Johann and Melina usually **meet** for dinner once a month.*
- *She often texts during dinner. It **annoys** her boyfriend.*
- *I **hate** going to parties by myself. I always **take** a friend.*

Note: adverbs of frequency come before the verb.

Present continuous

Question	Auxiliary	Subject	Verb phrase
What	are	you	doing here?
Where	is	he	going?

Use the **Present continuous** for:
1 actions in progress.
- *I'm chatting to my mom.*
2 future arrangements.
- *She isn't coming tonight.*

Note: do not use stative verbs in the Present continuous.
Do you understand me? NOT ~~*Are you understanding me?*~~

Present perfect

Subject	Auxiliary	Past participle
I / You / We / They	have / 've have not / haven't	hung out there before. gone there before.
He / She / It	has / 's has not / hasn't	spent time with him. been too hot today.

Form: *have / has* + past participle (for irregular participles list, see p. 158–159).

Use the **Present perfect** for:
1 past experiences without a specific time.
- *I've never **been** here before.*
2 completed actions from a past point in time to now.
- *We've just **eaten**.*
3 unfinished past: actions / states that began in the past and continue until now.
- *She's **had** three dates **since** she started speed dating.*

Yes / No questions	Short answers
Have you (ever) been on a meet-up?	Yes, I have. No, I haven't.
Have they (ever) broken up before?	Yes, they have. No, they haven't.
Has she (ever) lost her cell phone?	Yes, she has. No, she hasn't.

For short answers, do not contract the subject with the auxiliary.
Yes, I have NOT ~~*Yes, I've.*~~

1B Review of question forms

Yes / No questions

Auxiliary	Subject	Verb + object
Are	they	your workmates?
Do	you	know Natalie?
Have	you	been to London?
Can	you	play the piano?

Questions ending in prepositions

Question	Auxiliary	Subject	Verb phrase	Preposition
Who	do	you	want to speak	to?
Who	did	they	go to the party	with?

Object questions

Question	Auxiliary	Subject	Verb + object
What	do	you	want to eat?
Where	did	he	park the car?

Subject questions

Question (+ subject)	Verb + object
Which boy	won the prize?
Who	likes lemonade?

1C Emphatic forms

Subject	Auxiliary	Verb	Object
I	do	love	the sound of her voice.

Use auxiliary + verb to emphasize agreement / disagreement.
- *"You don't seem to like him."*
- *"That's not true. I **do** like him."*

Use adverbs before the verb to emphasize an opinion or agreement / disagreement.
- *I **really** don't think he's going to show up!*
- *I **definitely** want to meet him sometime.*

Note: emphatic auxiliaries and adverbs are more common in speech than in writing.

1A

1 Complete 1–6 with the *Simple present* or *Present continuous* of the verbs in parentheses.

1 He _____ with his friends this weekend. (travel)

2 Mara always _____ impatient when she _____ in long lines. (get / stand)

3 They _____ every night because they _____ classes. (not go out / have)

4 Ben and Amy _____ right now—I think they often _____. (not get along / argue)

5 You really _____ bored by this TV show. (seem)

6 So, how _____ him? (you know)

2 Use the phrases to describe each picture a–c. Try to use the *Simple present*, *Present continuous*, or *Present perfect*.

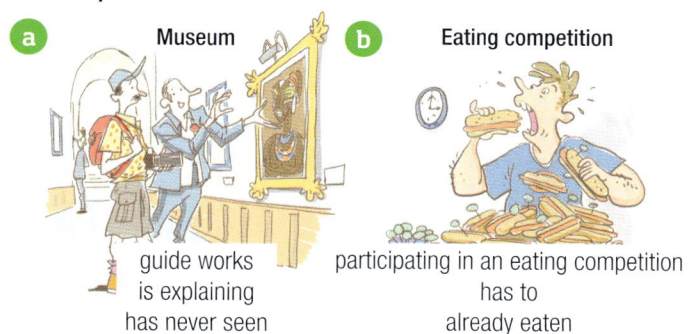

a Museum

guide works
is explaining
has never seen

b Eating competition

participating in an eating competition
has to
already eaten

c Skateboard park

hang out every Saturday
has started
is waiting

3 ⬤ **Make it personal** Describe where you've been lately, what you do every weekend, and what you're planning to do next weekend.

I always go to the same restaurants every weekend, so I have decided to try new places.
I've been to that new restaurant that's just opened. The Japanese place. And next weekend my friends and I are visiting a Turkish restaurant.

1B

1 Write *yes / no* questions for these answers.

1 He likes this city.

2 They are good at soccer.

3 She can drive a truck.

4 The baby is awake.

2 Circle the correct preposition.

1 What were you waiting **to / for**?

2 Who are you so angry **with / of**?

3 What is she spending all her money **in / on**?

4 Which line are you standing **in / at**?

3 Write one subject and one object question for each sentence.

1 Joanna loves taking photographs.

2 The kids went into the yard.

3 Chris has lost his keys.

4 Marie likes George.

4 Order the words in 1–5 to make questions.

1 time / in / which / city / some / would / spend / like / you / to / ?

2 talking / what / been / about / the / gossip magazines / have / ?

3 learning / a / you / find / language / do / easy / ?

4 starred / who / watched / last / film / you / in / the / ?

5 you / talk / last / best / friend / to / when / did / your?

1C

1 Complete 1–6 with an emphatic auxiliary.

1 You know, she _____ look a little bit like Emma Stone.

2 Come to think of it, I _____ feel a bit tired.

3 Well, they couldn't make it to our party, but they _____ send us a card.

4 If I _____ seem stressed, it's only because of the thunderstorm.

5 It _____ sound too good to be true, doesn't it?

6 We _____ have to pay something to use this site—it's not free, you know.

2 Complete 1–5 with the best adverb below.

absolutely   certainly   definitely   really   sure

1 Are you _____ going to wear that orange shirt with those pants?

2 Well, she _____ told me she was getting the afternoon flight.

3 They _____ look as if they're having fun.

4 He _____ is a quiet sort of guy, isn't he?

5 I'm telling you, I'm _____, 100 percent certain I've seen him before!

Grammar Unit 2

2A Adjectives from verbs and nouns

- *I only use recharge**able** batteries in my devices.*
- *She bought a very space-**efficient** apartment.*
- *This software is really user-**friendly**!*

Form adjectives by adding *-able*, *-efficient*, and *-friendly* to verbs and nouns.

-able means "can be done:" *drinkable, breakable, doable.*
Verbs ending in *-e* ➡ cut *-e* + *-able*.

- *reuse* ➡ *reusable*
- *recycle* ➡ *recyclable*
- *love* ➡ *lovable*

Exception: *rechargeable*

Use a hyphen between nouns and *-efficient* or *-friendly*.

- *She bought an energy-efficient washing machine.*
- *We took our nephews to a child-friendly restaurant.*

2B Present perfect continuous

Subject	*have / has*	*been + -ing*
I / You / We / They	have / haven't	been sitting here for hours.
He / She	has / hasn't	been waiting for the bus since 8:30.
It	has / hasn't	been raining all afternoon.

Form: *have / has* (not) + *been* + verb + *-ing*.
Use contractions: *have = 've / haven't, has = 's / hasn't*

Question	*have / has* + subject	*been + -ing*
What	have I / you / we / they	been talking about?
How long	has she / he / it	been doing it?

Use the **Present perfect continuous** with:

- ***since*** to indicate a point in time: *1989, eight o'clock, yesterday = a moment*
- ***for*** to indicate a period of time: *a few hours, six months, 20 years = a duration*

2C Present perfect vs. Present perfect continuous

You can often use **Present perfect** or **Present perfect continuous** interchangeably.

- *I've lived here since 2010.*
- *I've been living here since 2010.*

Present perfect

Use the **Present perfect** to describe activities that have or haven't been completed from a past point in time until now.

- *Agatha's written ten books in ten years.*

Present perfect continuous

Use the **Present perfect continuous** to emphasize the time a process or series of events took. It can also be used to describe an activity that is unfinished or temporary.

- *They've been hanging around with Mary lately.*
- *Agatha's been writing books since she was in her 20s.*

Don't use the Present perfect continuous with a stative verb (e.g. *be, have, know, understand*).

2D Simple past vs. Present perfect simple / continuous

Simple past

Subject	Past tense of verb	Object
I / You / He / She / It / You / We / They	traveled	to the North Pole.

Use the **Simple past** for completed actions in the past.

- *Jordan Romero **reached** the top of the Everest when he was only 16.*

Present perfect

Use the **Present perfect** to connect the past and present and to describe how much has been completed.

- *The explorer **has climbed** a lot of mountains in his life.*
- *The polar ice caps **have melted** over the past 30 years.*

Present perfect continuous

Use the **Present perfect continuous** to describe how long something has been happening.

- *He's **been exploring** exotic environments since he graduated from school.*
- *The polar ice caps **have been melting** since the 1980s.*

"According to this, you haven't been waiting long enough for treatment."

2A

1 Cross out the incorrect adjective in 1–5.

1 She always brings **recycling / recyclable** bottles to the store.
2 He likes the **usable / user-friendly** features of his new dishwasher.
3 We have **energy-efficiency / energy-efficient** lights in our house.
4 I only use **natural-friendly / nature-friendly** detergents.
5 **Disposing / Disposable** batteries are bad for the environment.

2 Describe photos a–d. Use adjectives from verbs and nouns.

Well, I guess it's child-friendly but …

2B

1 Complete 1–5 with the correct form of *have*.

1 _____ he been saving money for a new car?
2 What _____ you been doing all day?
3 Where _____ they been storing all those recyclable cans and boxes?
4 _____ you been listening to the news today?
5 _____ it been raining here?

2 Complete 1–5 with the *Present perfect continuous* of these verbs.

buy   collect   live   swim   work out

1 How long _____ you _____ watches?
2 They _____ in their new heated pool.
3 I _____ every day for the past three weeks.
4 Mario _____ next door for six years.
5 My mom _____ eco-friendly products since I was a kid.

3 🔵 Make it personal Describe what you've been doing lately at work / school / home.

I've been working out at the gym twice a week, but I haven't been running since I hurt my knee.

2C

1 Circle the correct option in 1–5.

1 She has **walked / been walking** to and from school every day since she was ten.
2 We've **tried / been trying** three different products and we still can't get this shirt clean.
3 He's never **traveled / been traveling** on a luxury cruise ship before.
4 They have **used / been using** energy-efficient appliances in their house recently.
5 I haven't **done / been doing** my housework as often as I should.

2 Complete the dialogues with the correct form of the verb in parentheses.

1 A: Where _____? There is mud all over your shoes. (walk)
   B: Oh, I _____ the garden and it _____ my shoes wet. (water / get)
2 A: I'm absolutely exhausted. I _____ since 8 a.m. (drive)
   B: Wow. You should let me drive for a while. I _____ at all. (not drive)
3 A: You _____ yourself enough time to get ready for work this morning. (not give)
   B: This old alarm clock _____ the right time for years! (keep)

2D

1 Order the words in 1–5 to make questions.

1 have / how / you / long / been / the / phone / using / you / that / bought / new / ?
2 flooding / has / any / been / there / you / where / live / ?
3 government / doing / to solve / has / the / been / problems / environmental / our / what / ?
4 know / the North Pole / did / that / global / you / has / warming / caused / at / melting / ?
5 since / the laws / enforced / been / about / pollution / have / they / made / were / ?

2 🔵 Make it personal Write your responses to the questions in **1**.

Grammar Unit 3

3A Past perfect

Subject	Auxiliary	Past participle
I / You He / She / It We / They	had / 'd	never been to Hong Kong before.
		already left by the time the suitcases appeared.
	had not / hadn't	had anything to eat for nearly 24 hours.
		ever been abroad until this trip.

Form:

● and ● = Subject + *had* (*not*) + past participle.
Use *'d* contractions for ● and ***hadn't*** for ● sentences.
❓ = *Had*(*n't*) + subject + past participle?

- ► ***Had*** you ***taken*** medicine before you flew?
- ► ***Hadn't*** you ever ***seen*** that before?
- ► What ***had*** you ***eaten*** before you got sick?

Note: when the main verb is *have*, *had* will appear twice, either together or separated by an adverbial expression.

- ► We ***had*** already ***had*** lunch when they called.
- ► Before I met her, I ***had had*** serious problems in my relationships.

Use the **Past perfect**:

1 for actions that happened before another past action.
- ► I didn't start studying English until after I***'d finished*** high school.

2 to express past wishes and expectations.
- ► My birthday party was better than anything I***'d expected***!
- ► The movie was more thrilling than they***'d hoped***!

Expressions like *already, before, by the time, never, until recently*, etc. indicate the duration of the event or when it happened.

- ► When the electricity went out, they'd ***already*** gone to bed.
- ► She'd never met a celebrity ***before***.
- ► ***Until recently,*** I hadn't used that website.

3B Past perfect continuous

Subject	Auxiliary	*been*	Verb + *-ing*
I / You He / She / It We / They	had / 'd	been	living there for a long time.
	had not / hadn't		standing in line for several hours.

Form:

● and ● = Subject + *had* (*not*) + *been* + verb *-ing*.
Use *'d* contractions for ● and ***hadn't*** for ● sentences.
❓ = *Had*(*n't*) + subject + *been* + verb *-ing*?

Use the **Past perfect continuous** to emphasize the duration of an action that was in progress before another past action.

- ► It ***had been raining*** for hours before the game started.
- ► We'd ***been walking*** in the park when we encountered our old friend.

Note: don't use the Past perfect continuous with stative verbs.

3C Narrative tenses

Simple past

Use the **Simple past** to talk about past actions and states.
- ► I ***graduated*** from high school and then I ***went*** to college.

Past continuous

Subject	*was / were*	Verb + *-ing*
I / He / She / It	was / wasn't	getting ready to go out.
You / We / They	were / weren't	listening to me.

Use the **Past continuous** to talk about actions in progress at a point in the past.
- ► I ***was working*** at a summer camp for three months.

Use the **Simple past** to talk about actions that interrupt actions in the **Past continuous**.
- ► I ***was walking*** home when I ***saw*** Julia.

Past perfect

Use the **Past perfect** to emphasize that one action happened before another in the past.
- ► He made breakfast after he ***had taken*** a shower.

If the sequence is clear, use the **Simple past**.
- ► He made breakfast after he took a shower.

Past perfect continuous

Use the **Past perfect continuous** to emphasize the duration of an action that was completed in the past.

- ► We'd ***been studying*** all afternoon before the examiner arrived.
- ► How long ***had you been dating*** before you got married?

3A

1 Complete the dialogues with the *Past perfect* or *Past simple* of the verbs in parentheses.

1 A: How was your trip to Italy? _____ you ever _____ there before? (be)

   B: It was great. I _____ there before. It was my first time. (be)

2 A: _____ you _____ Italian before you went there? (study)

   B: Yes, but I _____ more than a few words. (not learn)

3 A: _____ you _____ in time to see the festival? (arrive)

   B: No. By the time I got there, it _____ just _____. (end)

2 Describe the events in each of a–c in two or three sentences. Use the *Past perfect*.

3B

1 Complete 1–5 with the *Past perfect* or *Past perfect continuous* of the verbs in parentheses.

1 We _____ video games for almost two hours before the outage. (play)

2 Imagine if dinosaurs _____ because of climate change. (not die out)

3 She _____ for long when the lightning suddenly woke her up. (not sleep)

4 They _____ on coming to the party with us, but they had a family emergency at the last moment. (plan)

5 The tigers were pacing their cage because they _____ yet. (not eat)

2 Correct the mistakes in 1–5.

1 The manager had been warning him twice to stop using his cell in the theater.

2 They were towing our car because we had been parking in a tow-away zone.

3 She was still feeling confused even after the officer had gave her directions.

4 The law that all dogs must be on a leash had be in effect for thirty years.

5 Her wedding wasn't as perfect as she's hoped.

3 🔵 Make it personal   Describe five "first times", or things you had never done before. Use the topics from the box, plus any others you can think of.

(buy) your own computer, phone, or car   (drive) a car
plan a party   (ride) a horse or a bicycle   travel by plane

I had been living on the farm for one month but I hadn't ridden one of the horses ...

3C

1 Circle the correct alternatives to complete the anecdote.

Last Sunday, I ¹ **went / was going / had gone** to the cinema with my sisters. We ² **didn't drive / weren't driving / hadn't been driving** for very long when suddenly a small dog suddenly ³ **ran / was running / had run** out in front of us. It ⁴ **happened / was happening / had been happening** too fast, and I ⁵ **wasn't seeing / hadn't seen / hadn't been seeing** the dog before it ⁶ **ran / was running / had been running** out. We ⁷ **stopped / were stopping / had stopped** the car and ⁸ **got / were getting / had gotten** out. We ⁹ **were all feeling / had all felt / had all been feeling** very upset. We ¹⁰ **looked / was looking / had looked** under the car. Luckily, we ¹¹ **hadn't hit / weren't hitting / hadn't been hitting** the dog at all. It ¹² **hid / was hiding / had been hiding** under the car! We were very relieved!

2 🔵 Make it personal   Describe a time when you thought something bad had happened, but it ended happily.

Grammar Unit 4

4A too / enough

Use:

- *too* before an adjective when something is more than necessary.

▸ *Some students are **too** proud to ask for help.*

▸ *You're never **too** old to learn something new.*

- *enough* after an adjective / adverb, but before nouns when something is the necessary amount.

▸ *I didn't get to class early **enough** to get a good seat.*

▸ *There wasn't **enough** time to get everything done.*

Note: don't use *too* with adjectives + noun to mean *very*. *Her family are very nice people.* NOT ~~Her family are too nice people.~~

Use:

- *too many* before plural **C** nouns.

▸ *They have **too many** problems to deal with.*

- *too much* before **U** nouns.

▸ *There's **too much** pressure to get a high score on the exam.*

Note: when **U** nouns have a plural meaning or with *types of / kinds of*, use *too many*.

▸ *There are **too many** types of fish in this aquarium!*

4B should have

Use *should have* + Past participle:

1 to express a regret.

▸ *You **shouldn't have left** your drink near the computer.*

2 to speculate about the past.

▸ *We **should have known** there would be a test today.*

3 to give / ask advice about a past event.

▸ *What **should** I **have done** instead?*

Form:

Subject + *should* (not) + *have* + past participle.

Note: we often use the contraction *'ve* in spoken English.

▸ *She should**'ve** called to tell me she wasn't coming.*

▸ *I should**'ve** realized you would be late.*

▸ *You should**n't've** gone cycling without a helmet.*

4C First and second conditional

First conditional

If	Subject	Simple present	Subject	*will / won't*	Infinitive
If	I	have time,	I	will	buy some bread on the way home.
If	you	don't listen,	you	won't	know what to do.

Use the **First conditional** to talk about real and possible future situations.

Second conditional

If	Subject	Simple past	Subject	*will / won't*	Infinitive
If	I	could be anything I wanted,	I	would	be a lawyer.
If	they	didn't study so hard,	they	wouldn't	get such good grades.

Use the **Second conditional** to talk about "unreal" or imaginary situations.

The *if* clause can come first or second. Use a comma separating the clauses when the *if* clause comes first.

▸ *I'll buy some bread on the way home if I have time.*

▸ *They wouldn't get such good grades if they didn't study so hard.*

We can also use *when* or *as soon as* with the same sentence structure as with *if*.

▸ ***When** I get there, I'll call you.*

▸ *I'll call you **as soon as** I get there.*

We can use *can / could / may / might* instead of *would*.

▸ *If you studied a bit harder, you **might** get a higher score.*

4A

1 Circle the correct alternative in 1–5.

1 The print was **too / enough** small for her to read.
2 They've canceled the class because there weren't **too few / enough** people signed up.
3 The school was criticized because it didn't have **enough / too many** teachers.
4 Students complained that they were under **too much / enough** pressure to get good grades.
5 The educators thought the exams were **too / enough** hard for most students.

2 Complete 1–5 with *too much* or *enough*.

1 I don't have _____ time to read my notes before the test begins.
2 He has _____ time on his hands—he just plays video games all day.
3 Kindergarten children seem to get _____ homework.
4 I've got _____ money saved to buy a new tablet!
5 He hasn't done the dishes in days, so there aren't _____ cups for all of us.

3 ◯ Make it personal Describe these things. Use *too* and *enough* in your sentences.

apps on my phone   space in my room
free time   friends on Facebook   work
homework   hours in a day

I don't have enough free time!

"If you ask me, he's come too far too fast."

4B

1 Correct the mistakes in 1–6.

1 He should had organized his time better.
2 We should to have taken the bus instead of the subway.
3 They should have not given out their phone number.
4 You should listened to your father's advice.
5 It should've be easy to find his house with your GPS.
6 You should haven't left your wallet at the restaurant.

2 Order the words in 1–4 to make sentences. Then match 1–4 to a–d.

1 for / have / she / studied / should / more / exam / the / .
2 we / taken / road / that / should / have / not / .
3 pin / written / have / I / down / should / number / the / .
4 alarm / set / clock / have / should / they / their / .

a ☐ We got lost.
b ☐ I couldn't take out any money.
c ☐ They were late for class.
d ☐ She failed her test.

3 ◯ Make it personal Describe things you shouldn't have done or should've done differently.

I should've started learning English earlier. I still find it difficult.
I shouldn't have gone out last night. I'm exhausted.

4C

1 Check the correct ending for the sentences.

1 If you saw your favourite movie star,
   ☐ what will you do?
   ☐ what would you do?
2 If you are in trouble,
   ☐ I'll always help you.
   ☐ I'd always help you.
3 I'll see you later
   ☐ if you go to the party.
   ☐ if you went to the party.
4 I'd lend you my phone
   ☐ if you take care of it.
   ☐ if you took care of it.
5 If I knew the answer,
   ☐ I'll tell you.
   ☐ I'd tell you.
6 What would you do
   ☐ if you fail your exams?
   ☐ if you failed your exams?

2 ◯ Make it personal Complete the sentences so that they are true for you.

1 If I had one week left to live …
2 If I go out this weekend …
3 If I have enough money …
4 If I could go anywhere in the world …

5A Third conditional

If Clause			Result Clause			
If	I / you / he / she / we / they	had been on time,	I / you / he / she / we / they	would've		gotten a seat.
		'd read the book,		might've		understood the lecture.
		hadn't called,		wouldn't have		come to the party.

Use the **Third conditional** to express past wishes or possible past events and their probable results.

▸ *If you'd had more time, **what** would you have done?*

▸ ***How** would the world be different today if we'd had computers 100 years ago?*

Form:

If + subject + had (not) + past participle + subject + would have + past participle + phrase.

Note: use **might / could have** when the result is less sure.

▸ *If I'd lost some weight, I could have won the race.*

"Mom, would you have married Dad if you had seen him in high definition first?"

5B Modals of possibility / probability

Use *can / can't* or *could / couldn't* to show possibility.

▸ *You **can't** be serious.*

▸ *I thought you **could** do it.*

▸ *He **can't** be hungry again!*

▸ *It's midnight! Who **could** it be at the door?*

▸ *It **can't** be the kids! They're all in bed!*

Use *might* or *must* to show degrees of certainty or uncertainty.

▸ *I **might** go to the party tonight, but I'm not sure.*

▸ *You **must** be tired after your long flight.*

▸ *Yeah, I **may** just call in for half an hour.*

Note: you can use **may** instead of *might* or *could*.

5C Adjective order

▸ *It's a very **effective herbal** remedy.*

▸ *That **talented Spanish** actress is their new spokesperson.*

Fact adjectives follow this order:

size	age	shape	color	material	purpose	+ noun
little	old	square	red	brick	elementary	school

▸ *It was a **little, old, square, red, brick elementary** school.*

Note: try not to use more than three adjectives together.

▸ *He's a very **nice, smart, young** guy.*

Opinion adjectives (*amazing, friendly, good, interesting, nice, pretty*, etc.) usually come before fact adjectives (*American, metal, tall, young*, etc.).

A nice young man NOT *A young nice man*

Note: add a comma after each consecutive adjective.

Opinion	Fact	Noun
a delicious	square chocolate	brownie
a funny	new stand-up	comedian
an ugly	old plastic	bag

You can change the position of fact and opinion adjectives for emphasis. Put the most important adjective next to the noun.

▸ *It's a **boring, old** story.* → *It's the same **old, boring** story.*

▸ *He had an **ugly, large** bag.* → *He had a **large, ugly** bag.*

" Brilliant! A 3-D, holographic, pop-up annual report. Hopefully, no one will notice what a lousy year we had. "

5A

1 Match *If* clauses 1–6 to result clauses a–f.

1 If the alarm hadn't gone off,
2 If the Internet had been working,
3 If it had been an easier test,
4 If the sign hadn't been hidden,
5 If my phone hadn't run out of battery,
6 If we'd planned better,

a ☐ she wouldn't have missed the turn.
b ☐ there would've been enough food.
c ☐ I would've called you.
d ☐ he would've checked the schedule.
e ☐ more students might have passed it.
f ☐ you would've been really late.

2 Correct the mistakes in 1–5.

1 If you hadn't procrastinated, you'd had enough time to study.
2 I would've tell him if I would've seen him.
3 If you had bought a lottery ticket, you might win a lot of money.
4 We could been in the race if we'd sent our applications in on time.
5 If I hadn't found her when I did, she would lost.

3 🔵 **Make it personal** Describe what would have happened *if* ...

... you'd learned another language.
... you'd found some buried treasure.
... you'd been born the opposite gender.
... you'd been a professional athlete.

If I'd been a professional athlete, I would've been a soccer player.

5B

1 Match 1–5 to comments a–e.

1 I walked five miles to get here.
2 He hasn't eaten very much today.
3 Sorry, sir, you don't have enough money in your account.
4 There's no sound from the TV.
5 I heard thunder in the distance.

a ☐ He might be hungry. Offer him something.
b ☐ You can't be serious! How could that be?
c ☐ There may be a storm coming.
d ☐ You must be tired!
e ☐ It could be the speakers.

2 Circle the correct alternative in 1–5.

1 Studies show that lack of exercise **can / might** not lead to obesity.
2 Sugar-free chewing gum **can't / might not** be so good for your teeth.
3 He didn't realize that his car **could / must** get such good mileage.
4 It **might not / could** be so easy to find a replacement for that device.
5 It **can / must** be a really long wait for a table at this restaurant.

3 Complete 1–5 with *can't* or *must* and these verbs.

believe   imagine   keep   realize   think

1 I _____ _____ listened to her entire story again!
2 You _____ _____ that this is a controversial subject.
3 She _____ _____ how you got him to talk about it.
4 My friends _____ _____ I'm crazy to go out with him.
5 Don't tell her—she _____ _____ a secret.

5C

1 Order the words in 1–5 to make sentences.

1 wearing / long-sleeved / he / blue / was / a / T-shirt / cotton / .
2 new / we / car / washed / shiny / red / our / sports / .
3 the road / put / a / big / cone / plastic / the / construction / on / crew / orange / .
4 for / you / look / should / small / gray / house / wooden / old / a / .
5 scary / dressed up / monster / green / huge / a / like / he / .

2 Describe each photo using as many adjectives as you can.

3 🔵 **Make it personal** Describe what you are wearing. Use as many adjectives as you can.

I'm wearing a beautiful, blue and white cotton skirt.

Verbs

Irregular verbs

Irregular verbs can be difficult to remember. Try remembering them in groups with similar sounds, conjugation patterns, or spellings.

Simple past and Past participle are the same

Base form	Simple past	Past participle
bring	brought /brɔt/	brought
buy	bought	bought
catch	caught /cɔt/	caught
fight	fought	fought
teach	taught	taught
think	thought	thought
feed	fed	fed
feel	felt	felt
keep	kept	kept
leave	left	left
mean	meant /mɛnt/	meant
meet	met	met
sleep	slept	slept
lay	laid	laid
pay	paid	paid
sell	sold	sold
tell	told	told
send	sent	sent
spend	spent	spent
stand	stood /stʊd/	stood
understand	understood	understood
lose	lost	lost
shoot	shot	shot
can	could	could
will	would	would
build	built /bɪlt/	built
find	found /faʊnd/	found
hang	hung	hung
have	had	had
hear	heard /hɜrd/	heard
hold	held	held
make	made	made
say	said /sɛd/	said
sit	sat	sat
swing	swung /swʌŋ/	swung
win	won /wʌn/	won

Base form and Past participle are the same

Base form	Simple past	Past participle
become	became	become
come	came	come
run	ran	run

No changes across the three forms

Base form	Simple past	Past participle
cost	cost	cost
cut	cut	cut
hit	hit	hit
let	let	let
put	put /pʊt/	put
quit	quit /kwɪt/	quit
set	set	set
split	split	split

Special cases

Base form	Simple past	Past participle
be	was / were	been
draw	drew /dru:/	drawn /drɔn/
fly	flew /flu:/	flown /floʊn/
lie	lay	lain
read	read /rɛd/	read /rɛd/

Simple past + -*en*

Base form	Simple past	Past participle
beat	beat	beaten
bite	bit	bitten
break	broke	broken
choose	chose	chosen
forget	forgot	forgotten
freeze	froze	frozen
get	got	got / gotten
speak	spoke	spoken
steal	stole	stolen
wake	woke	woken

Simple past + -en

Base form	Simple past	Past participle
beat	beat	beaten
bite	bit	bitten
break	broke	broken
choose	chose	chosen
forget	forgot	forgotten
freeze	froze	frozen
get	got	got / gotten
speak	spoke	spoken
steal	stole	stolen
wake	woke	woken

Base form + -en

Base form	Simple past	Past participle
drive	drove	driven /drɪvən/
eat	ate	eaten
fall	fell	fallen
give	gave	given
ride	rode	ridden /rɪdən/
see	saw /sɔ/	seen
shake	shook	shaken
take	took	taken
write	wrote	written /rɪtən/

Base form ending in o + -ne

Base form	Simple past	Past participle
do	did	done /dʌn/
go	went	gone /gɔn/

i - a - u

Base form	Simple past	Past participle
begin	began	begun
drink	drank	drunk
ring	rang	rung
sing	sang	sung
swim	swam	swum

ow - ew - own

Base form	Simple past	Past participle
blow	blew /blu:/	blown
grow	grew	grown
know	knew	known
throw	threw	thrown

ear - ore - orn

Base form	Simple past	Past participle
swear	swore	sworn
tear /tɛr/	tore	torn
wear	wore	worn

Common stative verbs

Thinking / opinions

(dis)agree	imagine	realize	suppose
believe	know	recognize	think
depend	matter	remember	understand
guess	mean	seem	

Feelings / emotions

feel (=have an opinion)	(dis)like	prefer	wish
	love	promise	
hate	need	want	

Senses

see	taste	feel
hear	smell	

Others

belong	have	involve
contain	include	own

Use stative verbs:

▸ to describe states / opinions, not actions.
  I believe in God. I hate spiders.
▸ in the simple form, even for temporary situations.
  Sorry, we don't understand. NOT ~~We aren't understanding.~~

Note:
▸ Some verbs which are usually stative can be actions:
  I think that's a good idea. (opinion).
  It's lunchtime, so I'm thinking about food. (action)
  We're having a 10-minute break.
▸ A few, especially *like* and *love* are increasingly used in speech as "actions":
  I'm liking this burger.
  I've been loving you for so long …

Sounds and usual spellings

▶ To listen to these words and sounds, and to practice them, go to the pronunciation section on the Richmond Learning Platform.

Vowels

/iː/	three, tree, eat, receive, believe, key, B, C, D, E, G, P, T, V, Z
/ɪ/	six, mix, it, fifty, fish, trip, lip, fix
/ʊ/	book, cook, put, could, cook, woman
/uː/	two, shoe, food, new, soup, true, suit, Q, U, W
/ɛ/	pen, ten, heavy, then, again, men, F, L, M, N, S, X
/ə/	bananas, pajamas, family, photography
/ɜr/	shirt, skirt, work, turn, learn, verb
/ɔr/	four, door, north, fourth
/ɔ/	walk, saw, water, talk, author, law
/æ/	man, fan, bad, apple
/ʌ/	sun, run, cut, umbrella, country, love
/ɑ/	hot, not, on, clock, fall, tall
/ɑr/	car, star, far, start, party, artist, R

Diphthongs

/eɪ/	plane, train, made, stay, they, A, H, J, K
/aɪ/	nine, wine, night, my, pie, buy, eyes, I, Y
/aʊ/	house, mouse, town, cloud
/ɔɪ/	toys, boys, oil, coin
/oʊ/	nose, rose, home, know, toe, road, O

Voiced

Unvoiced

Consonants

TO MAKE THESE SOUNDS WE USE

our lips	p	b	m	w
our teeth + another articulator	f	v	θ	ð
the tip of the tongue	t	d	n	l
the front of the tongue	s	z	ʃ	ʒ
the back of the mouth	k	g	ŋ	h
the tooth ridge	tʃ	dʒ	r	j

/p/ pig, pie, open, top, apple
/b/ bike, bird, describe, able, club, rabbit
/m/ medal, monster, name, summer
/w/ web, watch, where, square, one
/f/ fish, feet, off, phone, enough
/v/ vet, van, five, have, video
/θ/ teeth, thief, thank, nothing, mouth
/ð/ mother, father, the, other
/t/ truck, taxi, hot, stop, attractive
/d/ dog, dress, made, adore, sad, middle
/n/ net, nurse, tennis, one, sign, know
/l/ lion, lips, long, all, old

/s/ snake, skate, kiss, city, science
/z/ zoo, zebra, size, jazz, lose
/ʃ/ shark, shorts, action, special, session, chef
/ʒ/ television, treasure, usual
/k/ cat, cake, back, quick
/g/ goal, girl, leg, guess, exist
/ŋ/ king, ring, single, bank
/h/ hand, hat, unhappy, who
/tʃ/ chair, cheese, kitchen, future, question
/dʒ/ jeans, jump, generous, bridge
/r/ red, rock, ride, married, write
/j/ yellow, yacht, university

Audioscript

Unit 1

▶1.1 Notice the word and sentence stress and the connections.

M = Mika C = Carlos

M How's_it going? Settling_into your **new home**? How's_the **new job**?

C It's going_**OK**, thanks! I've **met_a few** new **people** through **work**, but it'll_be nice to_**make** some **more friends**.

M Of **course**. I'm_**sure** you'll_start meeting **people** soon. It's_early days. Got_any **plans_for tonight**?

C Yup, I'm **going_on_a** "**meet-up**"! It's the **first** one I've ever been_on, **act**ually!

M You're **going_on_a what**?

C You **know**, a **meet-up**. It's like a **so**cial group for people who want to_make **new friends_and net**work, that kind_of thing. I've **org**anized_it through_an_**app**. You **down**load the_**app** or go on the **website**, **reg**ister, and write_a **pro**file about **your**self. **Up**load pictures_and **stuff**. The_**app** then **matches** you with **people** who_you've got **things_in common** with. Then you go_**on meet-ups**. It could be_a **restaurant**, **museum**, sports_**act**ivity ... **anything**!

M Oh, I **see**. I **haven't heard** about **that**. It sounds like_a **great_idea**, **though**! E**spe**cially when you're **new_in town**. **So**, what **happens** when you've **registered** and been **matched** with **people**?

C **Well**, then you_can **chat_online** and get_ to_**know** people_a bit **there first**. **Then** you **choose**_a **meet-up** to_**go to**. I've **met** some **nice** people_**on**line so **far**. I **guess** I'll_**see** how the **meeting-up**_part goes! We're **going**_ on_an_**org**anized **walk**_on **Sunday** and the **org**anizers_en**cour**age you to_**prepare** some **questions** to_**ask** to_**help** get_to_**know** people.

M **Really**? Like_an **interview**. So, uh, what **kind**_of **people** are you_**hoping** to_**meet**, then?

C Um, I'm just_**hoping**_to_make some new **friends** who_are_into the **same** things_as **me** and can show me_around the **city** a bit. It would be **good**_to_meet some new_**work** con**tacts**, too. Networking_is_**always good**!

M **Really**? So, you're going_on this **meet-up** to_ make **work** contacts?

C **No**, not really. You_**know**, I just want_to_meet some **cool** people and if_I **meet** someone who can help with **business**, that's_a **bonus**!

M Always **thinking**_about **work**, aren't_you?

C Well, **sure**, that's_why I **moved** here. But I'm ready to_make some **new** friends, too. What_about **you**? What's_going_on with ...?

▶1.2 Notice /w/, the connecting /w/ (caused by two vowel sounds connecting), and silent w.

C = Carlos J = Jenny

C Hi ... I'm Carlos. It's really nice to meet you. You are ...?

J Hi, Carlos! I'm Jenny. We chatted online a bit. Great to meet you in person!

C Oh yes, we did chat online, didn't we? I remember now.

J So, have you been to one of these things before? I remember you said you were new in town.

C No, I haven't. I've just moved here recently, so this is the first one. I'm feeling a bit nervous, to be honest.

J Don't worry. It's only natural. It can be a bit scary meeting lots of new people at once, can't it?

C It really can be! So, how ... er ... how ...

J Shall we have a look at our questions? Did you prepare some? That will give us something to talk about while we walk.

C Ah, yes. Good idea. I did prepare some.

J Great. I've still got mine, too. I bring them to every meet-up I come to. It might seem a bit strange, but it's a really good way to get to know someone.

C OK then! Why don't you go first?

▶1.3 Notice the intonation. ↗↘

C = Carlos J = Jenny

J How long have you lived here? ↘ Do you have a favorite part of town? ↗

C Ah, that's a difficult one. I've only been here for two months, so it's difficult to say. I love the square—what's it called? ↘ Queen's Square. It's really pretty.

J Yes, there are some really nice bars and shops there. I'm going there tomorrow evening, actually. I'm meeting some friends for coffee. You're welcome to join us if you like. Anyway, your turn ...

C Ah, thanks. That's really nice of you! So ... er ... tell me about your friends ... Who do you spend the most time with? ↘

J Well, I'm working so much at the moment, I spend most of my time with my cats! I've got three.

C Three cats! I have to admit, I'm more a dog person. I prefer dogs to cats.

J Well, I like dogs, too, but cats are easier to take care of.

C True.

J My turn. What about your parents? ↘ Who are you closer to—your mom or your dad? ↗

C Mom. Definitely. I haven't had any contact with my dad in years ... I don't want to talk about that if you don't mind.

J Oh, I'm sorry. Of course not.

C No need for you to be sorry. So, what are you doing this weekend? ↘

J This weekend, I'm visiting a friend for her birthday.

C That sounds like fun.

J It will be. OK. My turn. What celebrity would you enjoy having dinner with? ↘

C Hmm ... Let me think. I'd have to say Emma Stone ...

J Oh, me, too! She's the best. I've seen all of her movies.

C Really? Isn't she fantastic? ↗ So ... speaking of movies, what was the last movie that made you cry? ↗

J That's a good question ... Well, probably *A Street Cat Named Bob*. You know I love cats, and that cat was just amazing.

C No way! I cried like a baby watching that one, too.

J What's the first thing you do every morning? ↘

C That's easy! I throw my alarm clock on the floor. I hate the noise it makes!

J I see! Not a morning person, then. I love early mornings! It's the best time of day. Carlos, here's another question. What's the one thing you're most afraid of? ↘

C Promise you won't laugh? ↗ ... The dark.

J The dark? ↗ Oh, that's kind of cute.

C You think so? ↗

J Look at you! You're turning red! Are you a little bit embarrassed? ↗

▶1.5 Notice the final /t/ sounds and the connections with vowels.

I first met_Adam two years_ago. I used to walk my dog_in the park next to my house and he was_always there walking his dog, too. We just used to smile and say hello. Anyway, I was_attracted to him immediately. He has this really beautiful smile and ... one morning the dogs started playing together and he said something lame about the weather_or something and we started chatting and we got_along really well, so we swapped numbers. Then we went_out together a few times, you know, just for coffee and stuff. I thought he was funny and charming_and interesting. We started hanging out a lot more, going to restaurants and meeting each other's friends. We talked_about everything and got to know_each other really well. Things were great for about the first six months and then, you know, it was little things at first. I was working a lot_at the time and he couldn't understand why we weren't spending as much time together. We argued a lot and fell out_over stupid things like not returning each other's messages. It just wasn't working and eventually we broke_up. I got so angry with him that he couldn't_understand how important my career was to me. We were both really upset. After a few more months, I started to miss him, so I called and we talked_about stuff. He promised to be more understanding and I promised to make more time for him. Then we got back together! I think I ... I think I've fallen for him again! How weird is that? But who knows what_our future will bring!

▶1.7 Notice the false starts, repetitions, and uh pauses.

Kathy I think be realistic that you, our expectations sometimes are so high ... But most of marriage is lived in between the ups and the downs... And that it's hard work. And not all the time, but it's hard work.

Gene Uh, I think one of the pieces of advice that my dad gave me is, "Gene, always communicate. Always talk, talk things out." And I really believe that communication is so essential ... And that uh, you need to work out many different areas before you get married. Uh, I think you need to talk about money matters. I think you need to talk about child rearing. I think religion is important. I think sex takes care of itself ... Pretty much ... At least initially. But I really do think there are some topics or some areas that need to be hashed out, otherwise, it's conflict.

Karl You gotta learn to uh, give more than you take, or you'll never make it and uh, that, that's the bottom line.

Bonnie And you need, you need to, you know, grow together, uh, in what, in what you do ... Try new things, you know. Go out and start skiing if you haven't done it, do it as a couple. Do things together, you know, or as a family if you have a family. I think those are important things, too, you know. Don't you have your own hobbies and your husband or spouse have their own hobbies. That's not a real good way ...

Bill Every time, if you have a disagreement or a problem, you correct it before you go to bed. And uh, then, you never wake up, and uh, with a carry-over. And uh, that has—to me—always been good advice. I'm not sure that Kay and I have always followed that, but uh, you know, most of the time we have.

Kay I'd have to say those who play together stay together, instead of going your own separate ways and doing your own things.

▶ 1.9 Notice /ə/ and sentence stress.

Professor Robin Dunbar is an anthropologist and evolutionary psychologist at Oxford University. He is famous for calculating "Dunbar's Number," which is an estimate that the number of relationships humans are able to manage is 150. He believes that this number has been almost the same throughout human history. From small villages in the past all the way up to the modern age of international travel and social media. Dunbar's Number came from research Professor Dunbar did with primates in the 1990s. He discovered that there was a connection between the size of these animals' brains and the social groups they belonged to. By using the data he collected in his studies of primates, he estimated that humans should be able to handle only 150 relationships at any one time.

In order to build relationships, we need to remember details about people's lives, etc., so the size of our brains is an important factor. According to Dunbar, our brains can only hold enough information to maintain about 150 relationships. This number can be seen in lots of different situations: the size of villages, remote tribal groups, the number of Christmas cards we send, and the average number of Facebook friends we have.

Of course, within these 150 relationships, there are different levels. The first is made up of about five very close friends, the next 15 are good friends, 50 friends we see reasonably often, and then the remainder is acquaintances. This number is based on averages, so it's possible to have more or fewer people in your social circles. However, if we have more, it will be difficult to manage and the quality of the relationships will suffer. It seems that 150 is the best number. With this many people, we can maintain stable, honest relationships.

▶ 1.10 Notice /θ/, /ð/, and /d/.

J = Jamie A = Alison

J That's a nice picture! Are they your colleagues?
A Yes, they are. They're a great bunch. Luckily, we all get along really well.
J When did you take that one?
A That was taken at the Christmas party last year!
J Looks like you had fun! What about this one? Who's that?
A That's Lucy. She's my sister's best friend. She's a musician.
J Does she play professionally?
A Yes, she does. We often go to watch her.
J Can she play any other instruments?
A Sure! She's really talented; one of those people who can play anything!
J Oh, what a nice shot! Who took this one?
A My dad took it, I think. This is Dominic. We've known each other since kindergarten. He's great. The kind of person you can depend on.
J So, out of all these lovely people, who are you closest to?
A Hard to say, really. I love them all!

▶ 1.12 Notice the spellings of /k/.

A = Anna B = Betty

A So, who are you following on Insta these days? I want to find some new accounts to follow. Any good ones?

B Yes, sure. I've added some really cool ones recently. Do you want to see?
A OK, let's have a look.
B Right, well, I like to follow accounts that I find inspiring, funny, cute, etc. For example, travel accounts. Look at this one. This couple is traveling the world together. They take amazing photographs and they really inspire me. Each photo is so creative! I mean, who doesn't want to do what they're doing?!
A Oh, I see! Look at that picture. Wow! They sure look like they're having an amazing time. Where is that? Vietnam?
B I think so. They certainly are worth following, I think.
A OK, I'll add them! What else?
B I don't know about you, but I just love anything with cute animals, so I follow a few of these accounts. Look at this one! I mean, these instantly put me in a good mood.
A "Animal Addicts." Oh, look at the puppies! So cute!!
B And then there's this one. These guys rescue mistreated animals. It's so moving and inspiring.
A Ah, yeah. That one's definitely for me. I'll add it. Why would anyone ever want to hurt those animals? It's so touching to see those people with them!
B I know. I do love this one. It's one of my favorites. Want to see some more?
A Sure, this is fun!
B OK, I also like following accounts that post motivational quotes. Look, this one's called "Secret to Success." It's quotes from famous people.
A "Don't watch the clock. Do what it does. Keep going." I like that!
B It does make perfect sense.
A I'll follow that one, too. Thanks! I've got some great ones to follow now.

▶ 1.15 Notice the intonation. ↗↘

K = Kelly R = Roberto

K So ... How did it go last night? ↘
R You mean the date? ↗
K Yep. The one you met on that player.me app, right? ↗
R Yes, that's the one. Well, we arranged to meet at Starbucks on 57th. You know, the cozy one, great coffee ...
K Uh-huh.
R I got there a bit late because of the traffic and ... Well, anyway, I opened the door and, to my surprise ...
K Go on ... ↘
R I spotted her immediately. Sitting right in front of me, drinking coffee. It was obvious it was her even though I had no idea what she looked like. She was just perfect, you know? ↗
K Hold on a sec. You mean you hadn't seen her photo? ↗
R No! You see, she hadn't put a picture of herself on her profile. Just an image of the character she likes playing.
K No way! ↗
R Yeah, but I knew straightaway she was the girl I'd been chatting to on the app! I just knew.
K What happens next? ↘
R Our eyes meet, we shake hands and, you know, try to break the ice, talk about the coffee, the weather, the traffic ...
K And then ... ↘
R She gets up and leaves.
K What do you mean "leaves"? ↘

R She says, "Look, I don't think this is going to work out," leaves her share of the bill on the table, and walks away.
K Just like that? ↗
R Just like that. ↘
K Are you serious? ↗
R Yep. So there you go, one more disastrous date for my collection. How about that? ↘
K Oh, dear. Well, don't let it get to you, Roberto. You know, you'll meet someone else.
R Yeah, yeah ... Oh well.

Unit 2

▶ 2.4 Notice the silent letters.

It started out as an experiment. I wanted to see if I could leave no impact on the environment for an entire year, and I asked myself, "Was it possible I could become a happier person by reducing my impact on the environment?" And the answer I found out is a resounding "yes." So, I started by cutting out garbage, taxis, throw-away coffee cups ... I eliminated tomatoes in the middle of January, A/C in the dead of August, bottled water from France, and new clothing from who knows where. I saved money, lost weight, gained energy, improved my health, spent more quality time with my family and friends, renewed my relationship with my wife, and discovered an overall sense of freedom. I learned that, yes, sometimes less is more.

▶ 2.7 Notice the silent h and the /ə/ in the *How long* questions.

1 M Guess what! I go to the gym twice a week now! [beep]
  W Really? How long_have you been going there?
2 M I live near the park now, you know? [beep]
  W Really? How long_have you been living there?
3 M Susan's going out with Paulo. Can you believe that? [beep]
  W Really? How long_has she been going out with him?
4 M John's learning how to recycle glass. [beep]
  W Really? How long_has he been learning that?
5 M Rick plays the guitar really well. [beep]
  W Really? How long_has he been playing it?

▶ 2.9 Notice the short (/) and long (//) pauses.

1 The Earth is getting hotter, / not the sun. // In fact, / a number of independent measures of solar activity / indicate that the sun has cooled by a few degrees since 1960, / over the same period that global temperatures have been increasing. // Over the last 35 years of climate change, / sun and climate have been moving in opposite directions.
2 Some people say, / "Well, we've had ice ages and warmer periods, / so climate change is natural! / It's got nothing to do with us!" // This is like saying that forest fires have happened naturally in the past, / so any recent forest fires can't be caused by humans. // It just doesn't make sense.
3 Climate researchers have been publishing papers for years / saying that climate change is happening right now. // We can see the evidence in flooding and droughts all around the world. // We need to start making changes / immediately. // Around 97% of researchers agree on this. // There is no "Planet B."

4 Climate change deniers say the planet has been cooling down since a peak in 1998. // However, experts have shown that in a climate being warmed by man-made carbon emissions, / it is possible to have long periods of cooler temperatures. // This does not mean that climate change isn't happening. // In fact, / globally, / the hottest 12-month period ever recorded / was from June 2009 to May 2010.

5 A large number of ancient mass extinction events have been linked to global climate change. // Because the world's climate has been changing so rapidly, / the way species typically adapt / (for example, migration) / is, / in most cases, / simply not possible. // This, / along with poaching, etc., / does not help the world's threatened species.

▶ 2.12

1 Notice /ɪ/ and /iː/.
L = Lorna B = Beth

L Hi, Beth! You're looking well. Have you been on vacation?
B Hi! I wish. No, I haven't. Thank you, though.
L What have you been doing, then? I mean, you've obviously been doing something. You look great! You're really glowing!
B Well ... actually ... I've been trying this new dietary supplement.
L Ah, not another one of these "superfoods"?! They are such a load of nonsense!
B Yes, it is ...

2 Notice the connections in speech.
Z = Zach P = Pedro

Z Hey, Pedro, I tried_to call you, like, five times. Dude, where were you?
P Ah, Zach. Sorry bro. Not my fault. It's this thing_I bought ...
Z ... one_of those green models?
P Yeah, but, uh, I'm_taking_it back_to_the_store first thing tomorrow.
Z Oh yeah? How come?

3 Notice the /t/, /d/, and /ŋ/ endings.
B = Bruce T = Tom

T Are you still working for TechStars?
B I quit last month.
T Bruce! No! You loved that place.
B Yeah. I worked there for over ten years. But, like, you see, I ... I just couldn't handle the stress ...
T I know what you mean, sure. So, uh ... Have you found a job yet?
B Nope.
T So, like, let me try a different question. Have you been looking for a job?
B No ... You see, I spent the whole month away from Chicago ... just meditating, relaxing, and trying to find some peace of mind, you know?

▶ 2.13

1 Notice /s/ and /z/.
L = Lorna B = Beth

L Ah, not another one of these "superfoods"?! They are such a load of nonsense!
B Yes, it is. Moringa, have you heard of it?
L Mor ... what? No, I haven't. What is it?
B It's the leaves of the Moringa tree. They call it the "Miracle Tree." It's meant to be one of the healthiest things around.
L Well, it does seem to be working on you. What do you do with it?
B You just add it to drinks and food. It's really easy to use and I have to say, I've really noticed the benefits. I've got more energy, I'm sleeping better, and I'm not catching as many colds. It's really worth it!

L I can see. Let me know where you buy it. I'm definitely going to try it!

2 Notice the spelling of /uː/, /ʊ/, and /aʊ/.
Z = Zach P = Pedro

Z Oh yeah? How come?
P I've been trying to call you back for about an hour, and I haven't been able to get through. This thing is useless!
Z No kidding! It just doesn't connect to the network?
P No, it just keeps dying after an hour. What a waste of money! To think I threw away the old phone! I had my old Samsung for three years, and sure, it wasn't "green," but the battery life was much better.

3 Notice /ŋ/ and /n/ + consonant.
B = Bruce T = Tom

B No ... You see, I spent the whole month away from Chicago ... just meditating, relaxing and trying to find some peace of mind, you know?
T Wow! But where exactly did you go?
B I went to a meditation retreat up in the mountains. I was there for about a month, you know?
T And ...?
B I'm a brand new man.
T No way!
B Yeah. Never been happier.

▶ 2.17 Notice /r/ after vowels.
Our planet has some amazing species, but too many of them face extinction. Here are some of the rarest animals on earth. Perhaps the most famous rare animal is the giant panda. In 2014, scientists found fewer than 2,000 pandas in the bamboo forests of China, and there are only 300 pandas in our zoos, too. Imagine the world without pandas!

Next, one of the rarest marine animals. The Hawaiian monk seal only lives in the ocean around the beautiful islands of Hawaii, and fewer than 1,000 of these magnificent creatures remain.

OK, next up is the adorable golden lion tamarin from the Atlantic forests of Brazil. There are only around 3,000 of them left in the wild, although at least this number is now up from just 200 in 1980. Way to go, Brazil, keep up the great work!

It's not such good news for the mountain gorilla. They are under threat from poaching, war, and loss of habitat through deforestation. These gorillas were only discovered about 120 years ago, and now there are only about 800 left in the African mountains.

Another ocean mammal in extreme danger is the North Atlantic right whale. Mostly found along the Atlantic coast of North America, they are one of the most endangered of all large whales. Despite over 70 years of protection from hunting, fewer than 400 of these extraordinary creatures are still alive.

A similar sad story is the Javanese rhino. People have been killing this beautiful animal to make medicine for hundreds of years—and now there are approximately only 60 left, living in the Ujong Kulon National Park in Java, Indonesia.

And the worst story of all. Due to loss of habitat in their native forests of the southeastern United States, scientists believe that there are very few ivory-billed woodpeckers in the world, maybe even none. How awful is that?

Come on, people! Wake up! Let's finally learn from this and try to save what is left of our rich and varied wildlife—before it's too late. It's now or never ...

▶ 2.19 Notice /f/, /v/, and /b/.
Are we failing to communicate? Have we forgotten what first inspired our love of nature? All the

evidence shows that the single most important factor behind taking action is our childhood experience. The wellspring of our commitment comes from the emotional high we reach when in contact with nature. But how can this wonder be harnessed to change our behavior? Showing the loss of animals in faraway places may pull a few heartstrings—even attract donations. But does it really change our behavior? What if we were able to communicate to people the wonder of nature that surrounds them and promote education that leads to awareness of threatened species and the habitats they live in? In all parts of the world, we're beginning to see that public awareness does lead to change, where people can see the benefits from making their own contribution. It's not the depressing accounts of the wildlife we are losing that moves us. It's awe and wonder, enhanced by understanding, that can inspire us to take action. It's love, not loss.

▶ 2.20

1 Notice /w/ and /l/.
P = Phil L = Laura

P ... threatened species. Anyway, so Claire and I went on the Internet, accessed WWF.com, and we adopted a whale.
L Phil, why would you want to adopt a whale?
P Well, we paid 50 bucks and they ...
L Oh, Phil! Seriously. What is the point of spending money on an animal you will never see? Life's too short. Live a little.
P Honestly, Laura, don't you think ...

2 Notice /ʌ/ and /ʊ/.
W ... so, anyway, guess what. I've just created this brand-new blog to try to raise public awareness and I've been getting a lot of hits ...
M Oh yeah? Let's have a look. Hmm ... Wow, Brenda, you've put a huge effort into this. It looks really good. Keep up the good work.
W Thanks a lot! Yeah, I'm really pleased with it. I know it isn't much, but I need to follow my heart. The gorillas' lives are on the line here. And you know what ...

3 Notice the connecting /w/.
M1 ... and that's why, as I told you, we need to attract as many donations as we can.
M2 Uhmm ... And how exactly are you planning to do that?
M1 Well, I don't know. I've been thinking of going door to door.
M2 Door to door! Wow, you are determined! Good for you. Don't give up!

4 Notice the connections.
M Honey, I have_a little surprise for you.
W What?
M Look_over there.
W Oh, my God, don't tell me it's that new electric car you've been going_on_and_on about.
M Yep. Bought_it this morning. Wanna_go for_a ride?
W Honey, what's the use_of buying that when_you know nothing's gonna change? Look_around_ you! This must be the only electric car_in the neighborhood.

5 Notice /ʃ/, and /z/.
W1 ... so, since then, no more plastic bags. Ever. I've been using my own reusable bags whenever I go shopping.
W2 Every time? Way to go, Janet! I wish I had that kind of self- discipline.

Review 1

▶ R1.2 Notice the intonation ↗ on the short questions.

OK, now put each noun and adjective together. OK? ↗ So you should have three combinations, for example, an imaginative panda, an easy-going chicken, or an outgoing whale. Right, so let's find out what this means. Ready? ↗ The first combination is how you see yourself. Your self-image—OK? ↗ The second combination is how other people see you. Yeah, that's what they think of you. And, wait for it, the third combination is the truth, it's how you really are. That's you! Surprised? ↗ Or do you agree?

▶ R1.3 Notice /θ/ and /ð/.

Amazing Facts!

Fact one: Are you afraid to swim in the ocean? Sharks kill 8 to 12 people a year around the world, but really they should be scared of us. Scientists estimate that humans kill 100 million sharks annually.

Fact two: In 1990, 43% of the global population lived in poverty. By 2010, only 21% were living on less than $1.25 a day. The United Nations hopes to end extreme poverty by the year 2030. Let's hope they can!

Fact three: Edison Peña is one of the 33 miners who were stuck in a Chilean mine for 69 days in 2010. Edison ran 6 miles a day when he was in the mine and one month after escaping he ran the 42 kilometer New York marathon in just 5 hours and 40 minutes.

Unit 3

▶ 3.3 Notice the short (/) and long (//) pauses.

While people in Hong Kong are very familiar with western culture, / there are still unique social etiquettes that tourists should observe. // When greeting someone in Hong Kong, / a handshake is common, / but do it with a slight bow. // Kissing on the cheek and hugging is not practiced. // It is OK to gently push your way through the crowd as Hong Kong is so densely packed; // in fact, / if someone says they're sorry / while navigating the crowd, / it's considered impolite. // When giving gifts, / always give them with two hands. // Do not give clocks as the Chinese associate clocks with death. // And // gifts are never opened in front of the person that gave them. // When eating with others, / it's important to be aware of important table etiquette. // As a courtesy, / fill the tea cups of others / before pouring your own cup, / even if their cups are not empty. // When you need a refill, // keep the lid of the teapot half open, / and the waiter will get the hint. // Blowing on the soup is considered OK / to cool down the soup. // After you're done, / don't leave your chopsticks standing straight up, / as this signifies death. / Leave them flat on the table. // Tipping is customary, / a service tip of 10% is expected, // and tip the server directly, / as leaving a tip on the table is considered impolite. // Now you know a little bit more about Hong Kong. // This is Rosanna Wilcox, / informing you about Hong Kong.

▶ 3.7 Notice the silent final letters.

Raul I was studying full-time, had a part-time job to help with the student debt, I wasn't eating or sleeping properly, and my nonstop lifestyle was driving me crazy. I couldn't find that work-life balance. One day, I was studying in the middle of the night with the radio on and a classical tune came on that I used to play when I was a kid. It reminded me how much I missed playing the piano! The next morning, I sat down at my piano for the first time in years and started to play. I felt the stress just drain away from me. It's amazing how something so simple can have such a positive effect. Now, although I'm still just as busy, it doesn't really bother me as much. I always make time to sit down each day and play for ten minutes. Everything else melts away and I feel much better after. You should try it!

Tomiko I was getting up, drinking two cups of coffee, and grabbing an energy bar. Lunch was at my desk every day; a sandwich eaten in two minutes flat while working. I'd grab a takeout on the way home from work and in between there were more energy drinks and quick snacks. Food just didn't seem important, but I felt terrible and my energy levels were low. Things had to change! Now, I find it annoying if I don't have time to eat properly. I make sure that at least one meal a day is prepared with care. I plan what I'm going to eat, I go to the local farm shop and take time to enjoy the sights and sounds. I've made food more like a hobby. It takes more time, but I don't mind that. My health has improved and I'm hoping to start growing my own soon. I'm actually going on a beginner's gardening course this weekend.

André I first moved here five years ago for work. I didn't know anyone and I'd never lived alone before. Loneliness became a real problem for me. I couldn't stand coming home to an empty apartment every day. I could call my family and friends, of course, but it's not the same. I was walking home one day when this little cat started to follow me. She came right to the door and was still there a couple of hours later. Eventually, I let her in and that was it! We've been best friends ever since. It's just so nice to have someone to come home to in the evening. Even though I know she can't understand me, I still talk to her. It's just nice to have the company, you know. I still find the city a bit lonely at times, but I'm OK with it.

▶ 3.9 Notice how the similar sounds link.

Story 1

R = Rachel J = Juan

R You look a little bit depressed, Juan. What's wrong?

J Yeah, well, last Thursday I had a job interview—the third in a week.

R You poor thing!

J You see, I'd been trying to find a job as an architect for months, without success, of course, but I was really optimistic about that particular interview. Anyway, the big day finally came, and, hmm, guess what—there was a massive, massive traffic jam on the main avenue.

R Oh, no!

J Yep, but, you know, I wasn't too worried, since I'd woken up at six and left home at seven ... you know, just to be on the safe side.

R Right. What time was the interview?

J Eight thirty.

R Seems more than enough, doesn't it?

J Well, that's what I thought. At seven thirty, though, I was still stuck in exactly the same place, so I turned on the local traffic radio to see what was going on.

R And ...?

J Apparently, a bus had gone through a red light and crashed into three cars. On the day of my interview!

R Oh, no! Did you make it in time for the interview?

J Hmm ... Guess what time I got there. Eight fifty!

R You're joking! Gee! And how did it turn out?

J Surprise, surprise ... I didn't get the job I'd been dreaming of since I graduated! Darn it!

R Well, I'm sure something better will come along ... and next time be sure to rent a helicopter on the day of the interview.

J Ha, ha, very funny.

Story 2

S = Sandra E = Ethan

S [singing]

E I didn't know you liked Taylor Swift.

S Oh, I'm a huge fan. I'm crazy about her.

E Really? Have you ever seen her live?

S Yep. Well, sort of. E   Uh? What do you mean?

S Well, when I heard she was coming to Rio, I bought two tickets right away. Incredibly expensive, but I didn't care. Anyway, I spent the next two months anxiously waiting for the big day—the day I'd been waiting for since I was sixteen.

E Wow!

S On the day of the show, I left work two hours early and set off for São Paulo with a friend. She had arranged to pick me up in her car.

E OK, go on ...

S Well, we'd been driving for a little while when the car started making a weird noise. Then smoke started coming out from under the hood, so both of us started to freak out.

E No wonder! That sounds a bit scary.

S Yeah, I know ... We had to pull over. People were honking like crazy, but there was nothing we could do—the car broke down and we had to wait for road side assistance.

E So what happened in the end?

S Well, a mechanic arrived and told us we hadn't checked the oil. He fixed the car and we set off again. By the time we finally got to the stadium, she'd been singing for well over an hour. Thank goodness the security guards let us in.

E So you only caught—what—the last ten minutes of the show?

S Only the last few songs! But that was the best half hour of my life. I swear.

▶ 3.12 Notice the intonation in questions. ↗↘

1

A Excuse me ...

B Hang on a second, Julie. Yes? ↗

A Oh, hi ... uh ... Meditation 102 is about to begin.

B Yeah, I know. I'm in that group. Can't wait!

A Well, you see, we like to keep the school as quiet as possible, so ... uh ... I was wondering ... could you continue your conversation outside? ↗

B Oh, I'm sorry. Was I speaking too loud? ↗

A I'm afraid so.

B I'm sorry. I didn't realize that. Julie, gotta go, I'll catch up with you later.

2

C Excuse me ... Excuse me, miss.

D Yes? ↗

C Are you shopping with us? ↗

D Well, no, not now. Why? ↘

C Uh ... I'm afraid you can't park here.

D What do you mean I can't park here? ↘ Says who? ↘

C Just look at the sign over there.

D Oh, come on. Be reasonable. The parking lot's nearly empty and I ... and I just need to cash a check at the bank. Can I park here for just 10 minutes? ↗

C I'm afraid not.
D But I'm starving. I can bring you a muffin on my way back, how about that? ↘
C I'm sorry, miss. Our parking area's for patrons only. There's another parking lot right across the street and ...
D Well, I want to speak to the manager ...

3
E How may I help you, sir? ↘
F What do you mean "how may I help you"? ↘ Can't you see I'm going for my morning run? ↗
E I'm afraid this is private property, sir. You can't go beyond this point.
F Since when? ↘
E Since yesterday. Mr. Jobs just bought this whole area. You see the gate? ↗
F Well, I've been jogging here since 1999, so this is my area, too. They can't just close it off like that.
E Sir, I'm afraid I'm going to have to ask you to step back.

Unit 4

▶ 4.3 Notice the sentence stress and weak forms.

A I **can't** really **remember** the **last** time I had a **chance** to go in the **backyard** and just **run around**.
B School's just **so** much **pressure** that every day I **wake up dreading** it.
C I'm **afraid** that our **children** are going to **sue** us for **stealing** their **childhoods**.
D I would **spend six** hours a **night** on my **homework**.
E You **have** to get into the **top** schools.
F You **have** to **take tests** and do **interviews**.
G It's **gone way** to the **extreme**.
H We're **all caught up** in it.
I In **America**, if you don't **earn** a lot of **money**, **something** went **wrong**.
J The **pressure** comes from the **colleges**, from the **parents**, from the **government**, but it **has** to **stop**.
K You **have** to **do well** now, so you can get **into** a **good college**.
L **Everyone expects** us to be **superheroes**.
M You have a **fear** from the **parents** that my **kid** needs to be able to get a **job**.
N **How** do you **expect** us to do **well** when you **can't** even **make mistakes**?
O You're de**dicating** your **whole** life to your **grades**.
P You **have** to be **smart** and you have to be in**volved** in the **arts**.
Q I have **soccer** practice **every day**.
R **Plus** the **homework** on **top** of **that**.
S Pro**duce**, produce, produce ...
T It's im**possible**.
U I **couldn't cope**.

▶ 4.5 1 Notice the /ə/.

I = interviewer J = Justin
I Right, so you're basically saying that you hate the work you do.
J Well, I'm not sure about "hate."
I But you dislike engineering?
J Yeah ... I guess. I'm good at it, though.
I Oh, yeah?
J People at work say I'm really good at what I do, and ... they must be right.
I So ... Why exactly are you looking for a career change?
J 'Cause ... 'cause that's not where my heart is. I love music. Always have, always will.
I So, how come you majored in engineering, Justin?
J Well, Dad's an engineer and I'm an only child ... Do the math.

I And you've never considered getting a degree in music, arts, or something?
J Nope. Dad wanted me to follow in his footsteps, but I shouldn't have listened to him.
I Well, you're still young, you know. Have you thought about starting over?
J Nah. I'm way too old now. I should have gone to music school years ago.
I Well, I disagree. You see ...

2

I = interviewer Z = Zoe
I ... so, Zoe, you've come for some advice about your major, is that correct?
Z Uh-huh.
I Freshman?
Z Nope. I'm a sophomore.
I What seems to be the problem?
Z Well, I've been thinking of dropping out.
I Oh really? Why's that?
Z Well, basically, journalism's not my thing. I should have chosen another major.
I Right, but ... how can you be so sure that you've picked the wrong career?
Z Well, for starters, I can't stand writing and ...
I Oh ...
Z Yep. My writing really sucks. I can barely put two words together.
I I hear you, but ... um ... Did you enjoy writing at all when you were in high school? I mean, there's got to be a reason why you picked journalism.
Z Well, the truth is, I didn't want to lose touch with Kylie, Bonnie, Maria, and Tom.
I Excuse me?
Z My best friends. They all wanted to study journalism, so I ... hmmm ... I thought I'd learn how to like it eventually. Guess I was wrong ... Look, I know it was a stupid decision and I should have thought about it more carefully, but my question to you now is: Is it too late to switch majors?
I Hmm. Yes and no. You see ...

3

I = interviewer G = George
I ... so what is it that you do exactly, George?
G I'm a ... Roger, get out of here. I told you to wait outside, didn't I? Just go! Bad dog.
I You were saying ...
G I'm a dog walker.
I Uh-huh.
G The money's not bad and I ... I like dogs. But I'm 41 and ... you know, my wife thinks there is no future in it.
I Did you attend university at all?
G One year. Then I dropped out. You see, I really enjoyed college, but I just hated university, I didn't like being away from my family. But now I guess I'm paying the price. Every day I wake up and ask myself: Should I have persevered a little more?
I Well, yeah ... probably. But have you considered going back?
G Hmm ... Well, the thing is ...

▶ 4.8 Notice the short (/) and long (//) pauses.

1 One of my main goals is to get onto the property ladder as soon as possible. // Most people think I'm too young to be thinking about this kind of investment. At 22, / they think I should be going out partying and enjoying myself, / not working hard, / saving, / and putting all my money into real estate. // I'm still with my parents at the moment. // They are very supportive. // If I

didn't live at home, / I wouldn't be able to save anything. // My big dream / is to own lots of different apartments. // I'll buy them cheap, / do them up, and then sell them or rent them out. // If I work hard and save my money, / I'll see the benefits later. // My friends all think I'm a bit crazy, / but I'll be able to retire much earlier than them! //

2 I've always had itchy feet. // I never want to stay in one place. // There is a whole world out there to explore! // Imagine all of those different cultures and people and food // ... I have a big map on my wall at home and I put a pin in it every time I go somewhere new. // There aren't enough pins in there at the moment. // I've been to a few places in Europe, / but that's it so far. // My main wish is to reach all seven continents. // If there were nine or ten continents, / I would still want to visit each one! // I want to go in a hot air balloon over Cappadocia, / fly in a helicopter over the Grand Canyon, / dive on the Great Barrier Reef. // I know, I know, / all of this costs a lot of money. // If I save enough this year, / I'll go backpacking around Southeast Asia. // I can't wait! // So many places, / so little time! //

3 Earning this would mean everything to me. // It's taken me six years to get this far. // It means dedication, / perseverance. // You can't just give up. // In martial arts you have to be completely committed and dedicated to your sport. // Reaching that level is extremely difficult. // You have to go to every single class, / get beaten, / sweat, / cry. // All of this and still go to work or school! // If I pass this level, / I'll prove to myself that I can do anything I want. / To be honest, / if I didn't train in martial arts, // I wouldn't be the person I am now. / I feel more confident than ever before. / My ultimate aim is to become an instructor and have my own training school. //

▶ 4.12 Notice the connections and past forms of /t/, /d/, and /ɪd/.

1 His parents suspected he had a learning [beep] (disability).
2 He has trouble sleeping because he [beep] (constantly) sees numbers in his head.
3 By the age of three, Jacob could [beep] (easily) solve complex equations.
4 Jacob dropped out of [beep] (elementary) school.
5 At age eight, it was clear that his mathematical ability was [beep] (unusually) high.
6 He joined Purdue University and [beep] (eventually) became a paid researcher.

▶ 4.13 1 (with addition in ▶ 4.14) Notice the intonation of *What* and *Really*. ↗ ↘

I = Iris F = Fiona
I Hi, sorry I'm late. I missed the five o'clock bus.
F What happened to your car?
I Oh, you don't wanna know.
F What? ↗
I I drove into a tree.
F What? ↗
I Yep. A little dog ran out in front of me and I had to swerve quickly to avoid hitting it!
F Oh, my goodness! Well, look, at least you didn't get hurt. It could have been worse.

2

J = Josh B = Belinda
J Oh, no! Oh, no! Not again.
B What? ↘
J Seven hours of work gone to waste.
B What? ↗

J   Oh, you don't wanna know.
B   Know what? ↘
J   PC crashed again.
B   Don't tell me you had no backup. Josh, this is the third time this year! You should have known better.

3

G = Gina   J = Jay

G   I thought this was a new car.
J   It is.
G   Oh … uh … so …
J   Worst thing I've ever bought.
G   Oh, no. Really? ↗
J   Yeah, this is the second time it's broken down. And don't get me started on the price I paid.
G   Oh Jay, what a shame! You loved your last one like this. Well, what's done is done. You can always get rid of this one and get yourself a new model.

4

D = David   C = Carla   A = Anna

D   God, I hate this one.
C   What? ↗ No, you don't.
D   What do you mean? Look at this painting. My four-year-old could have done better.
C   David, shut up.
A   No, go on. I'm listening.
D   You know what I hate about it?
A   What? ↘
D   The use of colors. The whole thing's so primitive, you know? How can they call this art?
C   Listen, what my friend means is that …
A   Can you excuse me for a moment? There's somebody I've got to speak to.
C   David, are you out of your mind? She's the artist!
D   What? ↗ Oh, no!
C   What were you thinking?

Review 2

▶ **R2.2 Notice /w/ and /j/.**

M   Well, they arrived at the festival, but it had been canceled.
W   Yeah. I think it had been raining.
M   Yeah. It looks like it. And then they all stayed in one tent.
W   Uh-huh. The wind had taken the other tent.
M   Unlucky, huh? And what's this picture? They look cold.
W   Yeah, right. I guess they had been expecting hot weather because they are wearing T-shirts.

Unit 5

▶ **5.2 Notice /m/, /n/, and /ŋ/ endings and their spellings.**

P = presenter   N = Natalie

P   Hello and welcome to "Money-wise." Your weekly consumer program. This week we are talking to Natalie Dupont, a social media marketing expert. Welcome, Natalie.
N   Thank you.
P   On this program we're talking about the phenomenon of "shopping haul" videos. Natalie, can you explain for us?
N   Of course. YouTube "shopping haul" videos is a huge trend. A "haul" is a video of a vlogger unpacking and describing items they have bought.
P   OK, and why do people watch these?
N   For shopaholics, these videos are entertaining. It's strangely satisfying to see how people spend their money. There are millions of hauls posted on social media, and many companies have been using this user-generated content to

advertise their product. However, there is now a revolution. Vloggers are moving away from these materialistic videos and posting "anti-haul" videos.
P   What is an "anti-haul" video?
N   Basically, they encourage viewers to buy less. In the video they post, the vlogger gives a list of products they don't plan to buy because they think the products are useless or overpriced.
P   So, where did this trend for "anti-haul" videos come from?
N   Well, Beauty Vlogger Kimberly Clark started doing this in 2015. In her video, which has had over 100,000 views, Clark says we should "put the brakes on consumerism" and "stop shopping." She shows the viewer 14 products they don't need and shouldn't waste their money on. Clark's fans begged her to post more videos like this. This inspired other YouTube vloggers to post similar "anti-hauls" and there are now more than 850,000 online.
P   Really interesting. Why have they become so popular?
N   Because they talk to hardworking, underpaid shoppers. We have too many options and not enough money! Perhaps it's this generation. Millenials and Generation Z have grown up in a financial crisis. Students are in debt, there are fewer jobs. I think these videos speak to that generation. Research shows that Millennials would much rather buy experiences than stuff.
P   So, I guess the message is that you don't need most of the stuff marketed to you. Perhaps consumerism is finally going out of fashion!
N   Exactly!

▶ **5.3 Notice /ə/ and sentence stress.**

I started getting into debt when I was 18. I was at college, like you, so I took out student loans and signed up for credit cards.

I was enjoying student life! Who doesn't, right?! I would go on shopping sprees, buying clothes and music. I paid the minimum back on my credit card per month and the repayments were huge! There was 25% interest on top, so it quickly got out of control. I was overspending without even thinking about it, but what was I supposed to do? Stay home all the time? I just thought, "If I get a good job later, I'll pay it all back. No problem!"

Five years later, I graduated and I was $12,000 in debt. I had wasted a lot of money! I got my first job with a salary of about $2,000 per month, but my rent was more than 50% of that! I had to use the credit cards to keep my head above water. I managed to pay back a bit every month, but not enough. I was permanently in my overdraft. I never had any money and I kept pretending it wasn't happening. I think if I'd listened to advice at this point, I wouldn't have gotten into the mess I did.

When I turned 25, I was in more than $20,000 worth of debt. I was working hard and all the money was going to pay off the loans and credit cards. Think about that. One day, I went to the ATM and I couldn't withdraw anything. It was a wake-up call. I realized I couldn't keep living a lifestyle I couldn't afford. I had completely run out of money.

I couldn't tell my parents. They would have gone crazy! I had to change and get myself out of debt. This is how I did it: I took out one large loan to pay off all the credit cards and then started to pay off the loan. I cut up the credit cards, so I couldn't spend much. I set up a direct debit, so money automatically transferred from my account to pay off the loan every month. Every time I spent money

on something nice, I "matched" it by paying the same amount off on my loan. This was one of the best tips I heard, because it made me think about how much I was spending.

If I could give you one piece of advice, I'd say, be realistic about your lifestyle. Yes, I was young, free, and single, but I couldn't afford to live the life I wanted. I set myself a goal to get out of debt by my 30th birthday and I did it! It was tough, but I did it. I haven't used a credit card for a long time, but I think I'm ready to start using one sensibly now. If I had known then what I know now, I would have been much more careful.

▶ **5.8 Notice the connections and /t/, /d/, and /ɪd/ endings.**

You might be surprised to learn crowdfunding has been around for a very long time. But where did it all start?

An early example is the Statue of Liberty. The statue was a gift from the people of France to the United States in 1886. But after the American Committee ran out of money to pay for the site where the statue would go, publisher Joseph Pulitzer started a campaign in his newspaper to raise the money they needed. In five months, over $100,000 was raised by 160,000 donors including children, street cleaners, and politicians.

Even before this, people used crowdfunding to raise money. In 1783, Mozart hoped to perform three piano concertos in Vienna. He published invitations offering copies of the composition in return for money to help put on the concert.

The basic concept of crowdfunding is still very much the same these days, but the introduction of the Internet and crowd funding websites such as Kickstarter means that people around the world can easily connect with each other and donate to projects.

Internet crowdfunding first became popular in the art and music industry. In 1997, the rock group Marillion funded a tour through online donations from fans. They have since also funded albums this way. Their fans must really love their music!

Probably the biggest crowdfunding success is Pebble Technology. Pebble raised an incredible thirty million dollars and broke the record for the fastest ever campaign to be fully funded. Supporters received a Pebble watch, one of the first smart watches on the market.

So, what is the future of crowdfunding? Critics complain that businesses now use it to market their new products to more people and it's not just used by new start-up companies. But crowdfunding is now so popular that sixteen point two billion dollars was raised in 2016. When you look at the statistics and the success stories, no matter what the critics say, it can't be bad for young entrepreneurs! Got a business idea? It could work for you!

▶ **5.11 Notice the intonation. ↗↘**

A = Alberto   L = Laura   E = Ernie
Mrs. A = Mrs. Andrews
T = Tony   W = woman   S = Susie   M = man

1

A   What would you like for dinner, Rico? ↘ Tuna or chicken? ↘ Oops, we're out of tuna, Rico. Sorry. You poor baby!

2

L   Help! Somebody help! Oh my God. Not now. I'm late for work. Can anybody hear me? ↗ Excuse me … hi … I'm stuck between the fourth and the fifth floor. Could you send someone, please? ↗ Quick!

3

E I swear I did it, Mrs. Andrews, I swear, but Bart ate it. I tried to stop him, but I couldn't. It won't happen again, I swear.

Mrs. A. "The dog ate my homework." Yeah, right. Pretty lame, Ernie. Pretty lame.

4

T [breathing]

W OK, great. Breathe in as you move your left leg, and breathe out as you move your right leg to the left. Is everybody OK? ↗ Now, feel the vital energy flowing to your arms and hands.

5

S OK ... done that. What should I do now? ↘ Really? ↗ Well, if you say so ... OK, I've closed the window, but I don't understand ... How will that help? ↘

M Ma'am, I asked you to close the computer window—your browser, you know—not your living room window.

S My computer has no windows. Or doors. What are you talking about? ↘

○ 5.13 Notice the intonation ↗↘ of the echo questions.

M You know, I just can't believe you bought that stuff.

W I bought it on impulse. It was pure madness, I know.

M You bet. It can't work the way they advertised it would! Was it expensive?

W Expensive? ↗ It cost a fortune. I felt really guilty afterward, of course.

M Buyer's remorse, huh? ↗

W Yeah, at the time it seemed like a wonderful product, but ... it was such a disappointment.

M Well, what would you expect from these awful infomercials?

W I know, yeah ... And I think this stuff is actually quite dangerous.

M Dangerous? ↗

W Mmm, it smelled awful. Like really strong chemicals.

M Goodness knows what it did to your skin.

W And that's not all! They go on and on in the infomercial about how "natural" it is. Well, if you like looking like an orange ...!

M Oh dear. Was it really that bad? ↗

W Yes, it was and I used it before going to Jessica's wedding, so not only did I smell weird, but I was bright orange!

M But, uh, why on earth did you want to look tanned anyway, Liz? You have gorgeous skin.

W I do? ↗ Thanks! I guess it's just so fashionable these days, I wanted to give it a go.

○ 5.16 Notice /dʒ/, /tʃ/, and the consonant clusters.

1 Choosing

C = customer, SC = store clerk

SC Hello. Do you see anything you like?

C Oh, hi. Yeah, I like these shoes. Can I try them on?

SC What size do you take?

C Do you have a size ten in stock?

SC A ten? Uh—I'm sorry, ma'am, we're sold out.

C Ah, that's such a shame! It seems impossible to find larger sizes. Can you email me when you have some in stock?

2 Paying

SC Next, please ... Hello. Just the jeans and these two T-shirts?

C Yes ... No, sorry, this dress, too.

SC OK, that looks very nice.

C Oh, it's for my girlfriend.

SC Very nice. So that's $174.70. Cash or charge?

C Uh, charge.

SC OK. Insert your card, please.

C Uh-huh.

SC Ah. I'm afraid your card has been declined. Um, do you have another card?

C Declined! I don't understand. It's a new card, and I know I'm not over my limit. There must be a problem with your card machine.

3 Complaining

C Hello, hello. Yes, I'd like to return this phone. I bought it here the other day and it's damaged.

SC I see. Uh ... What seems to be the problem?

C Well, I bought it on ... Thursday, and when I got it home, I took it out of the box and ... well, you can see. The screen has a scratch on it.

SC Oh, oh yes. Well, uh, unfortunately, we can't give you a refund, but we'd be happy to exchange it for another one.

C Oh, that's great. Thank you so much.

SC Sure. Uh, I just need to see your receipt.

C Yes, of course. Uh, it's in here somewhere. Here it is.

PAUL SELIGSON
TOM ABRAHAM
CRIS GONTOW

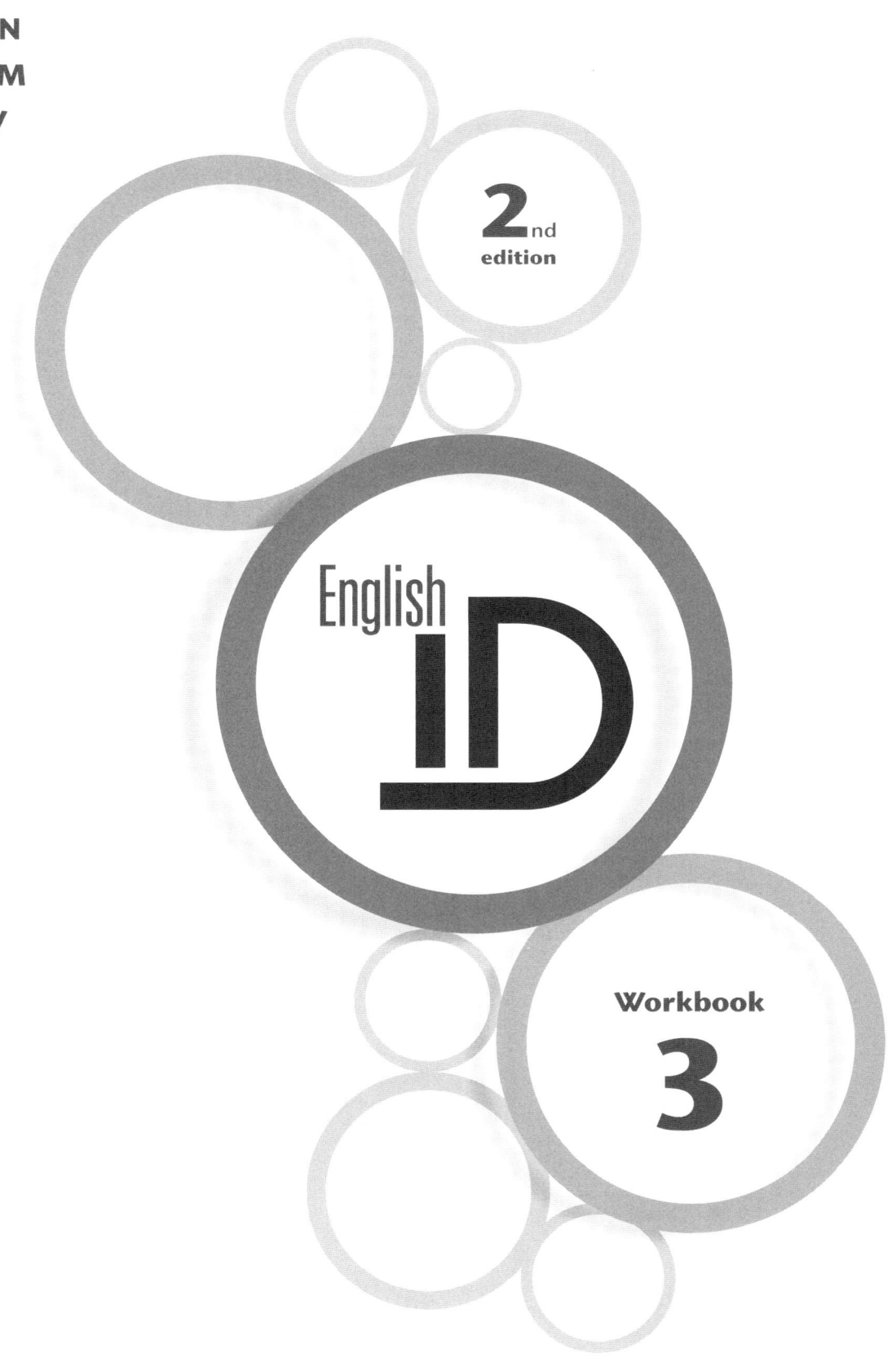

2nd edition

English **ID**

Workbook **3**

Richmond

1

1.1 Do you know all your classmates?

1 Match speed-friending events 1–3 to people a–g.

1 Come to the iD party!

New at school? Don't worry!
Speed-friending is a great way to meet new people and practice your speaking!
When: Friday, September 28th 8.30 p.m
Where: The iD Social Club

First 20 to register get a free snack!

For more info, contact the Students' Social Officer.

2 The Volunteer Society
Speed-friending for people who care

Want to make the world a better place?
Come and share ideas with people who feel the same as you.

Monday, December 7th
7.30 p.m - 9.30 p.m.
@Greenton Hall, St. Luke's Street.
Register by emailing bigheart@volunteerone.com.

3 East End Speed-friending and raffle

Come and meet your neighbors in the East End!

Wednesday, May 5th
6.00 p.m. - 8.00 p.m.
Boone Community Center

Spend a few minutes with each person, and get to know them all. Bring some food, too; it's a great conversation starter!
There will be a raffle at the end of the evening and we have some great prizes!
Contact Mrs. Hilary Dunn for more information.

a ☐ I've just moved into the East End.

b ☐ I just hate the silly, superficial small talk typical of speed-friending.

c ☐ I'm a language student, and I love parties.

d ☐ I'm free on September 28th

e ☐ My friends and I do volunteer work for a couple of charities when we can.

f ☐ Cooking is something I'm really good at.

g ☐ It's three weeks to Xmas. I don't want to spend the holidays alone.

2 Order the words in a–g to form questions. Be careful, there's one extra word in each.

a Facebook / have / do / How / you / you / many / friends / ?

b most / Who / do / makes / laugh / you / ?

c at / you / What / good / on / are / really / ?

d nervous / What / you / makes / are / ?

e last / did / do / does / What / vacation / you / ?

f speed-friending / Would / go / like / you / to / to / event / a / to / ?

g just / without / do / something / What's / live / you / can't / ?

3 Match questions a–g from **2** to these answers.

1 My cell phone, for sure.
2 Yes, I think they look fun.
3 I went to a water park with my cousins. We had a great time.
4 First dates. I never know what to say!
5 Reading and writing. I'm not very good at speaking or listening.
6 I have no idea! Too many to remember, that's for sure.
7 My friend Jack. He's such a funny guy.

4 🎧 **Make it personal** ▶1.1 Listen to the questions and answer using these words.

laptop	sports	first dates
mom	the National Park	

a What's something you just can't live without?

Well, let's see …

b What are you good at?

That's a difficult one. Er …

c What makes you nervous?

That's a good question. Well …

d Who are you closer to, your mom or your dad?

Hmm, let me think …

e What's the most fun place you've been to?

Hmm, I'm not sure …

1.2 How do couples meet?

1 Three authors made notes for a love story. Complete the notes with one word in each gap.

Love Story 1	Love Story 2	Love Story 3
They meet.	• They met.	They start hanging _____.
They fall _____ love.	• They got _____ really well.	She falls _____ him.
They _____ engaged.	• They fell _____ each other.	They move _____ together.
They get married.	• _____ _____ engaged.	He'll cheat _____ her.
They drift _____.	• They _____ married.	They'll break _____.
They get divorced.	• They lived happily ever after.	They'll get _____ together.

2 Match the stories in **1** to their views: a, b, or c.

a A fairy tale. **b** A boomerang relationship. **c** An extinguished candle.

3 Read the summary of *Romeo and Juliet*. Number the events in the correct order, 1–9.

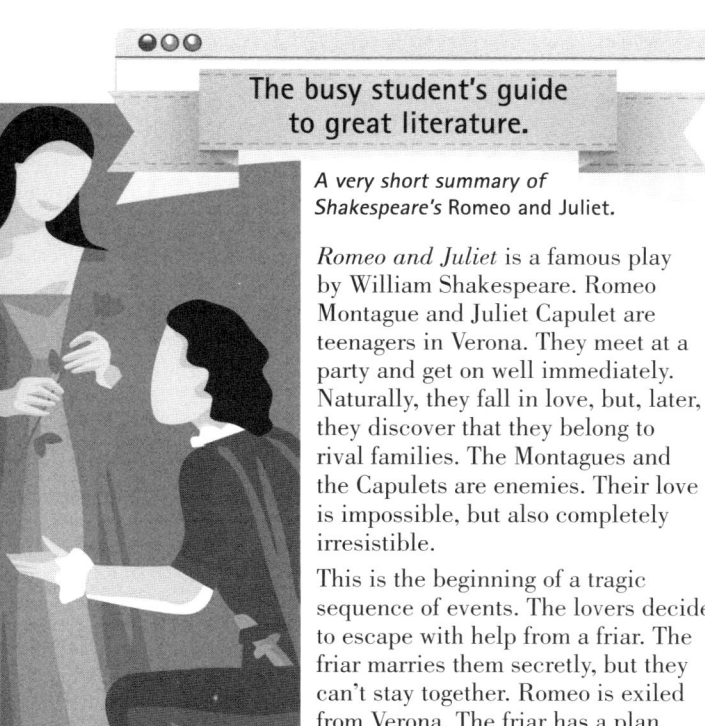

The busy student's guide to great literature.

A very short summary of Shakespeare's Romeo and Juliet.

Romeo and Juliet is a famous play by William Shakespeare. Romeo Montague and Juliet Capulet are teenagers in Verona. They meet at a party and get on well immediately. Naturally, they fall in love, but, later, they discover that they belong to rival families. The Montagues and the Capulets are enemies. Their love is impossible, but also completely irresistible.

This is the beginning of a tragic sequence of events. The lovers decide to escape with help from a friar. The friar marries them secretly, but they can't stay together. Romeo is exiled from Verona. The friar has a plan. He gives Juliet a herbal drink. She will "sleep" for 42 hours, enough for everyone to think she is dead. Then they will get together and leave Verona. Sadly, Romeo hears about Juliet's death, but doesn't know about the plan. He can't live without Juliet. He buys some poison, finds Juliet, and kills himself. Juliet wakes up and, finding Romeo dead, she takes his dagger and kills herself too. This classic romance has been an inspiration for generations of authors since.

4 ▶1.2 **Listen to the summary of** *Romeo and Juliet* **without reading. Check how much you understood.**

☐ 10–20% ☐ 30–50% ☐ 60–80% ☐ 90–100%

5 ▶1.3 **Look at the sound picture for the schwa, /ə/. Listen and repeat the sound and the words.**

6 ▶1.4 **Listen to extracts a–d and underline the schwas in each line. The number is in parentheses.**

a They meet at a party and get along well immediately. (4)

b Their love is impossible but also irresistible. (2)

c The friar marries them secretly. (4)

d ... but they can't stay together. (2)

7 🔊 **Make it personal** Find a simple summary of a well-known love story online. Exchange links with a study buddy and decide which you both prefer.

☐ Romeo dies
☐ escape
☐ meet
☐ Juliet dies
☐ get married secretly
☐ find out their families are enemies
☐ fall for each other
☐ get along well
☐ realize their love is impossible

1.3 How many Facebook friends do you have?

1 ▶1.5 **Order the words in italics to complete definitions a–d. Listen to check.**

a Acquaintances generally aren't *can / on / count / people / you /* .

b Friends are *usually / people / are / in / with / contact / you /* .

c Good friends are *along / people / get / with / you / and / hang / out / with /* .

d Very close friends are *always / rely / people / can / on / you / the /* .

2 ▶1.6 **Listen to a podcast about National UnFriend Day. What is it?**

3 ▶1.6 **Listen again. According to the podcast, which two things define a true friend? Someone who ...**

- ☐ is on your Facebook.
- ☐ helps you move house.
- ☐ shares his / her routine with you.
- ☐ has seen you recently.
- ☐ asks curious questions about you.
- ☐ is very good and nice.

4 Complete the Facebook comments.

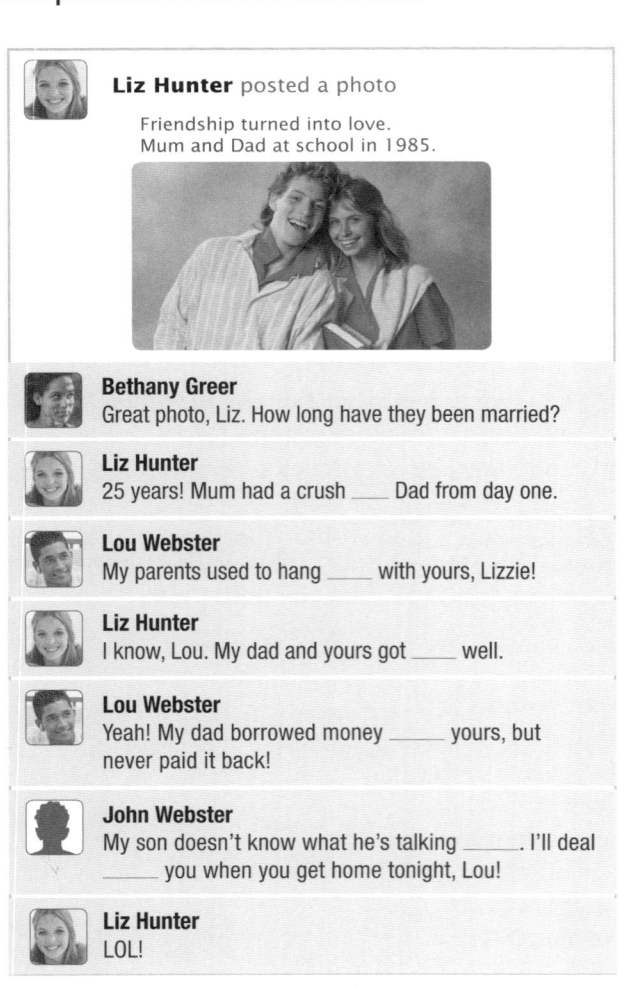

Liz Hunter posted a photo

Friendship turned into love.
Mum and Dad at school in 1985.

Bethany Greer
Great photo, Liz. How long have they been married?

Liz Hunter
25 years! Mum had a crush ____ Dad from day one.

Lou Webster
My parents used to hang ____ with yours, Lizzie!

Liz Hunter
I know, Lou. My dad and yours got ____ well.

Lou Webster
Yeah! My dad borrowed money ____ yours, but never paid it back!

John Webster
My son doesn't know what he's talking ____ . I'll deal ____ you when you get home tonight, Lou!

Liz Hunter
LOL!

5 ▶1.7 **Listen to a–f and check the correct column, acquaintances (A), friends (F), or very close friends (V).**

	A	F	V
a Tom and Lucy			
b Ben and Lou			
c J J and Bill			
d Sue and Rob			
e Joe and Pete			
f Meg and Amy			

6 🔵 **Make it personal** Think of someone you're attracted to and do the quiz. Write yes (Y) or no (N) in the first box.

Will it be love?

a ☐☐ Does this person give you intense looks?

b ☐☐ Does he or she often hold your hand or hug you?

c ☐☐ Have you spent more time together lately?

d ☐☐ Is your heart beating faster as you answer these questions?

e ☐☐ Do you spend more time with this person than with other friends?

f ☐☐ Do you like to talk with this person before you go to sleep every night?

g ☐☐ Have you and your friend felt jealous of each other lately?

h ☐☐ Are you going on holiday together any time soon?

Mostly Yes? Are you already married to this person?
50 / 50? Try a bit harder; he or she might be interested in you, too.
Mostly No? Give up and find someone else.

7 ▶1.8 **Listen to Gwen doing the quiz. Check / Cross her answers in the second box. What should she do?**

8 🔊 **Connect**

Create a quiz with questions about you. Email it to a friend and find out how well they know you.

1.4 Do you have many social media profiles?

1 Match words 1–10 with words / suffixes a–h to make personality adjectives.

1	adventure	a	minded
2	easy	b	loving
3	fun	c	seeking
4	knowledge	d	ful
5	like	e	iable
6	open	f	going
7	out	g	able
8	self	h	centered
9	soc		
10	thought		

2 Look at the selfies. Which adjectives from **1** can you use to describe each person? More than one adjective might be possible.

> adventure-seeking   easygoing   fun-loving
> knowledgeable   like-minded   open-minded
> outgoing   self-centered   sociable   thoughtful

3 ▶1.9 Complete Chloe and Jake's conversation about people to follow on social media with emphatic forms of the words in parentheses. Listen to check.

Jake: Oh, look at him. He looks quite boring and self-centered.

Chloe: Yes, that one _____ not for me. (**definitely / be**)

Jake: What about this one? They _____ very sociable. (**sure / look**)

Chloe: Yes, they look fun. And I _____ people who are a bit silly. I'll follow them. (**like**)

Jake: Ah, look at this one. What a cute couple.

Chloe: Hmm, yes they _____ in love. (**certainly / be**) But they're a bit over the top, don't you think? I _____ it when people are like that. (**hate**)

Jake: Ha! Yes, I know what you mean!

4 ▶1.10 Listen and copy the stress and intonation in extracts a–e.

5 Match questions 1–5 to opinions a–e.

1 What's important to you in a friend?
2 What do you think about people who post lots of selfies on social media?
3 Do you think we use social media too much?
4 What's the best social media app? Why?
5 How can you stay safe online?

a I do believe we use it a lot, but I don't think it's a problem.
b It's definitely important not to share too much information about yourself.
c I do think we should be like-minded.
d They sure are self-centered, but I don't mind. I like posting them myself.
e I don't know. I like them all!

6 🔵 **Make it personal** ▶1.11 Listen to check and email your opinion to your teacher.

1.5 How much time do you spend online?

1 People a–j have met through a dating service. Read and decide what each person wants after their first date.

Friendship

Nothing

Love

- a Jerry about Wang: "I had a good time with Wang. We both like *Star Trek* movies, but that's not enough for me."
- b Wang about Jerry: "Jerry's such a charming guy. I hope he'll ask me out again."
- c Zoe about Joe: "Joe is the most handsome guy I've ever met. He's totally gorgeous!"
- d Joe about Zoe: "Zoe is great! I'd love to date her."
- e Bernie about Lilly: "Lilly and I just didn't click at all."
- f Lilly about Bernie: "Bernie and I didn't get along. Scientific matching isn't perfect after all."
- g Marney about Ben: "Ben and I had fabulous chemistry for a blind date! He could be the one!"
- h Ben about Marney: "I can't wait to see Marney again. She's such fun, but only as a friend, sadly."
- i Hannah about Caleb: "Well, he is fun to be with, I guess, but there was no attraction between us."
- j Caleb about Hannah: "It was a little embarrassing. She's great, but not the one for me."

2 ▶1.12 Classify italic words in a–h: noun (N), adjective (ADJ), adverb (ADV), or verb (V). Listen and copy the stress and intonation.

- a Montagues and Capulets were *rival* families. _ADJ_
- b Romeo and Juliet fell for each other *immediately* when they met. _____
- c Romeo and Juliet's was an *impossible* love. _____
- d Good *communication* is essential in both friendship and love. _____
- e The hardest thing about marriage is learning to *communicate* with each other. _____
- f When Jo and I met, there was instant mutual *attraction* between us. _____
- g *Respect* is the most important thing in any relationship if it's going to last. _____
- h I got a divorce because my ex didn't *respect* me at all. And he was cheating on me, too. _____

3 ▶1.13 Listen and order the story of Antony and Cleopatra, 1–6.

PRODUCTION: Antony and Cleopatra
SCENE: Caesar and Antony fight to control Egypt. TAKE:

PRODUCTION: Antony and Cleopatra
SCENE: Antony cheats on his wife, Fulvia. TAKE: 1

PRODUCTION: Antony and Cleopatra
SCENE: Antony goes back to Egypt and Cleopatra. TAKE:

PRODUCTION: Antony and Cleopatra
SCENE: Antony marries Caesar's sister, Octavia. TAKE:

PRODUCTION: Antony and Cleopatra
SCENE: Antony and Cleopatra both die. TAKE:

PRODUCTION: Antony and Cleopatra
SCENE: Fulvia dies and Antony goes back to Rome. TAKE:

4 ▶1.14 Follow the model. React to the stories you hear.

So, Antony is married to Flavia.

You mean Fulvia, right?

- a You mean Fulvia, right?
- b No way! With Cleopatra, right?
- c So what happens next?
- d Hang on a sec! He marries Caesar's sister?
- e Are you serious? He cheats on her, too?
- f And then?
- g Whoa! What a crazy story!

Can you remember ...

> 3 verb forms for the present? SB→p. 7
> 6 phrasal verbs for relationships? SB→p. 8
> 6 compound adjectives for personality? SB→p. 12
> when auxiliary verbs are stressed? SB→p. 13
> 10 personality adjectives? SB→p. 13

2.1 How green are you?

1 Read the start of the article and check the correct meaning of "go off the grid".

- [ ] not use regular electricity
- [ ] ride a bike (cycle)
- [ ] turn the lights off

Pedal! For how long?

Physics teacher John Cornell's classroom at Henleigh High School will "go off the grid" for a day this Friday. But that does not mean they can't use any electrical items. Instead, there'll be pedal power to generate electricity.

2 Read the rest of the article. True (T) or False (F)? Correct the false statements.

Cornell and another teacher connected a bike to a power generator two weeks ago. As students pedal, their energy is converted into electricity that is stored in a car battery in the classroom.

"Students have been coming into our classroom an hour before class and staying for another hour after school to power the generator by cycling", Cornell said. When the battery's full, the students will vote for what they want to use the electricity for. Students will then calculate how much energy they'll need to do whatever they want to do.

For example, to watch a movie, they'll need to cycle for 72 minutes in order to power the TV and DVD player. To make waffles, they'll need much more energy and more pedaling. "This project is great fun and we've learned a lot," a student commented. "To get electricity you have to do hard work. I unplug my laptop and cell phone charger when I'm not using them now," another confirmed.

a Cornell is a chemistry teacher who started this idea on his own.

b The generator and battery are in different rooms.

c Students have been generating electricity on their own time.

d The teacher tells them how much energy each item needs.

e Watching a movie in class uses more energy than powering a waffle maker.

f At least one of John's students has learned to be greener.

3 Add one word to complete comments a–g. Are the speakers green (G) or not green (NG)?

a Yeah! We won't use plastic cups in this office anymore.

b What? Three thousand dollars for couple of solar panels? Forget it!

c Can have a couple more plastic bags, please?

d It's pretty simple be eco-friendly. I just try to reuse, reduce, and recycle.

e What? Recycling? It's useless. Forget!

f Are you joking? Why take the stairs when you can take elevator?

g I work in same office as my neighbor, Bill. Sometimes he drives me; other days I drive him.

4 ▶2.1 Match a–g in **3** to replies 1–7. Listen to check.

1 Yes, but you will save a lot more money than that on electricity bills.

2 I'm so glad. Those cups take 500 years to decompose.

3 I know. The three Rs. But it's not so easy!

4 No, it isn't. Think of all the trash you create when you throw things away.

5 Can I join you? That'd make it cheaper for the three of us.

6 Because the exercise is good for you and it will save energy.

7 Here you are. Would you like to buy a reusable bag?

5 Complete the sentences with a word from box 1 and a suffix from box 2.

1	2
energy fuel pet recharge reuse	able efficient friendly

a This product is _____, so it won't harm your dog.

b Let's get an _____ light bulb to put in that lamp.

c Hybrid cars are more _____ than traditional cars.

d Can I get a _____ bag for my groceries, please?

e It's got a _____ battery, you just need to remember to charge it!

6 Order the words to form green survey questions.

a plastic / home / you / do / recycle / at / ?
   Do you recycle plastic at home?

b flexitarianism / practice / you / ever / do / ?

c you / have / home / energy-efficient / light bulbs / do / at / ?

d transportation / using / of / you / to / walked / have / or cycled / work / lately / instead / private / ?

e when / appliances / using / you're / you / do / turn off / not / them / ?

f use / do / you / eco-friendly / products / cleaning / ?

g have / plastic / reusable / changed / from / you / to / cloth bags / ?

7 ▶2.2 Match a–d to the responses. Find four examples of /ɑ/ or /oʊ/ in each pair. Listen to check.

a Is the hotel down the road open?

b Don't go alone. I'll come with you.

c Has John gone to the vet?

d Hey, that's a nice orange top!

- [ ] Yeah. His dog stopped eating.
- [ ] Thanks a lot. I got it at the new store.
- [ ] Yes, I think so.
- [ ] Great! Get your coat.

8 🎤 **Make it personal** Record your answers to the questions in **6**, then share them with a classmate.

9

2.2 How long have you been studying here?

1 Amir made a list of "green" resolutions on January 1st. Use the notes to complete his blog with the present perfect continuous + or −. There is one extra note.

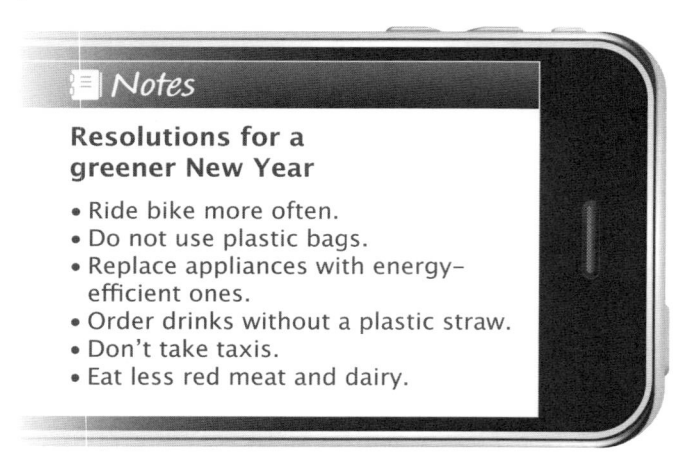

Notes

Resolutions for a greener New Year

- Ride bike more often.
- Do not use plastic bags.
- Replace appliances with energy-efficient ones.
- Order drinks without a plastic straw.
- Don't take taxis.
- Eat less red meat and dairy.

posts | about | contact

June 30th

I've been trying to go green for the last six months. It hasn't been easy, but I feel truly proud of myself. So far, I've managed to change quite a few things for the better. So, first of all [1]I've been bike riding to work twice a week. The exercise is good for me and I feel a lot healthier now, but it isn't much fun when it's windy and worse when it rains! ☹ And also on transportation, [2]_____ . It makes it hard to get home at night, but I'm saving a lot of money.

I'm shopping differently at the moment, too. [3]_____, because this type of plastic isn't recyclable and is filling up our seas, damaging the wildlife. Instead I take my own reusable bag. In cafés and restaurants, [4]_____, too. It's unnecessary and produces so much plastic waste. [5]_____, too, because raising cattle isn't very environment-friendly and uses up lots of the earth's valuable resources. I don't really miss it much to be honest, and I'm eating a lot more healthy now.

2 Reread and answer a–f.
- a How does Amir feel about his achievement? [1]
- b What's the disadvantage of cycling to work?
- c What's the advantage of not taking taxis?
- d What problems does using plastic create?
- e How does he feel eating less red meat and dairy?
- f Does Amir's blog encourage you to do the same?

3 ▶2.3 Many countries have been going green lately. Read changes a–h and predict which country is doing each. Listen to check.

Austria	Brazil	Costa Rica	France
Iceland	Norway	Sweden	Switzerland

- a In _____, architects have been building energy-efficient houses.
- b _____ has been using clean electricity from geothermal energy.
- c _____ has been building national Alpine parks.
- d _____ has been planting millions of trees to reduce deforestation.
- e _____ has been using more water and wind power for electricity.
- f _____ has been collaborating with Sweden to produce clean energy.
- g _____ has been producing a lot of its fuel from sugar cane.
- h In _____, more families have been installing solar panels at home.

4 Correct two mistakes in each of a–g.
- a The office have been really busy. We've been worked like crazy.
- b I like your shoes. I've been trying find a pair like that last year.
- c So sorry! Have you been waited for a long?
- d Hey! I've been trying to call you yesterday. Where was you?
- e He's been studied English for year.
- f They've been playing the soccer before.
- g Joan been managing the company advertising since 2012.

5 ▶2.4 Make sentences with the present perfect continuous. Follow the model.

Model: *Try to call you.*
You: *I've been trying to call you.*

6 👤 **Make it personal** What have you done this year to be "green"? Make a list of things you've done.

7 📶 **Connect**
Use your phone to record your answers and share them with a classmate.

2.3 How has the climate been changing?

1 Order the letters to spell environment phrases.

a NGIAOPCH
b RDUGOHTS
c OSLDFO
d NSEDROFATOIET
e NGIRSI ESA VLEESL

f PNGIUDM FO EESTWA
g TNHERTDEAE PCEISES
h LFSOSI LSEFU
i MEATLIC NECAGH

2 ▶2.5 Listen to two students and check the four problems in **1** they mention.

3 ▶2.5 Listen again and answer a–f.
a Does their city suffer from floods or droughts?
b Were Lucy and Mikaela personally affected?
c Have the authorities repaired all of the damage?
d When was the last time it rained in the north?
e What percentage of the earth is water?
f Which country does Lucy give as an example?

4 ▶2.6 Imagine significant progress is made in the next 50 years to protect the environment. Read the future news, and write the verbs in the present perfect or perfect continuous. Listen to check.

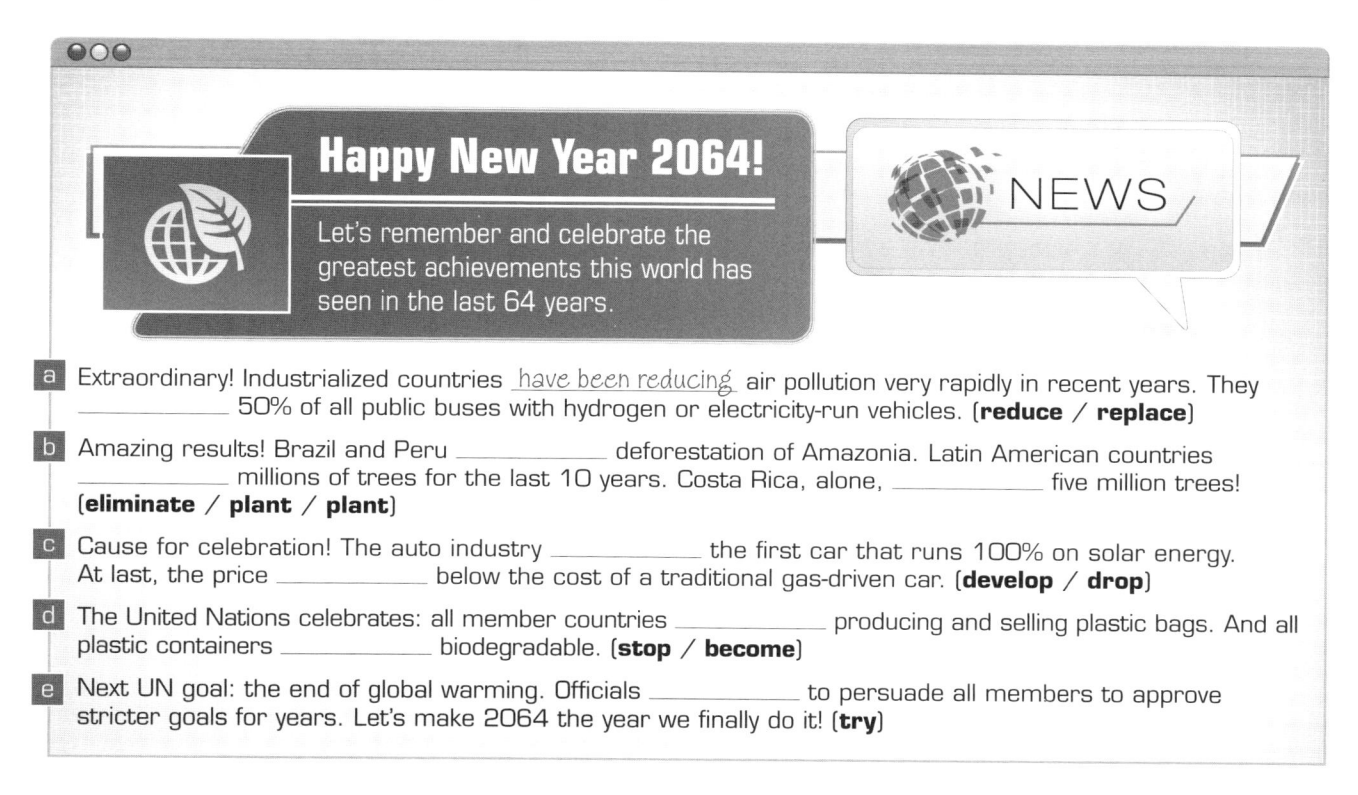

Happy New Year 2064!

Let's remember and celebrate the greatest achievements this world has seen in the last 64 years.

NEWS

a Extraordinary! Industrialized countries _have been reducing_ air pollution very rapidly in recent years. They _____ 50% of all public buses with hydrogen or electricity-run vehicles. (**reduce** / **replace**)

b Amazing results! Brazil and Peru _____ deforestation of Amazonia. Latin American countries _____ millions of trees for the last 10 years. Costa Rica, alone, _____ five million trees! (**eliminate** / **plant** / **plant**)

c Cause for celebration! The auto industry _____ the first car that runs 100% on solar energy. At last, the price _____ below the cost of a traditional gas-driven car. (**develop** / **drop**)

d The United Nations celebrates: all member countries _____ producing and selling plastic bags. And all plastic containers _____ biodegradable. (**stop** / **become**)

e Next UN goal: the end of global warming. Officials _____ to persuade all members to approve stricter goals for years. Let's make 2064 the year we finally do it! (**try**)

5 ▶2.7 Write present perfect questions a–h. Use the continuous form where possible. Listen to check.
a How long / you / know / your best friend?
b You / work hard / recently?
c You / ever / live / in a different city?
d How long / you / study / today?

e How much bread / you / eat / today?
f How far / you / walk / today?
g How many cups of coffee / you / drink / today?
h You / exercise / a lot / lately?

6 🔵 **Make it personal** Share your answers to **5** with a classmate. Any surprises?

2.4 What's the best ad you've seen recently?

1 Read and match pop-up adverts 1–5 to Internet users a–e.

a I'm a qualified young woman with no previous experience. I need to get a job fast.
b We're soccer fans and we're tired of adverts on TV.
c I'm a senior manager working for a multinational company. I am looking for an agent who can help me manage my career.
d I'm a sales representative for a large consumer goods company that hopes to export to Asian countries.
e I'm a Mac user with a slow, slow laptop. Get me out of here!

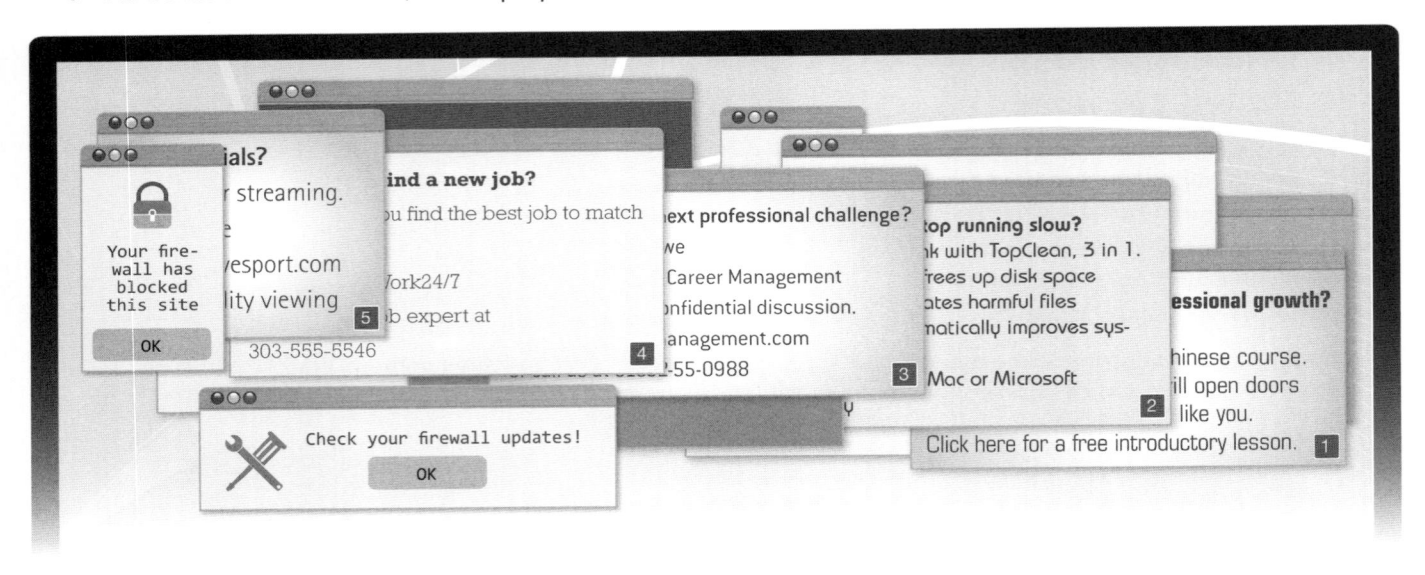

2 ▶2.8 **Predict and write the words you can't see. Listen to check. Would you contact any of these companies?**

3 Add the missing words to make complete questions.

a Ready for professional growth?
b Laptop running slow?
c Looking for your next professional challenge?
d Want to find a new job?
e Tired of commercials?

4 ▶2.9 **Listen to three calls to the companies in 1 and answer a–f. Mia (M), Cal (C), or Jake (J)?**

Which caller …
a has not contacted the company before?
b has never met a representative of the company before?
c has been waiting the longest?
d received a guarantee?
e leaves contact details?
f currently has no work?

5 ▶2.9 **Complete extracts a–f with the correct form of the verbs in parentheses. Listen again to check.**

a I _____ in for an interview a couple of weeks ago. (**come**)
b It _____ two weeks and I _____ anything from you. (**be / not hear**)
c Hello. You _____ the offices of Grabowsky and Loewe. (**reach**)
d I _____ in the oil industry for 17 years now. (**work**)
e I _____ a copy of *Selling in China for Beginners* and, er, it _____ yet. (**order / not arrive**)
f I _____ my bank account and I _____ five weeks ago, so I _____ for 35 days. (**check / pay / wait**)

6 Correct the mistake in each sentence.

a I've started this course in February.
b I've been having my job for five years.
c Our teacher has given us lots of homework last week.
d I've been learning 10 new words this lesson.
e I haven't gone out last night.

7 🔵 Make it personal Which of the sentences in **6** are true for you? Change the others so they're true.

2.5 Do you support any charities?

1 ▶2.10 **Listen to four dialogues and identify the animals mentioned in each.**

> Giant panda   Golden lion tamarin   Monk seal   Ivory-billed woodpecker
> Javanese rhino   Mountain gorilla   North Atlantic right whale

2 ▶2.11 **These extracts are in phonetics. Can you decipher them? Listen to check and notice the /ə/.**
a /aɪm gəʊɪŋ tə teɪk ə fəʊtəgræf/
b /aɪ kən siː ðæt ðeɪ ə(r) iːtɪŋ fruːt/
c /hələʊ ənd welkəm tə zuː ətlæntə/
d /mʌðə(r) ənd tʃaɪld trævəlɪŋ əlɒŋ/

3 ▶2.12 **Order the words in a–e to form questions. Cross out the extra word in each. Listen, check, and answer.**
a animal / you / have / ever / endangered / a / seen / an / in / wild / the / ?
b a / you / have / a / ever / one / seen / in / zoo / ?
c animal / sick / looked / on / have / after / you / ever / a / ?
d given / never / have / you / an / money / for / animal / ever / cause / ?
e NGO / an / have / ever / considered / you / it / working / for / animal / protection / ?

4 **Read the charity ad and change the underlined expressions to percentages (%).**

> _A third_ of all our food depends on bees and other insects pollinating the plants it grows from.
>
> The number of bees in Europe has fallen drastically in recent years, and now _a tenth_ of bees face extinction.
>
> Because of intense farming over the last century, _hardly any_ of their natural environments now remain.

5 ▶2.13 _Dictation_. **Listen and complete a–e with four or five words each. Encouragement (E) or discouragement (D)?**
a _____ you'll get there.
b _____ doing that?
c Keep going. You'll _____.
d _____ succeed, try, try again.
e Do you really think _____?

6 ▶2.14 **Listen to two short dialogues and check the phrases in 5 that you hear. What does each person want to do?**

7 🔊 Make it personal **Which of the animals in this lesson would you adopt (i.e., give money to a charity to save)?**

Can you remember ...

➤ 7 "green" adjectives using -able, -efficient, and -friendly? SB→p.19

➤ 3 words that rhyme with go and 3 that rhyme with hot? SB→p.19

➤ 4 frequency expressions, 4 quantity expressions, and 8 time expressions? SB→p.21

➤ 9 environmental disasters / problems? SB→p.22

➤ 2 differences between the present perfect and the present perfect continuous? SB→p.23

➤ 7 species of animals we may never see again? SB→p.26

➤ 3 encouragement and 3 discouragement expressions? SB→p.27

3

3.1 Which city would you most like to visit?

1 Use the clues to complete the crossword with adjectives to describe cities.

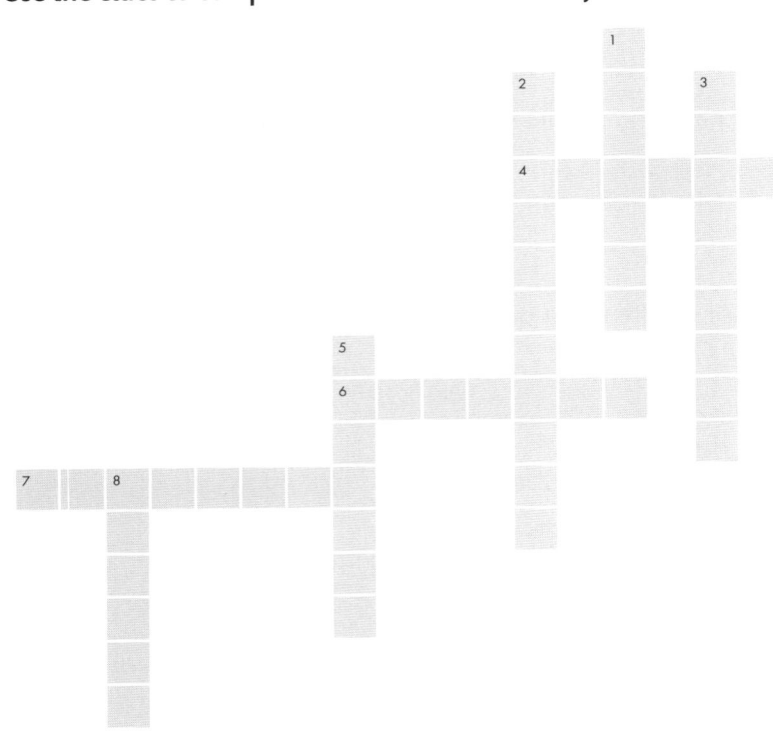

Across:
4 When the air is dirty with a mixture of smoke and fog.
6 An area of a city where people with a lot of money live.
7 When the air / sea is dirty from traffic and industry.

Down:
1 When everything is very busy and confusing.
2 An area of the city where lots of people want to live.
3 An area which hasn't had much care or maintenance.
5 An area in a very bad state.
8 An area which is busy and where people have fun.

2 Complete the sentences with words from **1**.
a I live in a _____ neighborhood. Everyone wants to live there.
b This used to be a nice part of town, but nowadays it's looking _____ because most of the buildings are old and damaged.
c After an accident at the chemical factory, the river became very _____ .
d Have you tried driving in the downtown area? It's _____!
e In rush hour there's a lot of traffic so the air becomes very _____ .
f If you want to have fun, go to Lapa. It's a really _____ part of the city.

3 ▶3.1 **Order the words in a–d. Complete the answers with *a* or *the*. Listen to check. What city is it?**
a you / like / city / how / your / do / ?
It's _____ truly awesome city; _____ city that never sleeps; _____ capital of _____ world.
b way / it / easy / is / to / your / around / find / ?
It is really easy to find your way around because _____ streets are numbered.
c your / what's / landmark / favorite / ?
Well, in _____ city of skyscrapers, I guess it's _____ Chrysler Building.
d spots / are / the / what / most / tourist / popular / ?
Central Park, Greenwich Village, 5th Avenue, One World Trade Center, and so many others.

4 ▶3.2 **Listen and repeat. Pronounce the underlined sounds correctly.**

It's a pity our pretty city is now littered with little bits of plastic.

/ɪ/

Three sleepy sheep on a beach, each eating a piece of green cheese.

/iː/

5 🅐 **Make it personal** Answer the questions from **3** for yourself. Share your answers with a classmate. Do you agree?

3.2 Was your last vacation as much fun as you'd hoped?

1 Chris is in Mumbai to meet his fiancée's family. He's arranged to meet a friend, Roni, first. Read Roni's texts and mark a–f True (T), False (F), or not mentioned (N).

> Finally made it to the hotel, but you'd left. Sorry! Good luck with your in-laws. R
> Sent 17:31

> Remember not to kiss your girlfriend in front of her parents. Terrible manners in India! R
> Sent 17:35

> Almost forgot. Hug her brothers if you want to, but don't kiss them on the cheek, OK? R
> Sent 17:42

> One more: don't greet servants as you do with the family. Just nod. Can u reply, pls? R
> Sent 17:45

> Aha! Can't see my texts 'cause u turned off your cell phone as I told you. ☺ R
> Sent 18:36

a By the time Roni got to the hotel, Chris had gone.
b Chris sent five texts to Roni.
c Roni had told Chris to turn his phone off while visiting his future in-laws.
d Chris told Roni that he had turned his phone off.
e Indian men don't greet other men with kisses.
f You're not supposed to shake hands with the servants.

2 Complete Chris' email to his family with the past perfect form of these verbs.

break	(not) hug	kiss	make
mistake	send	shake	tell

Dear Mom and Dad,

Greetings from a really rainy Mumbai—I thought it'd be hot and dry. Last night I met Diya's parents. After a tense couple of hours I got back to the hotel, turned my cell phone back on (Roni ᵃ_____ me to switch it off), and found several text messages with advice from Roni. Too late! He ᵇ_____ those messages while my phone was off. As I read them I realized I ᶜ_____ so many terrible mistakes at Diya's. To begin with, I had kissed her in front of her parents, apparently a big no-no in India. To make matters worse, I ᵈ_____ her brothers, too — males usually don't. Worse still, I ᵉ_____ them as you're supposed to. Worst of all, I ᶠ_____ one of the servants for a member of the family and ᵍ_____ hands with her. In India, you greet people from different social backgrounds differently. In other words, I discovered I ʰ_____ practically every cultural rule in the book. I just hope they'll give me another chance. Wish me luck! I'll write again soon. Hope Dad's feeling a little better now.

Love,

Chris xx

3 Correct one mistake in each of a–e.
a Did you know the Romans had spoken Latin?
b After we had arrived home, we made some sandwiches.
c By the time we got home, the TV show finished.
d When I had lunch, I had a short nap.
e We had bought our car five years ago.

4 Choose the correct past participle.
a Chris had been / gone by the time Roni arrived.
b Chris had never been / gone to Mumbai before.
c Roni had been / gone to India several times.
d By the time Chris saw Roni's messages, he'd already been / gone to his in-laws'.

5 ▶3.3 Watch / Listen to the host and underline the word(s) with the strongest stress in a–f. The number of stressed words is in parentheses.

a Hi, this is your travel host. (4)
b I'd like to show you the top ten attractions of Madrid, Spain. (8)
c Number ten, Plaza de Cibeles. Madrid is known for many beautiful squares like this one. (9)
d The Cibeles fountain is an important symbol of this city. (5)
e Number nine. Almudena Cathedral. It took more than a hundred years to complete its construction in 1993. (8)
f The original site was occupied by Madrid's first mosque. (6)

6 ▶3.4 Listen and copy the sentence stress.

7 **Make it personal** Write a short review of a hotel, restaurant, or attraction you know well. Share it with a friend. Do they agree?

3.3 Do you ever want to get away from it all?

1 Read comments from four people about where they live. Match the topics in the box to each person.

> crime   driving   money   noise

○○○

Carlos

I've sold my car recently and now I only use public transportation. I hated it because I always got stuck in ¹_____ jams and could never find a parking ²_____ . Also, there's a lot of car ³_____ so I was always afraid I'd lose it one day.

Anya

There's a lot of ⁴_____ . round here, you can see it everywhere, from broken windows to graffiti. There's also a lot of ⁵_____ on the buses, especially when it's crowded. It's a constant worry, you have to keep your hands on your bags and pockets to stop people stealing from you. The crime ⁶_____ in general is very high.

Mike

My city isn't a quiet place. People are always ⁷_____ their horns loudly, it makes me mad. Sometimes I just want to get away from all the ⁸_____ pollution and hide on a quiet beach forever!

Margaret

I live in a small town, where most of the young people have left to work in big cities. It's become very poor, and most people here are in ⁹_____ .They're struggling to pay their bills most of the time, so they don't have much of a work–life ¹⁰_____ .

2 Complete the comments in **1** with the words in the box. There are two extra words.

> balance   debt   honking   noise
> pickpocketing   rate   spot   construction
> theft   trash   traffic   vandalism

3 Match phrases 1–10 to endings a–j to make phrases describing urban problems.

1	constantly	a loneliness
2	go through	b balance
3	suffer from	c parking spot
4	get stuck	d connected
5	find a	e theft
6	be in	f pollution
7	crime	g red lights
8	work–life	h in traffic jams
9	noise	i rate
10	car	j debt

4 Which of the urban problems do each of these sentences describe?

a Oh, no! Someone's stolen my car!

b I wish I had more friends, I hardly ever leave the house.

c I never get any free time any more. I just seem to work all the time.

d I don't know how I'm going to pay my bills this month.

e Uh-oh, it looks like the parking lot is full.

f You're never off your phone!

5 🔵 Make it personal   Complete sentences a–c. Use words and phrases from this unit to help you. Then share your answers with a friend.

a I don't mind ..., but ... really annoys me.

b I wouldn't live in a city where / which ... .

c In big cities, it's difficult to ... .

3.4 Have you ever missed any important dates?

1 Complete the conversations with one word.

a A: I was petrified watching that movie.
B: No _____! It's a very scary movie.

b A: We had a really good day in the end.
B: Oh, yeah? How did it _____ out in the end?

c A: I hate using taxis.
B: What do you _____? I thought you used them all the time.

d A: I had a nightmare at work today.
B: You _____ thing! What happened?

e A: That concert was boring.
B: You're _____! I thought it was fantastic!

2 ▶ 3.5 Listen to problems a–g and match them to these sentences.

- [ ] He'd been locked out of the house.
- [a] He'd been stuck in a traffic jam.
- [ ] They'd been stuck in a subway train.
- [ ] They'd been stuck in an elevator.
- [ ] They'd been locked out of their car.
- [ ] They'd been stuck at the top of a building.
- [ ] They'd been stuck in a line for hours.

3 ▶ 3.6 What had they been doing? Listen, choose the correct verb, and write your guesses below.

dance	do exercise	fight	fly	speed

a Bill and Jim _____.
b Meg and her boyfriend _____.
c Betty and Pete _____.
d Joe and his girlfriend _____.
e Suki _____.

4 Complete a–e with the verbs in parentheses in the past perfect or past perfect continuous.

a Marge watched her husband come in and collapse on the couch. He _____ with his friends in the bar. (**hang out**)

b As he walked through the door, he knew Wilma _____ his favorite brontosaurus rib pie. (**make**)

c When Stan reached the top of the hill, he realized his friend _____ there a few minutes before. (**get**)

d He was almost sick when he found out his roommate Leonard and his neighbor Penny _____ secretly for some time. (**date**)

e In the end we find out that Severus Snape _____ Albus Dumbledore. (**kill**)

5 Two of sentences a–g are correct; the others have one mistake each. Correct them.

a I had to sit down because I'd stood all day.

b We got lost because we hadn't been understanding the directions.

c Julio failed the exam because he hadn't studied enough.

d Vera had been visiting Turkey before so she knew the best places.

e Until yesterday night, I'd never been eating meat before.

f Luigi only got married because he'd been living with his mother for 40 years.

g How long were you waiting when the doors opened?

6 😀 **Make it personal** Have you ever had any of the experiences in **5**? Tell a friend what happened.

3.5 Do you always follow the rules?

1 Match signs a–f to the places 1–6 you might see them.

a
> Speed limit 20 MPH

b
> Please do not distract the driver

c
> DEEP WATER—No swimming

d
> Strictly no parking!

e
> Please do not feed the animals

f
> No photography allowed

1 on a bus
2 at a zoo
3 at a lake
4 in an art gallery
5 on a street
6 in front of someone's house

2 Match the two parts of the signs, and complete them with prepositions.

a Danger! No _____
b Kindly refrain _____
c Park here _____
d Please clean _____
e Tow _____
f Vehicles will be _____

☐ _____ after your pet.
☐ zone. Do not stop here.
☐ towed _____ owner's expense.
☐ your own risk.
☐ lifeguard _____ duty.
☐ _____ smoking.

3 ▶3.7 Listen to the sound effects and make rules with *can't* after the beep. Follow the model.

Excuse me. I'm afraid you can't take photos here.

4 ▶3.8 Match the two parts of the quotes. Listen to check.

a The golden rule is
b Life is short. Break the rules. Forgive quickly. Kiss slowly.
c Know the rules well,
d If you obey all the rules,
e You have to learn the rules of the game.
f There are three rules for writing a novel.

☐ Unfortunately no one knows what they are. Somerset Maugham
☐ so you can break them effectively. Dalai Lama XIV
☐ And then you have to play better than anyone else. Albert Einstein
☐ that there are no golden rules. George Bernard Shaw
☐ you miss all the fun. Katharine Hepburn
☐ Laugh uncontrollably. And never regret anything that makes you smile. Mark Twain

5 🔵 Make it personal Which of the quotes do you most agree with? Share your ideas with a classmate.

Can you remember ...

➤ 8 words for features of a city? SB→p. 32
➤ 9 customs in Hong Kong? SB→p. 34
➤ how to use the past perfect? SB→p. 34
➤ 10 urban problems? SB→p. 36
➤ 5 phrases to show you are listening? SB→p. 38
➤ the difference between past perfect and past perfect continuous? SB→p. 39
➤ 2 people, 4 verbs, and 4 preposition phrases from signs? SB→p. 40

4.1 Does your school system work well?   **4**

1 Add vowels to the school subjects. Circle three /dʒ/ sounds and underline one /tʃ/.

L		T	R	T	R

	R	T

G			G	R		P	H	Y

M		T	H

H		S	T		R	Y

L		N	G			G		S

C	H		M		S	T	R	Y

P	H	Y	S		C	S

B			L		G	Y

2 ▶ 4.1 **Listen to two teachers. Who said it? Ruth (R) or Dan (D)?**

a I think schools need to teach 21st century skills.

b I believe we should concentrate on reading, writing, and arithmetic.

c I think kids have to learn how to solve problems creatively.

d In my opinion, smart phones can be a useful learning tool in class.

e Smart phones shouldn't be allowed in class.

f I don't think students should look for information online. It's useless.

g Teachers should teach students to find information on the Internet that they can trust.

3 ▶ 4.2 **Listen and match a–g in 2 to the agree / disagree responses.**

Agree	Disagree
I think so, too.	I don't think so.
I completely agree with you.	I don't agree with you.
Yeah, you're right.	Oh, come on!

4 ▶ 4.3 **Listen to the sentence stress. Then follow the model.**

● ● ● ●

Model: *I think so, too.*

You: *I think so, too.*

5 Complete the mind maps with these words.

badly   a difference   an exam
an exercise   feedback   good grades
homework   into trouble   kicked out
mistakes   photos   progress
a report card   a test   well

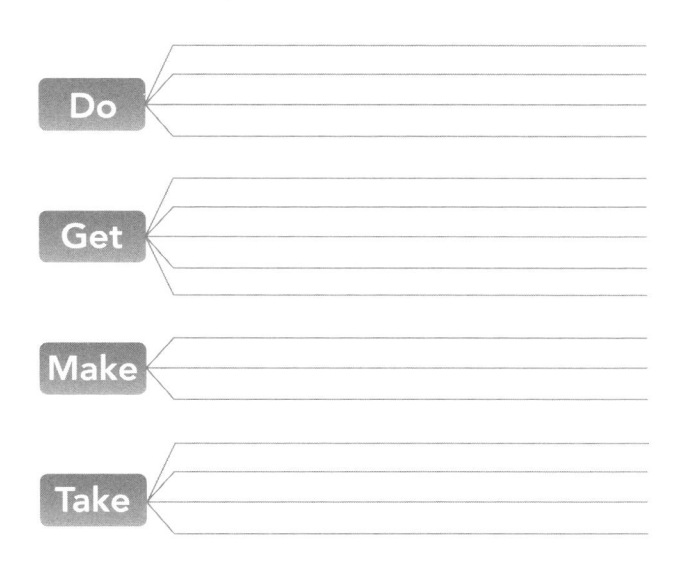

Do

Get

Make

Take

6 Match 1–7 to a–g to make sentences. Underline the phrases you don't use a lot in English.

1 I haven't done

2 I'm under a lot of pressure to pass

3 Who would have guessed I'd get kicked

4 I know I should get a

5 The only way to do

6 It's really no secret that I must get

7 The career advisor told me it takes

a degree if I want to get a decent job.

b out of school for cheating on a test.

c excellent grades if I want to get a scholarship.

d over five years to train to be a vet.

e as well as I expected in school this year.

f my exams so I can get into college.

g well in school is to do homework and revise for tests.

7 🔵 **Make it personal**   What subjects are / were you best / worst at? Why? Discuss with a classmate.

4.2 What's the ideal age to go to college?

1 Read a teacher's social media updates and circle the correct choice.

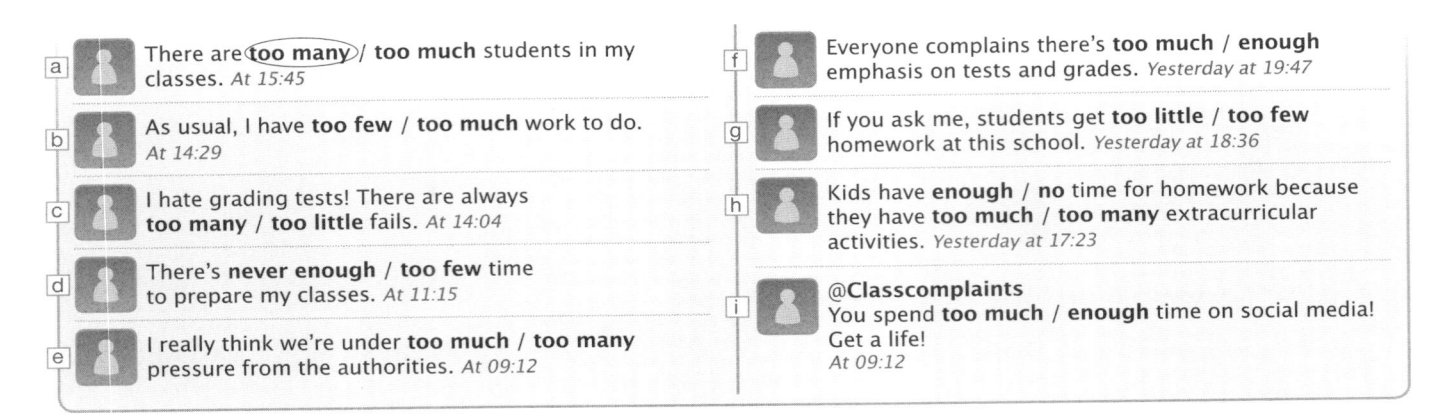

a There are (too many) / too much students in my classes. *At 15:45*

b As usual, I have too few / too much work to do. *At 14:29*

c I hate grading tests! There are always too many / too little fails. *At 14:04*

d There's never enough / too few time to prepare my classes. *At 11:15*

e I really think we're under too much / too many pressure from the authorities. *At 09:12*

f Everyone complains there's too much / enough emphasis on tests and grades. *Yesterday at 19:47*

g If you ask me, students get too little / too few homework at this school. *Yesterday at 18:36*

h Kids have enough / no time for homework because they have too much / too many extracurricular activities. *Yesterday at 17:23*

i @Classcomplaints You spend too much / enough time on social media! Get a life! *At 09:12*

2 Cross out the wrong option in a–c.

a I haven't got enough **energy** / **money** / **rich** / **time** to …
b I've got too much **work** / **pressure** / **problems** / **stress** from …
c There are too many **distractions** / **noise** / **people** / **rules** at …

3 ▶ 4.4 Listen and repeat a and b. How fast can you go? Be careful to pronounce the /ʊ/ correctly every time.

a The woman could cook because she read the book.
b Hey! Look where you're putting your foot!

4 ▶ 4.5 Listen to a joke and circle the words you hear.

Three language students are **talking outside** / **walking to school** for their listening class.

"It's **Wednesday** / **windy**," says Yolanda.

"No, it isn't, it's **Thursday** / **thirsty**," says Jaime.

"Me, too," says Petra, "Forget class, let's find **a café** / **a coffee**!"

5 🅞 Make it personal   What jokes do you know in English? Tell a classmate.

4.3 What do you regret not having done?

1 Look at the people in photos a–c. What do you think they regret?

2 Match what the people say to the photos in **1**.

1 *I should have studied harder at school. I didn't take it seriously at the time, but now, doing this job, I realize how important it was.*

2 *I shouldn't have chosen political science as my major. I thought it would be interesting, but it isn't.*

3 *I shouldn't have gone out with my friends at the weekend. I should have studied for my test this morning.*

3 Rewrite a–f as if you were regretting your choice.

a "I didn't think carefully about my options."
   I should have thought more carefully about my options.

b "Truth is I didn't get into law school 'cause I didn't work hard enough." I should have …

c "Choosing engineering instead of art was a big mistake." I should have …

d "Everybody says I didn't get the job because I didn't dress appropriately for the interview." I should have …

e "My career just isn't taking off 'cause I didn't go to music school when I had the chance, I guess." I should have …

f "I dropped out of college 'cause I wanted to make money straight away. Now I'm stuck in this boring, badly paid job." I shouldn't have …

4 ▶ 4.6 Listen and express regrets. Follow the model.

It was a mistake to drop out.

I shouldn't have dropped out.

5 ▶ 4.7 Order the phrases, 1–5, to make three dialogues a–c. Listen to check.

a ☐ Really? What did you do?
   ☐ I was in 5th grade, I think, and I stuck the teacher's purse to a table.
   ☐ I have no idea. I really don't know.
   ☐ Why did you do such a thing?
   ☐1 I did something terrible at school once.

b ☐ I looked my mother in the eye and told her that I hated her with all my heart.
   ☐ Really? What did you say?
   ☐ Yep! I don't really know where that came from.
   ☐ I said something really mean once.
   ☐ What a terrible thing to say!

c ☐ So I hit it off with my hand, but it hit the wall and broke into a thousand pieces. And I realized it wasn't an insect. It was some kind of brooch.
   ☐ Oh, no! What a silly thing to do!
   ☐ I did the most embarrassing thing a while ago.
   ☐ This teacher came up to me and there was this insect on her blouse.
   ☐ Really? What did you do?

6 ▶ 4.8 Listen to extracts a–c, choose the correct option and react after the beep.

a Really? What did you **say / do**?

b Why would you **say / do** such a thing?

c What a silly thing to **say / do**!

7 🔵 **Make it personal** Is there anything about your school life that you regret? Discuss with a classmate.

4.4 What would you do if you won a million dollars?

1 Aisha is a college student, majoring in technology. She's thinking about her future goals and aspirations. Match actions 1–6 to the results.

1 I'll probably graduate next year,
2 I think I'll move to San Francisco,
3 I might find a good job quickly,
4 I'd really like to travel the world,
5 I want a better computer
6 I have a big nose

a but it usually takes a long time.
b because I can't write very good apps.
c but I don't have enough money for tickets.
d and the first thing I'll do is look for a job with a tech company.
e and I hate it!
f it's a good place to find a tech job.

2 ▶ 4.9 Complete Aisha's goals and aspirations with the verbs. Listen to check and repeat.

a If I graduate from college next year, I _____ a job with a tech company. (**look for**)
b If I _____ to San Francisco, I'll find a good tech job. (**move**)
c I _____ surprised if I find a good job quickly. (**be**)
d If I _____ the lottery, I'd travel the world. (**win**)
e I could write better apps if I _____ a better computer. (**have**)
f If I _____ change one thing about myself, I'd have a smaller nose. (**can**)

3 Which of the sentences in exercise **2** are first conditional, and which are second?

4 ▶ 4.10 Match the words to the sound pictures. Listen to check.

blue   book   cook   could   moon
moved   pool   school   should
through   true   woman

_____
_____
_____
_____
_____
_____

5 🔵 Make it personal Write a first and second conditional sentence for each of the situations below.

a Your national soccer team is in the semi-final of the World Cup. The team they're playing is very bad, but the team they'll play in the final is very good and it's unlikely they'll win.

If my team wins the semi-final, they'll go to the final.

If my team won the World Cup, ...

b You really want to buy a new car, but you don't have any money.

_____
_____

c You live in a big house, but it needs some work.

_____
_____

d You might go out this weekend.

_____
_____

e You're thinking of becoming a politician.

_____
_____

4.5 What makes someone a genius?

1 ▶ 4.11 **Read movie reviews 1–3 and complete them with *a*, *an*, or *the*. Listen to check.**

Movie list #4: Geniuses

1 Gifted

Marc Webb directs __ movie about __ intellectually gifted seven-year-old girl and her uncle and grandmother's fight to have custody of her. The girl, Mary Adler, is played by __ actor Mckenna Grace, who gives __ outstanding performance. Mary lives with her uncle Frank, played by __ actor Chris Evans, but her grandmother wants to take her away and provide her with __ special tutor so as to exploit __ gift that she has. __ movie follows the battle between the uncle and the grandmother.

2 Magnus

Magnus is __ documentary movie by director Benjamin Ree, which follows __ fascinating journey of Magnus Carlsen to becoming chess grandmaster at __ age of 13. __ movie shows how __ strong interest in numbers when he was five years old led __ boy to become interested in chess, as well as his drive, devotion, and passion throughout __ journey.

3 Hidden Figures

Hidden Figures is __ biographical drama which tells __ incredible true story of three African–American women who worked at NASA in __ early 1960s. Each woman was __ brilliant mathematician and together they were __ brains who put astronaut John Glenn into space. __ story shows how __ women overcame strong gender and racial barriers and inspired many others.

2 **Reread and answer a–d.**

a How many actors are mentioned in the three reviews?
b Which movie(s) is / are about child geniuses?
c Which movie is about a legal battle?
d Which movie is about people who faced discrimination?

3 **Order the words in a–g and write sympathy (S) or criticism (C).**

a done / is / what's / done / .
b thinking / were / what / you / ?
c end / world / the / not / it's / the / of / .
d better / you / known / should've / .
e such / could / do / how / you / thing / a / ?
f you / get / let / don't / it / down / .
g you / will / learn / ever / ?

4 ▶ 4.12 **Listen to problems 1–7 and react using expressions from 3. Follow the model.**

"I didn't get the scholarship because I didn't prepare for the interview."

Model: *g*
You: *Will you ever learn?*

5 ▶ 4.13 **Complete the two sentences for each problem a–e. Listen to check.**

a I didn't get the scholarship because I didn't prepare for the interview.
You (**should**)/ **shouldn't**) _____

_____

If you (**'d**)/ **hadn't**) _____

_____

b I failed the test because I didn't study.
You (**should** / **shouldn't**) _____ .
If you (**'d** / **hadn't**) _____ .

c I got really bad grades because I was absent a lot this semester.
You (**should** / **shouldn't**) _____ .
If you (**'d** / **hadn't**) _____ .

d I got kicked out of school because I cheated on a final exam.
You (**should** / **shouldn't**) _____ .
If you (**'d** / **hadn't**) _____ .

e My parents were upset because I couldn't get into college.
You (**should** / **shouldn't**) _____ .
If you (**'d** / **hadn't**) _____ .

6 🔒 **Make it personal** **In pairs. Think about something you have done that you wish had been different. Share your experiences with a partner. Use expressions to show sympathy.**

Can you remember ...

➤ 8 school words? SB→p. 44
➤ 13 school subjects? SB→p.44
➤ 2 expressions with *do*, 2 with *get*, 1 with *make*, and 1 with *take*? SB→p. 45
➤ how to use *too* and *enough* with adjectives? SB→p. 46
➤ ⊕, ⊖, and ❷ for *should have*? SB→p. 48
➤ ⊕ and ⊖ for the first and second conditional? SB→p. 51
➤ which syllable is stressed in three, four, or five-syllable words ending in *-y*? SB→p. 52
➤ 4 phrases for sympathy and 4 for criticism? SB→p. 53

5.1 Are you a shopaholic?

1 Read the advertisement and match three of the headings a–e to paragraphs 1–3.

a You can cut costs.
b You can expand your business.
c You can use cutting-edge technology.
d You can take time off.
e You can get customers to your store.

Join us at Gen-Z Mall in 2020 and take your business into the future.

Coming in spring of 2020, the new Gen-Z Mall in downtown Austin will be the first of its kind. We are embracing the technology and shopping habits of Generation Z to bring you the best business possible. Here are three reasons why you should move your retail business here:

1 _____

We are providing _____ to all businesses and customers throughout and outside the mall, so everyone can access the Internet without paying. There will also be _____ throughout the mall so customers don't have to worry if their mobile devices lose power. We can also provide screens for _____ in clothing stores to save customers time and help them decide what clothes will look like before they buy.

2 _____

We've created a system where we provide _____ for customers to get special deals and discounts throughout the mall. These will only be valid if customers do _____ rather than buying online, though, so you can expect to see much more traffic into your business.

3 _____

We provide _____ terminals which will help you reduce staff costs while customers process their own purchases. We also actively encourage _____ by showing videos on large screens of products available in the mall. This will help you build _____ and so make sure your customers return.

2 Reread and complete with these words / phrases.

> brand loyalty   charging stations   coupons
> free Wi-Fi   self-checkout   in-store shopping
> virtual try-ons   user-generated content

3 Find 15 (3↘, 6→, 6↓) clothes and accessories in the word puzzle.

E	S	U	N	G	L	A	S	S	E	S
B	H	U	V	C	O	H	W	A	A	H
J	O	Z	I	O	U	C	E	V	R	O
K	R	F	Q	T	J	T	A	B	R	E
T	T	B	S	C	W	A	T	J	I	S
S	S	C	A	R	F	J	E	A	N	S
A	X	H	P	G	F	K	R	C	G	U
N	E	B	I	K	I	N	I	K	S	W
D	T	I	A	R	O	S	W	E	E	T
A	S	Y	N	E	T	A	A	T	R	T
L	J	E	W	E	L	R	Y	L	T	O
S	A	D	J	D	P	P	A	N	T	S

4 Which items from **3** complete phrases a–c?

a I bought <u>a new pair of</u> _____ last week. (7 items)
b I really want to buy <u>some</u> new _____. (8 items)
c That's <u>a</u> nice _____. (7 items)

5 ▶5.1 Listen to six short phrases and write down the question you hear.

6 🔵 Make it personal   Read the cartoon and think about your answers to the questions. Then share your ideas with a friend.

a Do you ever compare prices online while you're in a store?
b What types of things do you always / never buy online?
c What's the best thing about buying things in-store?

5.2 What shouldn't you have spent money on?

1 Complete the conversations with the missing prepositions.

1. A: Why do you look so happy?
   B: I've finally paid ... my loan!
2. A: What did you do on the weekend?
   B: I went ... a shopping spree and bought lots of new clothes.
3. A: Do you think you earn enough money in your job?
   B: Not really. I always run ... of money before the end of the month.
4. A: It was hard financially, being a student. I had to take ... a loan.
   B: Me, too. In the end I got ... a lot of debt.

2 ⏵5.2 Listen to Jia and Andreas and answer the questions.

1. How much was the loan that Andreas applied for?
2. How much does Andreas earn?
3. Who agreed to help Andreas?
4. How much interest will he pay?
5. When is his first payment due?

3 ⏵5.3 Listen to extracts a–d and circle the word you hear.

a. If I'd planned my application more carefully, they **would** / **might** / **could** have accepted it.
b. If I **hadn't** / **haven't** / **wouldn't** gone on vacation twice this year, I wouldn't have got into debt.
c. If you'd told me, I would **of** / **had** / **have** helped you.
d. So if she hadn't died, I **didn't** / **wouldn't** / **hadn't** have received it.

4 ⏵5.4 Listen and repeat a–d twice. Try to join the words together.

5 ⏵5.5 Put the words in the columns. Listen to check.

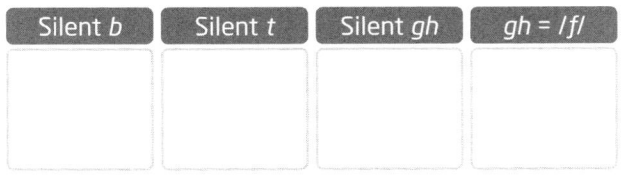

bought	doubt	enough	fasten
laugh	listen	though	thumb

Silent *b*	Silent *t*	Silent *gh*	*gh* = /f/

6 Complete signs and adverts a–e with words from **5**.

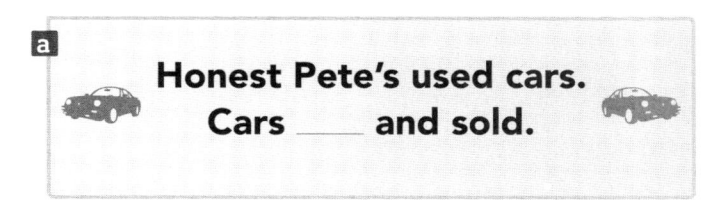

a Honest Pete's used cars. Cars _____ and sold.

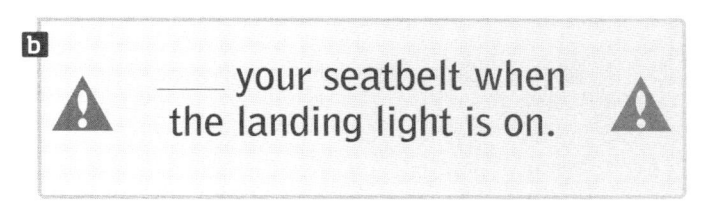

b _____ your seatbelt when the landing light is on.

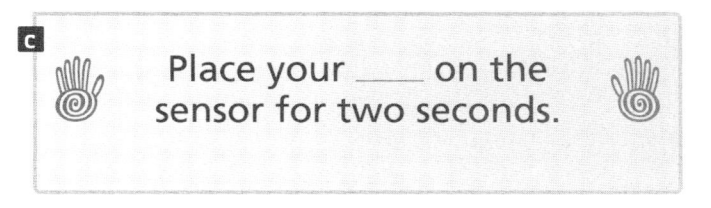

c Place your _____ on the sensor for two seconds.

d College Comedy night. Look, _____, and _____!

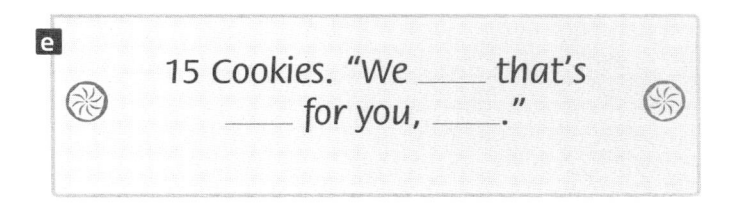

e 15 Cookies. "We _____ that's _____ for you, _____."

7 🔵 **Make it personal** Interview a classmate about their shopping habits e.g. *Where do you normally buy your clothes – online or in-store?* Do you agree?

5.3 Have you ever borrowed money from a relative?

1 Read the riddles a–e and complete the guesses.

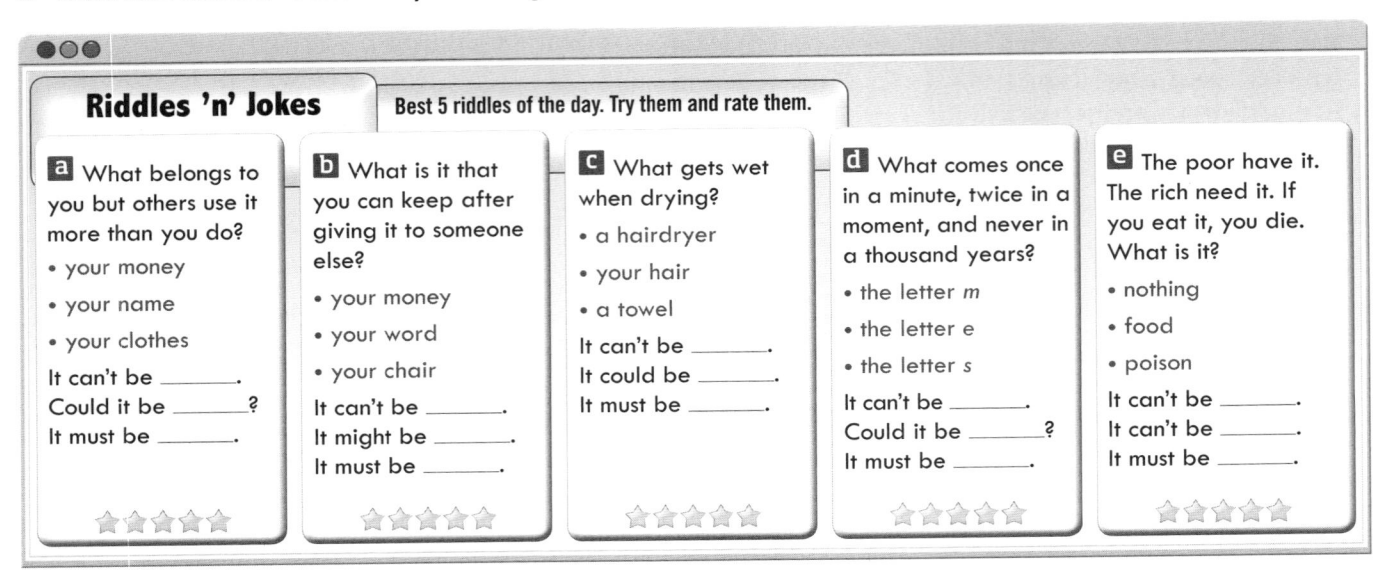

Riddles 'n' Jokes | Best 5 riddles of the day. Try them and rate them.

a What belongs to you but others use it more than you do?
- your money
- your name
- your clothes

It can't be _____.
Could it be _____?
It must be _____.

b What is it that you can keep after giving it to someone else?
- your money
- your word
- your chair

It can't be _____.
It might be _____.
It must be _____.

c What gets wet when drying?
- a hairdryer
- your hair
- a towel

It can't be _____.
It could be _____.
It must be _____.

d What comes once in a minute, twice in a moment, and never in a thousand years?
- the letter *m*
- the letter *e*
- the letter *s*

It can't be _____.
Could it be _____?
It must be _____.

e The poor have it. The rich need it. If you eat it, you die. What is it?
- nothing
- food
- poison

It can't be _____.
It can't be _____.
It must be _____.

2 ▶5.6 Listen and match 1–3 to three of the signs a–e.

a American Airlines — Check-in Economy
b MacArthur High School — Teacher's Meeting Room 3
c MacArthur High School — Class of 2014
d Gate 37 — Now boarding
e Live Show — Studio 4

3 Match statements 1–6 to responses a–f.

1 There are figs on the menu.
2 I've just run 20 km.
3 Did you know that Lara doesn't drink milk?
4 The boss asked to speak with me in her office.
5 My credit card statement says I paid $60 for a pizza!
6 Have you seen that new movie? Absolutely terrible!

a Really? I guess she may be allergic or something.
b It could be a promotion. Good luck!
c That must mean that summer is nearly over.
d Come on! It got four stars. It can't be that bad.
e You must be exhausted. Come and sit down.
f What?! That can't be right.

4 Complete the mind maps with expressions from the box.

be insane | ~~be joking~~ | be serious | be out of your mind | seriously expect me / us to believe that

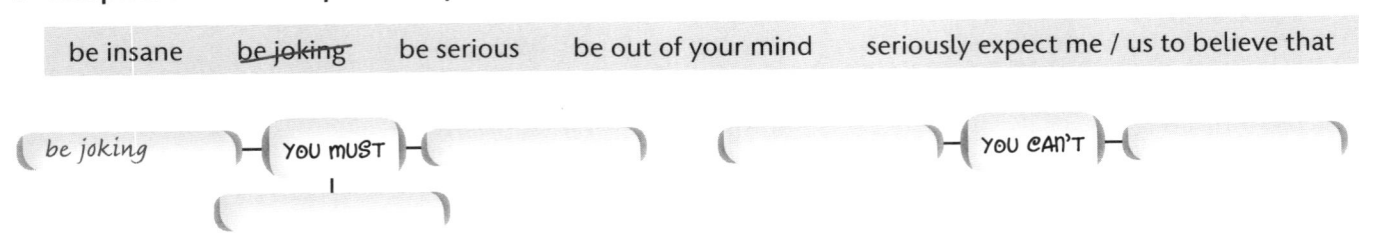

be joking — YOU MUST

YOU CAN'T

5 ▶5.7 Listen and check the phrases from **4** you hear. Pay special attention to the way final *t* and *d* almost disappear before consonants.

6 ▶5.8 *Express surprise.* Listen and express surprise with the prompts. Follow the model.
Model: *I just spent three thousand dollars on a designer bag. / be serious.*
You: *Three thousand dollars? You can't be serious!*

7 🅠 **Make it personal** Write down three names, places, or objects that are important to you. Then have a classmate speculate on why you have chosen them.

5.4 Have you ever bought a useless product?

1 Quickly read the article and match photos a–d to the four sale items.

Into bargain-hunting online? Here are a few examples of the most bizarre things ever sold on eBay's auction site:

WEIRD STUFF

for sale

The owner of an F/A-18 Hornet fighter jet had bought it second-hand and had offered to have the plane restored for an incredibly low price of $9,000,000. After hearing of the **auction**, the FBI contacted the seller to **notify** him that he could only sell the plane to an American citizen residing in the United States. On top of that, the plane could not leave U.S. airspace; it was a matter of national **security**. Under these circumstances, nobody was prepared to participate in the auction.

After Britney Spears had her hair cut off **completely**, the hair salon put it on eBay. The seller obviously saw the **opportunity** to make a small fortune. However, due to eBay's policy, the **ambitious** seller was not able to complete the **transaction**.

One of the most interesting auctions happened in November 2005 when the original 1923 Hollywood sign was sold on eBay. The owner at the time wanted to sell it because he needed the money to finance a Hollywood project. A prospective buyer had a team of experts brought in to **certify** that it was indeed an original. **Luckily** it was, and the transaction was completed successfully.

There are many **unbelievable** stories. A citizen of Australia tried to sell the country of New Zealand once. **Ridiculous**! There were a couple of bidders that day, but the auction suddenly stopped because it violated eBay's policy. I guess it's **impossible** to sell a country unless its people agree to it.

2 Reread. How many of the items were actually sold?

3 ▶5.9 Complete the suffix table with the 12 words in bold in **1**. Circle the stress. Listen to check.

Nouns		Verbs	Adjectives		Adverbs
ability	solution	purify	gorgeous	remarkable	desperately

4 Complete a–f with the correct form of the words in parentheses.
   a Dial 1-800 334717 to _____ your reservation now. (**security**)
   b I'd never used such a _____ product before. (**marvel**)
   c The thing turned out to be a complete _____. (**disappoint**)
   d The label said it was _____, but I guess I should've had it dry-cleaned. (**wash**)
   e I love to see all those shirts _____ arranged on the shelves. (**nice**)
   f The sales clerk said the cream would _____ my skin. (**pure**)

5 Are the adjectives in the statements in the correct order? Correct them if not.
   a Last weekend I bought a beautiful, green dress at the mall.
   b My grandfather is an old, kind man.
   c I love my shampoo. It gives me shiny, gorgeous hair.
   d I never really wear fashionable, new clothes.
   e I live in a big, lovely house.

6 🅐 **Make it personal** Which of the statements in **5** are true for you? Change the ones that aren't.

7 🔊 **Connect**
   Try to find the weirdest item you can on eBay in five minutes. Send it to a classmate and ask them if they would buy it, and why / why not?

5.5 Do you often buy things on impulse?

1 Read the three headings in the article and choose the best title, a–c. Then read enough to confirm your choice.

a How grocery stores get you to spend more.

b How grocery stores get you to spend more – and what you can do.

c The history of the grocery store.

It's all in the layout

Fruit and vegetables are usually the first thing you see when you enter the grocery store, but not the best thing to put at the bottom of your shopping cart. They do this so that you feel healthy after selecting them and then spend more on higher-priced, less healthy products. Have you ever gone to the store to buy some milk and come out with bags full of stuff? Essentials like bread and milk are usually hidden in corners, so that you pass by lots of other attractive produce when looking for them. With this in mind, get to know your grocery store's layout and plan where to visit first and last.

They attack your senses

Many grocery stores play slow, peaceful music as it makes you go round more slowly. Wear your headphones and listen to fast music when you shop. Grocery stores also use smells to attract you to certain areas. How often do you walk past the bakery section and think of delicious, fresh bread? Never go shopping when you're hungry. It won't affect you so much. Premium, expensive products are usually placed at eye-level, so make sure you look up and down when selecting what to buy.

Complicated pricing strategies

Grocery stores often use different measurements for products so that they look cheaper than they are. Always check the price per unit, in smaller text, on the shelf to compare prices. Also, that "3 for 2" offer may sound like a great deal, but remember that two products will always cost more than the one you went in there for.

2 Reread **1** carefully and circle the correct choice in a–f.

a Fruit and vegetables are usually **near** / **far from** the entrance.

b Bread and milk are usually **easy** / **difficult** to find.

c Grocery stores want you to do your shopping **quickly** / **slowly**.

d You should go shopping **before** / **after** you've eaten.

e The **cheapest** / **most expensive** products are at the same height as your head.

f You should check the **price** / **price per unit** to compare prices.

3 ▶5.10 Order sentences a–f. Write customer (C) or sales clerk (SC). Listen to check.

☐ I just need to see your receipt, please.

☐ Can I exchange it for the 256 GB?

☐ I bought this flash drive yesterday and realized it's only 63 GB instead of the 256 GB I paid for.

☐ In that case I'm afraid there's nothing I can do.

☐ Seriously? But look, I have the bag.

☐ That's the thing. I threw it away, you see.

4 ▶5.11 Complete the dialogue with five words from the box. Listen to check.

card	cash	declined	exchange	insert
refund	stock	afraid	thanks	

SA _____ or charge?

C Charge, please.

SA Thank you. _____ your _____, please.

C There you go.

SA I'm _____ it has been _____.

C I don't understand. Can you try this one?

SA It worked this time. There you are.

C Ah! At last!

5 ▶5.12 *Dictation*. Listen and write down the dialogue. Check your answer in ▶5.12 on page 59.

6 🔊 **Make it personal** When was the last time you returned something to a store? Discuss with a classmate.

Can you remember ...

➤ 6 technology words about shopping? SB→p.58

➤ 3 things you can pay off? SB→p.60

➤ ⊕ and ⊖ for the third conditional? SB→p.61

➤ 5 modals of probability? SB→p.62

➤ 2 examples of words with the suffixes -*ous*, -*ment*, and -*ness*? SB→p.65

➤ adjective order? SB→p.65

➤ three shopping problems SB→p.67

Audioscript

Unit 1

▶ 1.1

a What's something you just can't live without?

b What are you good at?

c What makes you nervous?

d Who are you closer to, your mom or your dad?

e What's the most fun place you've been to?

▶ 1.2

Romeo and Juliet is a famous play by William Shakespeare. Romeo Montague and Juliet Capulet are teenagers in Verona. They meet at a party and get along well immediately. Naturally, they fall in love, but, later, they discover that they belong to rival families. The Montagues and the Capulets are enemies. Their love is impossible, but also completely irresistible. This is the beginning of a tragic sequence of events. The lovers decide to escape with help from a friar. The friar marries them secretly, but they can't stay together. Romeo is exiled from Verona. The friar has a plan. He gives Juliet an herbal drink. She will "sleep" for 42 hours, enough for everyone to think she is dead. Then they will get together and leave Verona. Sadly, Romeo hears about Juliet's death, but doesn't know about the plan. He can't live without Juliet. He buys some poison, finds Juliet and kills himself. Juliet wakes up and, finding Romeo dead, she takes his dagger and kills herself, too. This classic romance has been an inspiration for generations of authors since.

▶ 1.3

B = Ben   M = Matthew

B I just couldn't finish reading *Antony and Cleopatra*. All those difficult words, bro.

M OK, here's the idiots' summary of the play. Caesar, Antony and Lepidus rule the Roman Empire.

B The three guys, right?

M So Antony is married to Flavia …

B You mean Fulvia, right?

M Uh, yeah. Fulvia. So Antony is married to Fulvia, but they don't get along very well. She lives in Rome, he lives in Alexandria, Egypt, and cheats on his wife with Cleopatra, Queen of Egypt.

B Right! Antony and Cleopatra hang out together in Egypt. Woohoo …

M Then Antony's wife, Fulvia, dies and he goes back to help Caesar fight the enemies of Rome.

B Then Antony and Caesar's sister get married. What's her name?

M Octavia. Right. But they soon drift apart and Antony goes back to Egypt and Cleopatra.

B I bet Caesar didn't like that!

M He didn't like it for sure. So Caesar and Antony fall out and start to fight for control of Egypt.

B What happened in the end?

M Antony heard false news of Cleopatra's death and killed himself. When Cleopatra heard the love of her life was dead, she committed suicide, too …

B … with small black poisonous snakes. Got it! Thanks a lot, man.

▶ 1.5

a Acquaintances generally aren't people you can count on.

b Friends are people you are usually in contact with.

c Good friends are people you hang out with and get along with. OR Good friends are people you get along with and hang out with.

d Very close friends are the people you can always rely on.

▶ 1.6

Here's something I've been giving a lot of thought to lately: friendship. Friendship is a sacred thing and I believe Facebook is cheapening it. I go on this Facebook, I see people with thousands of what they call friends, which is impossible. You can't have a thousand friends. Here's how you can tell who on Facebook is really your friend. Let's say on Friday, post a status update that says "I'm moving this weekend and I need help." The people that respond, those are your friends. Everyone else isn't. I would like people to start whittling this down. Here's an example of someone who has 545 friends: her name is Gina. Every five seconds, Gina has something to say—"100 degrees in San Diego, ugh," "Gina is eating other people's food," "Coffee," "Gina is watching *Weeds*," "Listen to Patti, people," "I should be watching *Oprah* right now," "Yay, my weekend just started," "Robin Thicke and mashed potatoes. Hollah!", "Can the time please change already?", "Who am I to come between a girl and her nose?", "It's November, yay!" and "Cinnamon hazelnut!" This woman cannot possibly have 545 friends. If she has five, I'd be shocked. So I say unfriend her. Unfriend Gina, unfriend all the Ginas of the world. They're not your friends. Tonight I'm planning to launch a new holiday. Two weeks from today, November 17th will heretofore be known as National Unfriend Day. On National Unfriend Day, I encourage you to cut out some of the friend fat in your life. A friend is someone you have a special relationship with. It's not someone who asks which *Harry Potter* character are you.

So, and then remember five years ago when no one was on Facebook and didn't know what the guy you took high school biology with was having for lunch. Remember how that was … fine. Let's go back to that. National Unfriend Day. November 17th. Spread the word. And for more on National Unfriend Day, here's William Shatner.

WS Hello, I'm William Shatner. These people on Facebook, they are not your friends.

William Shatner speaking. And let me tell you something about William Shatner, very nice guy, good guy, not my friend.

▶ 1.7

a We only just met. She seems nice.

b We've known each other for many years. We get along really well.

c We drifted apart for a few months this year, but now we text each other many times a day and go out every weekend. I know I can rely on JJ.

d His name is Rob. Or Bob? I think.

e I haven't seen Joe in forever, but we email from time to time and I'm going to invite him to my wedding next month. It'll be good to see him again.

f Amy and I have a lot of fun together when we meet. Uh, we're going out on Saturday for some pizza and gossip. I haven't seen her for a while, so we'll have a lot to talk about.

▶ 1.8

Mmmmhhh, OK. A: "Does this person give you intense looks?" Wow, he does, too! B: He doesn't hug me that often. Well, not more than other people. Huh! OK … Now, C: "Have you spent more time together lately?" Have we? Uh … No, not really. I wish! Next, D: "Is your heart beating faster as you answer these questions?" Can't everybody hear it? Faster and louder! Fine. E: "Do you spend more time with this person than with other friends?" Hmmm. I don't really. I don't … spend that much time with him. No. OK. F: I do! I do, I do! I love to talk before we go to bed. Now, G: I'm jealous of … everyone! Hope he is, too, but … who knows, right? H: "Are you going on holiday together any time soon?" Sadly no. That's it. Let's see what it says here …

Audioscript

▶ 1.9

J = Jake   C = Chloe

J   Oh, look at him. He looks quite boring and self-centered.

C   Yes, that one definitely is not for me.

J   What about this one? They sure do look very sociable.

C   Yes, they look fun. And I do like people who are a bit silly. I'll follow them.

J   Ah, look at this one. What a cute couple.

C   Hmm, yes they certainly are in love. But they're a bit over the top, don't you think? I do hate it when people are like that.

J   Ha! Yes, I know what you mean!

▶ 1.10

a   So, Lena does seem very smart.

b   She certainly does. She's just too knowledgeable for my taste, though.

c   How do you like Gamester?

d   I do like to relax, but I'm not crazy about online games.

e   You certainly aren't.

▶ 1.11

1   What's important to you in a friend?
    I do think we should be like-minded.

2   What do you think about people who post lots of selfies on social media?
    They sure are self-centered, but I don't mind. I like posting them myself.

3   Do you think we use social media too much?
    I do believe we use it a lot, but I don't think it's a problem.

4   What's the best social media app? Why?
    I don't know. I like them all!

5   How can you stay safe online?
    It's definitely important not to share too much information about yourself.

▶ 1.12

a   Montagues and Capulets were rival families.

b   Romeo and Juliet fell for each other immediately when they met.

c   Romeo and Juliet's was an impossible love.

d   Good communication is essential in both friendship and love.

e   The hardest thing about marriage is learning to communicate with each other.

f   When Jo and I met, there was instant mutual attraction between us.

g   Respect is the most important thing in any relationship if it's going to last.

h   I got a divorce because my ex didn't respect me at all. And he was cheating on me, too.

▶ 1.14

b   But Antony cheats on his wife, Fulvia.
    No way! With Cleopatra, right?

c   Exactly. He falls for Cleopatra in Egypt. So what happens next?

d   Back in Rome, his wife dies and he marries Caesar's sister, Octavia.
    Hang on a sec! He marries Caesar's sister?

e   He marries her and then goes back to Cleopatra.
    Are you serious? He cheats on her, too?

f   He cheats on Caesar's sister, That's right. And then?

g   In the end, Antony and Cleopatra die. Whoa! What a crazy story!

Unit 2

▶ 2.1

a   Yeah! We won't use plastic cups in this office anymore.
    I'm so glad. Those cups take 500 years to decompose.

b   What? Three thousand dollars for a couple of solar panels? Forget it!
    Yes, but you will save a lot more money than that on electricity bills.

c   Can I have a couple more plastic bags, please?
    Here you are. Would you like to buy a reusable bag?

d   It's pretty simple to be eco-friendly. I just try to reuse, reduce, and recycle.
    I know. The three Rs. But it's not so easy!

e   What? Recycling? It's useless. Forget it!
    No, it isn't. Think of all the trash you create when you throw things away.

f   Are you joking? Why take the stairs when you can take an elevator?
    Because the exercise is good for you and it will save energy.

g   I work in the same office as my neighbor, Bill. Sometimes he drives me; other days I drive him.
    Can I join you? That'd make it cheaper for the three of us.

▶ 2.2

a   Is the hotel down the road open?
    Yes, I think so.

b   Don't go alone. I'll come with you.
    Great! Get your coat.

c   Has John gone to the vet?
    Yeah. His dog stopped eating.

d   Hey, that's a nice orange top.
    Thanks a lot. I got it at the new store.

▶ 2.3

a   In Austria, architects have been building energy-efficient houses.

b   Iceland has been using clean electricity from geothermal energy.

c   Switzerland has been building national Alpine parks.

d   Costa Rica has been planting millions of trees to reduce deforestation.

e   Sweden has been using more water and wind power for electricity.

f   Norway has been collaborating with Sweden to produce clean energy.

g   Brazil has been producing a lot of its fuel from sugar cane.

h   In France, more families have been installing solar panels at home.

▶ 2.5

M = Mikaela   L = Lucy

M   So, Lucy, which of these do you think is worse?

L   That's a tough one. Ummm ... Well, I guess maybe floods. They caused a lot of damage in the city last year.

M   Well, yeah, but, you know ... my house wasn't damaged. And Mikaela, your house was OK too, so ...

L   Well that's not really the point. I mean, it caused a lot of problems for other people, and, for example, the government still hasn't fixed the old bridge. We still can't use it.

M   Yeah, OK, OK. But what about food? I mean the guys in the north have been waiting, what, three, four months for the rain and, you know, all the land is dry and ...

L   That's true. But, you know, I think we can solve that problem. Look, I mean, the earth is something like 80% water and ...

M   Yeah, OK, but most of that is salt water or ice. You know, we can't just put the ocean on the desert and solve the problem, I mean, that's crazy.

L   Ah! Well, that's where you're wrong. Scientists have been working on this and in, like, Israel I think, yeah, in Israel they've been using water from the oceans for many, many years.

M   Really? Huh. That's interesting.

L   Yeah, so you see, our problem isn't lack of water, like in a drought, it's really having too much water, like in a flood. So, if you look at it like that, floods are a bigger problem. And, you know, a lot of flooding problems are made worse by deforestation and global warming so,

Audioscript

you know, there are things we can do to help stop flooding and ...

2.8

1 Ready for professional growth? Congratulations! You've won a free online Chinese course. Learn the language that will open doors for intelligent sales people like you. Click here for a free introductory lesson.

2 Your laptop running slow? Clean up tons of junk with Top Clean 3 in 1. 1-click cleaner frees up disk space. Security Plus eliminates harmful files. Performance automatically improves system preferences. Top Clean 3.1 for Mac or Microsoft.

3 Looking for your next professional challenge? Grabowski and Lowe Career Management. Contact us for a confidential discussion: www. gandlcareermanagement.com or call us at 212-555-0988.

4 Want to find a new job? We can help you find the best job to match your strengths. Call Work24/7. Speak to a job expert at 303-555-5546.

5 Tired of commercials? Try soccer streaming. 100% free. Only at livesport. com. High-quality viewing.

2.9

R = recorded message   C = Cal

1 R Work 24/7! Finding jobs for you whatever you do. Please press one to speak to an expert. Press two ... The expert is busy right now. Please leave a message.

  C Hello, Mr. Connie. It's Cal Taylor here. I don't know if you remember me, I came in for an interview a couple of weeks ago. Uh, I'm looking for a job, uh, any job and ... Well, look, it's been two weeks and I haven't heard anything from you, or from any potential employers. Your website guaranteed I would only wait a week. I'm going to come into the office tomorrow and I want to talk about this with somebody. Good-bye.

R = recorded message   M = Mia

2 R Hello. You've reached the offices of Grabowski and Lowe, specialists in career advice. We apologize that there is nobody to take your call right now, so please leave a message after the tone.

  M Hi, Ms. Grabowski? Mia Stromboli here. You gave me your card at the conference in Seattle last Thursday. I'd like to arrange an appointment to discuss my career with you at some

point. Uh, a little about me. I've been working in the oil industry for 17 years now, both overseas and in the U.S. Uh, I have a lot of management experience and uh ... Well, maybe I should tell you this when we meet. So, uh, please call me back at 736-555-8191. Look forward to hearing from you. Bye.

R = recorded message   J = Jake

3 R Welcome to Five Star Chinese courses for professionals. Please press one to order your copy of our book. Press two for a quick language test. Press three to leave a message.

  J Hello? Hello. Yes, uh ... Look, I ordered a copy of *Selling in China for Beginners* and, uh, it hasn't arrived yet. Uh, the order number was, uh ... Let's see ... It was SCB3020. Now, I checked ... Oh, my name is Jake Powers. Now, look, I checked my bank account and I paid five weeks ago, so I've been waiting for 35 days. Even with 28 days for delivery, the package is still a week late. Now, I know there were no promises about the mail, but this really isn't good enough. Now, you have my contact details and I want you to call me back before the end of the day so we can figure this out. OK?

2.10

G = guide   T = tourist   Z = zoo owner

1 G Oh my goodness! Look! There in front of us. I haven't seen one of those for years, they are extremely rare. Oh, isn't he amazing?

  T Is that a ... is that ... Oh gee! Martha, pass the camera, I'm going to take a photograph.

  G No! Don't open the door. Stay in the Jeep. We're safe in here, he thinks we're one big animal, just like him. If you get out, he might attack you. He can run faster than you think, and that thing on his nose isn't just for decoration.

2 G Shhh! We have to stay very quiet. Just 20 feet in front of me, and up in the trees. I can see ... I can see that they're eating fruit, and I don't think they know we're here. Ah! These beautiful golden animals! They are very much at home here in the Brazilian Atlantic forest.

3 Z Hello, and welcome to Zoo Atlanta. Uh, I know you're all very anxious to meet our new arrivals, but, uh, first I'd like to take this, uh, this opportunity to thank our colleagues in China. We have worked very closely with them over a number of years to, uh, to

protect this iconic species and to, uh, to reach this success. The mother, Lun Lun, is doing very well and so are the twins.

4 G From our position, here in the helicopter, we can look down and see a fantastic sight. Mother and child traveling along next to each other, completely unaware of us, flying above them. These two will continue their migration along the eastern coast of the United States, from the warm waters in the south to cold feeding grounds of the north.

2.11

a I'm going to take a photograph.
b I can see that they are eating fruit.
c Hello and welcome to Zoo Atlanta.
d Mother and child traveling along.

2.12

a Have you ever seen an endangered animal in the wild?
b Have you ever seen one in a zoo?
c Have you ever looked after a sick animal?
d Have you ever given money for an animal cause?
e Have you ever considered working for an animal protection NGO?

2.13

a Work hard at it and you'll get there.
b What's the point of doing that?
c Keep going. You'll get there in the end.
d If at first you don't succeed, try, try again.
e Do you really think that's a good idea?

2.14

M = man   W = woman

1 M Oh, I can't believe it! Another "no" letter. This must be the fifth job this month. I'm never going to get a job as a journalist!

  W Hey, listen. You have to believe in yourself. Work hard at it, and you'll get there. I know you can do it!

  M Huh. That's easy for you to say.

2 W Oh, here's my paycheck! Yeah! I've almost saved enough money for my trip!

  M Your trip? What are you talking about?

  W Duh! I've been talking about it, like, forever! Hannah and I are going to take a gap year. We're going to go backpacking and camping across the country and ...

  M Wait a minute. You and *Hannah*? Hannah that can't stand spiders? That

Audioscript

Hannah? Do you really think that's a good idea?

W Oh come on, she's not that bad. And anyway, it'll be fun.

Unit 3

▶ 3.1

a How do you like your city?

It's a truly awesome city; the city that never sleeps; the capital of the world.

b Is it easy to find your way around?

It is really easy to find your way around because the streets are numbered.

c What's your favorite landmark?

Well, in a city of skyscrapers, I guess it's the Chrysler Building.

d What are the most popular tourist spots?

Central Park, Greenwich Village, 5th Avenue, the World Trade Center, and so many others.

▶ 3.5

a The honking went on for hours until we slowly started moving.

b The firefighters finally opened the door and helped each one of us up to the 15th floor.

c I walked out in my pajamas to get the paper and the wind blew the door shut behind me.

d When we got back to the parking lot, I realized I'd left the keys somewhere.

e Almost 12 hours to buy tickets for a show sounds crazy, doesn't it?

f We couldn't get out because we were between stations.

g The observation deck was so full with people we couldn't get to the door to get down again.

▶ 3.6

a Wow. My whole body hurts.

Well, you hadn't been to the gym in a long time, had you?

b So how did it go last night?

It was just perfect. Chad and me, the music, the lights, everything.

c My neck hurt for a couple of days. And Betty's ears hurt.

That's what a 12-hour trip does to you.

d So what happened in the end?

I told her I was sorry and she accepted my apology. I think we're going to be ok now.

e He asked to see my driver's license.

Did he give you a ticket?

▶ 3.8

a The golden rule is that there are no golden rules.

b Life is short. Break the rules. Forgive quickly. Kiss slowly. Laugh uncontrollably. And never regret anything that makes you smile.

c Know the rules well, so you can break them effectively.

d If you obey all the rules, you miss all the fun.

e You have to learn the rules of the game. And then you have to play better than anyone else.

f There are three rules for writing a novel. Unfortunately no one knows what they are.

Unit 4

▶ 4.1

R = Ruth   D = Dan

R I'm reading this fabulous book about 21st century skills.

D Not another book telling us to teach kids collaboration and creativity, is it?

R Yes, among other important skills. It's a collection of papers by 21 different authors.

D Do any of the authors tell us how to motivate kids to learn reading, writing and arithmetic these days?

R Well, Dan, kids need much more than that to succeed in the 21st century. People need to be able to work together well to solve really complex problems, to show initiative and come up with ideas that have value to others, you know, being creative. Reading, writing, and math are just tools.

D It's all very well for theorists to say that, but how do you keep a group of teenagers engaged in a classroom these days? When everybody is texting everybody, or checking their Facebook timeline, or even gaming during classroom time?

R Precisely! Everyone's connected by technology and, suddenly, that has to stop when they enter a classroom. It's not natural! I really think we are right to use as much information technology in our schools as possible. That's how we prepare kids for a future we can't even imagine. Let them use their cell phones to learn. Let them look for information on the web and share it with everyone in class.

D Let them use their cell phones in class? You can't be serious! How do you know they're not texting their friends?

R Frankly, Dan ... Because you negotiate the rules with your students from the start.

D Fine, let's say they do use their smartphones to look up information for a project. You know as well as I do that the Internet is full of garbage.

R Well, then you teach kids how to find information they can trust. That's a 21st century skill.

▶ 4.2

R = Ruth   D = Dan   C1 = colleague 1
C2 = colleague 2

a R I think schools need to teach 21st century skills.

C1 Do you think so? I mean, they learn those things at home. School is where they should learn what they can't learn in other places. So, no, I don't agree with you.

b D I believe we should concentrate on reading, writing and arithmetic.

C2 I don't think so. Well, not only those things. What about art, or history, or music?

c R I think kids have to learn how to solve problems creatively.

C1 No, I don't think so. They should learn rules, rules, rules.

d R In my opinion, smart phones can be a useful learning tool in class.

C2 Yeah, you're right. I use them all the time.

e D Smart phones shouldn't be allowed in class.

C1 Oh, I think so too. They really annoy me. All that beeping.

f D I don't think students should look for information online. It's useless.

C2 Oh, come on! You think that? The Internet is part of our lives now.

g R Teachers should teach students to find information on the Internet that they can trust.

C2 That's absolutely right! Yes, I completely agree with you!

▶ 4.7

A

I did something terrible at school once.

Really? What did you do?

I was in 5th grade, I think, and I stuck the teacher's purse to a table.

Why did you do such a thing?

I have no idea. I really don't know.

B

I said something really mean once.

Really? What did you say?

Audioscript

I looked my mother in the eye and told her that I hated her with all my heart.

What a terrible thing to say!

Yep! I don't really know where that came from.

C

I did the most embarrassing thing a while ago.

Really? What did you do?

This teacher came up to me and there was this insect on her blouse.

So I hit it off with my hand, but it hit the wall and broke into a thousand pieces. And I realized it wasn't an insect. It was some kind of brooch.

Oh no! What a silly thing to do!

▶ 4.9

a If I graduate from college next year, I will look for a job with a tech company.

b If I move to San Francisco, I'll find a good tech job.

c I will be surprised if I find a good job quickly.

d If I won the lottery, I'd travel the world.

e I could write better apps if I had a better computer.

f If I could change one thing about myself, I'd have a smaller nose.

▶ 4.10

a book – could

b blue – two

c could – should

d true – through

e moved– moon

f school – pool

g cook – woman

Unit 5

▶ 5.1

1 I bought a new pair of jeans last week. Do you like them?

2 That's a nice pair of sunglasses. Where did you get them?

3 I really want to buy some new sandals. Where can I get some?

4 So you gave your girlfriend some jewelry for her birthday. Did she like it?

5 I need a suit for my job interview. Where can I get one?

6 I bought a new T-shirt online. Do you like it?

▶ 5.2

A = Andreas   J = Jia

A My bank manager has just approved a 2,000-dollar loan for me.

J I thought you'd applied for three grand.

A I did, but they only approved two grand. I only make 500 bucks a week, you know.

J Did your brother agree to be your co-signer?

A Nope. The good news is my dad agreed.

J Good for him. Do you pay very high interest on the loan?

A 1.5 percent. I guess it's the standard rate for a three-year loan.

J Depends on the terms. When's your first payment due?

A July first.

J Will you be able to pay it off?

A I sure hope so.

▶ 5.3

a If I'd planned my application more carefully, they might have accepted it.

b If I hadn't gone on vacation twice this year, I wouldn't have got into debt.

c If you'd told me, I would have helped you.

d So if she hadn't died, I wouldn't have received it.

▶ 5.6

1 Ladies and gentlemen, we continue boarding American Airlines flight 542 with service to London through gate 37. At this time, we're ready to board passengers in group C. All other passengers, please remain seated. We'd like to invite passengers with "group C" on their boarding passes to board now through gate 37. Please, have your boarding passes ready and passports open at the picture page.

2 Directors, teachers, fellow classmates and families and friends, we are the graduating class of 2014! It is a great honor to be here to commemorate this major moment in my life and that of my fellow classmates. I think we've all been looking forward to today as our prize for the hard work of the last four years.

N = narrator   D = David

3 N In five, four, three, two, one. Ladies and gentlemen, from the top of New York's beautiful Rockefeller Center, we present the *David Perlman Show*. Please welcome your host: David Perlman.

D Good evening everybody. We have a great show for you tonight. Beautiful Miss Taylor Swift and Academy Award winner Jennifer Lawrence are here, ladies and gentlemen.

▶ 5.7

I just spent $3,000 on a designer bag.

$3,000? You can't be serious.

Yeah. And I have another one just like it at home.

Another one? You must be kidding.

I'm not kidding. I bought it last week.

Last week? You must be insane!

Aha. Worse thing is, I feel like buying one more.

One more? You must be out of your mind.

In fact, I'm going there right now.

Right now? You can't seriously expect me to believe that? You must be joking!

You're right. I'm joking.

Ha! I knew it!

▶ 5.9

1 He works as a security guard.
Security.

2 Don't miss this great opportunity.
Opportunity.

3 You have completed your transaction.
Transaction.

4 I got it in an online auction.
Auction.

5 We will notify you by mail.
Notify.

6 You have to certify your documents.
Certify.

7 She's very ambitious.
Ambitious.

8 That hat is ridiculous.
Ridiculous.

9 No way. That's unbelievable!
Unbelievable.

10 Nothing is impossible if you try.
Impossible.

11 A car suddenly stopped in front of us.
Suddenly.

12 Luckily, we were wearing seatbelts.
Luckily.

▶ 5.10

C = customer   SA = sales clerk

C I bought this flash drive yesterday and realized it's only 63 GB instead of the 256 GB I paid for. Can I exchange it for the 256 GB?

SA I just need to see your receipt, please.

C That's the thing. I threw it away, you see.

SA In that case, I'm afraid there's nothing I can do.

C Seriously? But look, I have the bag.

▶ 5.11

C = customer   SA = sales clerk

SA Cash or charge?

C Charge, please.

SA Thank you. Insert your card, please.

C There you go.

SA I'm afraid it has been declined.

C   I don't understand. Can you try this one?

SA It worked this time. There you are.

C   Ah! At last!

 5.12

C = customer   SA = sales clerk

C   I like these shoes. Can I try them on?

SA Sure. What size do you wear?

C   Size 12.

SA I'm sorry. We're sold out.

C   Do you have the same shoe in brown?

SA A size 12 in brown, right?

C   Yep. Wait! Forget it. I'm really late as it is. Thanks.

SA You're welcome sir. Good-bye.

C   Good-bye.

Answer key

Unit 1

1.1

1 a3 b2 c1 d1 e2 f3 g2

2 a How many Facebook friends do you have / ~~you~~?
  b Who makes you laugh most? / ~~do~~
  c What are you really good at? / ~~on~~
  d What makes you nervous? / ~~are~~
  e What did you do last vacation? / ~~does~~
  f Would you like to go to a speed-friending event? / ~~to~~
  g What's something you just can't live without? / ~~do~~

3 a6 b7 c5 d4 e3 f2 g1

1.2

1 Love Story 1: in, get, apart
Love Story 2: along, for, They got, got
Love Story 3: out, for, in, on, up, back

2 a2 b3 c1

3 (8) Romeo dies, (6) escape, (1) meet, (9) Juliet dies, (7) get married secretly, (4) find out their families are enemies, (3) fall for each other, (2) get along well, (5) realize their love is impossible

4 Personal answers.

6 a They meet at a party and get on well immediately.
  b Their love is impossible but also irresistible.
  c The friar marries them secretly.
  d ... but they can't stay together.

1.3

1 a people you can count on.
  b people you are usually in contact with.
  c people you get along with and hang out with.
  d the people you can always rely on.

2 National UnFriend Day is a day for removing unnecessary people from Facebook.

3 helps you move house / has seen you recently

4 on, out, along, from, about, with

5 a acquaintances
  b very close friends
  c very close friends
  d acquaintances
  e friends
  f friends

6 Personal answers.

7 aY bN cN dY eN fY gY hN
She should try a bit harder.

1.4

1 1c 2f 3b 4g 5a 6a 7f 8h 9e 10d

2 Personal answers.

3 definitely is / sure do look / really do like / certainly are / do hate

5 1c 2d 3a 4e 5b

1.5

1 a Friendship b Love c Love d Love
  e Nothing f Nothing g Love
  h Friendship i Nothing j Nothing

2 b ADV c ADJ d N eV f N gN hV

3 1 Antony cheats on his wife, Fulvia.
  2 Fulvia dies and Antony goes back to Rome.
  3 Antony marries Caesar's sister, Octavia.
  4 Antony goes back to Egypt and Cleopatra.
  5 Caesar and Antony fight to control Egypt.
  6 Antony and Cleopatra both die.

Unit 2

2.1

1 Not use regular electricity.

2 aF bF cT dF eF fT

3 a G (cups in this) b NG (for a couple)
  c NG (Can I have) d G (simple to be)
  e NG (Forget it) f NG (take an elevator)
  g G (in the same)

4 1b 2a 3d 4e 5g 6f 7c

5 a pet-friendly b energy-efficient
  c fuel-efficient d reusable e rechargeable

6 b Do you ever practice flexitarianism?
  c Do you have energy-efficient light bulbs at home?
  d Have you walked or cycled to work lately instead of using private transportation?
  e Do you turn off appliances when you're not using them?
  f Do you use eco-friendly cleaning products?
  g Have you changed from plastic to reusable cloth bags?

7 a (hotel, road, open, so) b (Don't, go, alone, coat) c (John, gone, dog, stopped) d (orange, top, lot, got)

2.2

1 2 I haven't been taking taxis
  3 I haven't been using plastic bags
  4 I've been ordering drinks without a plastic straw
  5 I've been eating less red meat and dairy

2 a Proud.
  b Wind and rain.
  c He is saving money.
  d It fills the seas and damages wildlife.
  e He feels more healthy.
  f Personal answer.

3 a Austria
  b Iceland
  c Switzerland
  d Costa Rica
  e Sweden
  f Norway
  g Brazil
  h France

4 a The office **has** been really busy. We've been **working** like crazy.
  b I like your shoes. I've been trying **to** find a pair like that **since** last year.
    OR I **was** trying **to** find a pair like that last year.

  c So sorry! Have you been **waiting** for long?
  d Hey! I've been trying to call you **since** yesterday. Where **were** you?
    OR I **was** trying to call you yesterday.
  e He's been **studying** English for **years**.
    OR ... English for **a** year.
  f They've been playing soccer.
    OR They **were** playing soccer before.
  g Joan**'s / has** been managing **the advertising company** since 2012.

2.3

1 a POACHING
  b DROUGHTS
  c FLOODS
  d DEFORESTATION
  e RISING SEA LEVELS
  f DUMPING OF E-WASTE
  g THREATENED SPECIES
  h FOSSIL FUELS
  i CLIMATE CHANGE

2 Floods, droughts, deforestation, climate change.

3 a Floods.
  b No.
  c No.
  d 3 or 4 months ago.
  e 80%.
  f Israel.

4 a have replaced b have eliminated / have been planting / has planted c has developed / has dropped d have stopped / have become e have been trying

5 a How long have you known your best friend?
  b Have you been working hard recently?
  c Have you ever lived in a different city?
  d How long have you been studying today?
  e How much bread have you eaten today?
  f How far have you walked today?
  g How many cups of coffee have you drunk today?
  h Have you been exercising a lot lately?

2.4

1 a 4
  b 5
  c 3
  d 1
  e 2

2 See ▶2.8.

3 a **Are you** ready for professional growth?
  b **Is your** laptop running slow?
  c **Are you** looking for **your** next professional challenge?
  d **Do you** want to find a new job?
  e **Are you** tired of commercials?

4 a M bJ cJ dC eM fC

5 a came
  b 's been / haven't heard
  c 've reached
  d 've been working
  e ordered / hasn't arrived
  f checked / paid / 've been waiting

6 a I started this course in February.
  b I've had my job for five years.

0# Answer key

c Our teacher gave us lots of homework last week.

d I've learnt 10 new words this lesson.

e I didn't go out last night.

2.5

1 1 Javanese rhino 2 Golden lion tamarin
3 Giant panda 4 North Atlantic right whale

2 a I'm going to take a photograph.
b I can see that they are eating fruit.
c Hello and welcome to Zoo Atlanta.
d Mother and child travelling along.

3 a Have you ever seen an endangered animal in the wild? / a
b Have you ever seen one in a zoo? / a
c Have you ever looked after a sick animal? / on
d Have you ever given money for an animal cause? / never
e Have you ever considered working for an animal protection NGO? / it

4 33%, 10%, nearly 0%

5 a Work hard at it and you'll get there. (E)
b What's the point of doing that? (D)
c Keep going. You'll get there in the end. (E)
d If at first you don't succeed, try, try again. (E)
e Do you really think that's a good idea? (D)

6 Person 1 wants to get a new job (phrase a).
Person 2 wants to take a gap year (phrase e).

Unit 3

3.1

1

Across	Down
4 smoggy	1 chaotic
6 upscale	2 fashionable
7 polluted	3 neglected
	5 rundown
	8 lively

2 a fashionable b rundown c polluted
d chaotic e smoggy f lively

3 a How do you like your city?
a / the / the / the
b Is it easy to find your way around?
the
c What's your favorite landmark?
a / the
d What are the most popular tourist spots?
They are talking about New York City.

3.2

1 a T b F c T d N e T f T

2 a had told b had sent c had made
d had kissed e hadn't hugged
f had mistaken g had shaken h had broken

3 a Did you know the Romans **spoke** Latin?
b After we **arrived** home, we made some sandwiches.
c By the time we got home, the TV show **had** finished.
d When I had **had** lunch, I had a short nap.
e We **bought** our car five years ago.

4 a gone b been c been d been

5 a Hi, this is your travel host.
b I'd like to show you the top ten attractions of Madrid, Spain.
c Number ten. Plaza de Cibeles. Madrid is known for many beautiful squares like this one.
d The Cibeles fountain is an important symbol of this city.
e Number nine. Almudena Cathedral. It took more than a hundred years to complete its construction in 1993.
f The original site was occupied by Madrid's first mosque.

3.3

1 Carlos driving. Anya crime. Mike noise. Margaret money.

2 1 traffic
2 spot
3 theft
4 vandalism
5 pickpocketing
6 rate
7 honking
8 noise
9 debt
10 balance

3 1 d 2 g 3 a 4 h 5 c 6 j 7 i 8 b
9 f 10 e

4 a car theft
b suffer from loneliness
c work–life balance
d be in debt
e find a parking spot
f constantly connected

5 Personal answers.

3.4

1 a wonder
b turn
c mean
d poor
e joking

2 c, a, f, b, d, g, e

3 a had been doing exercise
b had been dancing
c had been flying
d had been fighting
e had been speeding

4 a had been hanging out
b had made / had been making
c had gotten
d had been dating
e had killed

5 a I had to sit down because I'd been standing all day.
b We got lost because we hadn't understood the directions.
c OK
d Vera had visited Turkey before so she knew the best places.
e Until yesterday night, I had never eaten meat before.
f OK
g How long had you been waiting when the doors opened?

3.5

1 a 5 b 1 c 3 d 6 e 2 f 4

2 a Danger! No lifeguard **on** duty.
b Kindly refrain **from** smoking.
c Park here **at** your own risk.
d Please clean **up** after your pet.
e Tow **away** zone. Do not stop here.
f Vehicles will be towed **at** owner's expense.

4 f, c, e, a, d, b

Unit 4

4.1

1 literature, art, geography, math, history, languages, chemistry, physics, biology

2 a R b D c R d R e D f D g R

3

Agree	Disagree
e	b, c
g	a
d	f

5 Do: badly, an exercise, homework, well
Get: feedback, good grades, into trouble, kicked out, a report card
Make: a difference, mistakes, progress
Take: an exam, photos, a test

6 1 e 2 f 3 b 4 a 5 g 6 c 7 d

4.2

1 b too much c too many d never enough
e too much f too much g too little
h no / too many i too much

2 a rich
b problems
c noise

4 walking to school / windy / Thursday / a café

4.3

1 Personal answers

2 1 b 2 c 3 a

3 b ... worked harder.
c ... chosen art.
d ... have dressed appropriately for the interview.
e ... gone to music school when I had the chance.
f ... have dropped out of college.

5 a 2, 3, 5, 4, 1
b 3, 2, 5, 1, 4
c 4, 5, 1, 3, 2

6 a do b say c do

4.4

1 1 d 2 f 3 a 4 c 5 b 6 e

2 a will look for
b move
c will be
d won
e had
f could

3 first conditional: a, b, c
second conditional: d, e, f

Answer Key

4 /uː/ blue, true, through, moved, moon, school, pool
/ʊ/ book, could, should, would, cook, woman

4.5

1 1 a, an, the, an, the, a, the, The
2 a, the, the, The, a, the, the
3 a, the, the, a, the, The, the

2 a Two
b *Gifted* and *Magnus*
c *Gifted*
d *Hidden Figures*

3 a What's done is done. (S)
b What were you thinking? (C)
c It's not the end of the world. (S)
d You should've known better. (C)
e How could you do such a thing? (C)
f Don't let it get you down. (S)
g Will you ever learn? (C)

5 a You should have prepared for the interview.
If you'd prepared for the interview, you would've gotten the scholarship.
b You should've studied for the test.
If you'd studied for the test, you wouldn't have failed.
c You shouldn't have been absent a lot.
If you hadn't been absent a lot, you wouldn't have got bad grades.
d You shouldn't have cheated on a final exam.
If you hadn't cheated on a final exam, you wouldn't have been kicked out of school.
e You should've got into college.
If you'd got into college, your parents wouldn't have been upset.

Unit 5

5.1

1 1 c 2 e 3 a 6 f (*b* and *d* are not used.)

2 1 free Wi-Fi, charging stations, virtual try-ons
2 coupons, in-store shopping
3 self-checkout, user-generated content, brand loyalty

3

S	U	N	G	L	A	S	S	E	S
H	U					W		A	H
O	I					E		R	O
R		T				A		R	E
T	T	B				T	J	I	S
S	S	C	A	R	F	J	E	A	N	S
A	H	G				R	C	G	
N	B	I	K	I	N	I	K	S	
D			R				E		
A			T				T		
L	J	E	W	E	L	R	Y		
S						P	A	N	T	S

4 a sunglasses, jeans, pants, sandals, shorts, earrings, shoes
b sunglasses, jeans, pants, sandals, shorts, earrings, shoes, jewelry
c scarf, bikini, sweater, jacket, T-shirt, suit, bag

5 1 Do you like them?
2 Where did you get them?
3 Where can I get some?
4 Did she like it?
5 Where can I get one?
6 Do you like it?

5.2

1 1 off / back 2 on 3 out 4 out, into

2 1 $3,000
2 $500 a week
3 his father
4 1.5 %
5 July 1st

3 a might
b hadn't
c have
d wouldn't

5

Silent *b*	Silent *t*	Silent *gh*	*gh* = /f/
doubt	fasten	bought	enough
thumb	listen	though	laugh

6 a bought
b Fasten
c thumb
d listen / laugh
e doubt / enough / though

5.3

1 a your clothes / your money / your name
b your money / your chair / your word
c your hair / a hairdryer / a towel
d the letter *e* / the letter *s* / the letter *m*
e food / poison / nothing

2 1 d 2 c 3 e

3 1 c 2 e 3 a 4 b 5 f 6 d

4 You must: be insane, be joking, be out of your mind
You can't: seriously expect me / us to believe that

5 can't be serious, must be joking, must be insane, must be out of your mind, can't seriously expect me to believe that

5.4

1 a, c, b, d

2 Only the Hollywood sign.

3

Nouns		Verbs
security	transaction	notify
opportunity	auction	certify

Adjectives		Adverbs
ambitious	unbelievable	completely
ridiculous	impossible	luckily

4 a secure
b marvelous
c disappointment
d washable
e nicely
f purify

5 a OK
b kind, old
c gorgeous, shiny
d OK
e lovely, big

5.5

1 b

2 a near
b difficult
c slowly
d after
e most expensive
f price per unit

3 c, b, a, e, f, d
SC, C, C, SC, C, C

4 Cash, Insert, card, afraid, declined

5 See ▶5.12.

Phrase Bank

This Phrase Bank is organized by topics.
► The audio is on the ID Richmond Learning Platform.

Getting to know people

Unit 1
Do you have any nicknames?
Are you usually more optimistic or pessimistic?
What's the first thing you notice when meeting someone new?
Where are you and your family from?
What are the three most important objects you have at home?
What did you want to be when you were a kid?
Which sports team do you and your family support?
What do you do to wake yourself up in the morning?
I don't know. Maybe join a sports club or take a course.
I guess one advantage is that you get to know a lot of different people.

Relationships

Unit 1
Have you met all your classmates?
Yes and no. I mean, I've seen them, but I haven't spoken to them all yet.
My sister broke up with her boyfriend last year, but they got back together after a week.
Oh yeah? Are they still together?
Taylor Swift and Calvin Harris broke up in 2016.
I'd never fall for someone who likes pop music – I can't stand it!
Justin Bieber met Selena Gomez in 2009 after his manager called her mom to arrange a meeting.
They dated on and off for years, but they finally broke up in 2018.
We've known each other since elementary school. We used to be really close.
I have a lot of very close friends.

Asking for and giving opinions

Unit 1
I think selfies show that someone cares a lot about what they look like.
I post a lot of group photos, but I definitely don't feel lonely!
My brother is always posting selfies, and he's incredibly self-centered.
I do believe that ...
People seem to ...
I do agree that ...
I definitely think that ...

Unit 2
I'd never try the Moringa stuff. I don't believe in all these "superfoods".
Hmm ... maybe I'd go to the retreat. I need a rest.

Unit 3
I feel most sorry for ... because ...
Our city has a lot of problems. I love it, though.
Really? I don't. I'm tired of living here.
How do you feel about ...?
What do you think of ...?

Unit 4
And I think uniforms are a good idea. It's one less decision to make in the morning.
No way! I love wearing my own clothes.

Reactions / Listening actively

Unit 1
You mean the date?
Go on.
Hold on a sec.
No way!
What happens next?
What do you mean "leaves"?
Are you sure?
Oh, dear!
So, I finish work and I'm walking to my car. I'm tired and really looking forward to getting home. I open ...
Uh-huh. Yeah. And then ...?

Unit 3
What do you mean?
You poor thing! Oh, no!
You're joking! Gee! And how did it turn out?
No wonder!
I was going to visit my grandparents once, and we got stuck on the highway for four hours.
Oh, no. You poor thing. What happened?
So, I was going for a job interview, I'd been looking for a job as an architect for ages, so I was really nervous.
Well, it was my cousin's birthday, and I'd been planning ...
Well, I'm sure something better will come along ...
What do you mean I can't park here? Says who?

Unit 4
Really? What did you do?
Why would you say such a thing?

Going green

Unit 2
Well, 1 is plastic bottles. I think it takes a lot of energy to produce them.
Yes, and then the oceans are full of plastic waste ...
Do you have water-efficient faucets in your home?
I have no idea!
I suppose I could try flexitarianism. I could be a vegetarian half the week.
That's a good idea. Vegetarianism is more animal-friendly and environment-friendly, too!
I do what I can, but it doesn't feel like it's changing anything.
Yeah, but we have to start somewhere. The real problem is education.

Talking about duration

Unit 2
I have been walking to work once a week.
I have been studying English all weekend.
Guess what! I go to the gym twice a week now.

Phrase Bank

Really? How long have you been going there?
Are you reading anything now?
Yeah, I'm reading a graded reader.
How long have you been reading it?
She's been trying a new superfood. It's made her feel much better.
I collect old vinyl pop records.
No way! How long have you been collecting them?
Well, it all started when ...

The environment

Unit 2
I feel a bit more optimistic about threatened species because there are lots of conservation groups trying to stop extinction.
I think the scientist who makes the first point will say climate change is also a problem right now.
Floods are a real problem in São Paulo.
And it's gotten worse recently.
I can't believe there are only about 800 gorillas left!
It makes me want to do something.
Me, too. I think it's actually worse. I heard recently we've lost more than half the world's wildlife since 1970!
We should be taught more about it at school.
I've been trying to walk more instead of driving everywhere.
Good for you. I should use my car less.
I think using hybrid cars will make a big difference.

Describing places

Unit 3
These two look like fashionable neighborhoods ...
There's a bridge in this one.
I'd say our city is chaotic. There's lots of traffic and millions of people.
We have a beautiful square in the heart of our town. It's a real tourist spot because it has great cafés and restaurants.
A dangerous, ancient, Asian, skyscraper.
The city I'd like to visit has beautiful beaches, great music, and some of the best colonial architecture in South America. It's well-known for its mix of European, African, and indigenous cultures. Famous landmarks include ...
Last year I went to this amazing place. I'd never been before, and to my surprise, it was completely empty. I'd expected it to be full!
I saw the pyramids in Egypt five years ago. I'd never seen anything so old before!
My home town, Trujillo, has some great colonial architecture.

Urban problems

Unit 3
I think the worst problem by far is the traffic.
No way! I'd say vandalism is a much more serious issue.
Littering bothers me a lot.
The traffic doesn't bother me..
In my neighborhood, there is trash everywhere.
All the traffic jams drive me crazy!

Making guesses and deductions

Unit 5
I think he must be talking to his son.
Hmm ... Not sure. I think he might be talking to a friend.
I think the first one might be true, but I'm not really sure.
Really? I actually think it could be bad for your teeth.
You look in shape. I think you might work out a lot in your free time.
Yeah, I saw you carrying a tennis racket the other day. You must play tennis.
I'd say it's probably about consumer behavior.

Reinforcing

Unit 3
I'm afraid so.
I'm afraid not.

Apologizing

Unit 3
I'm sorry. I didn't realize that.

School life

Unit 4
All the books remind me of my school bag. It was really heavy!
I used to hate math because the teacher couldn't explain it to us.
Maybe they have a lot of expensive private schools.
Yes, I guess the teachers are well qualified, too.
They have one-on-one tutoring sometimes. We don't get that if we fail a test.
It'd be a nice modern building. We would only do a little homework every day and not take a lot of tests. And I think uniforms are a good idea.
No way! I love wearing my own clothes.
At my school, students have too much homework. It takes me four or five hours a day.
Well, when I was in high school, I had a lot of homework, too.
I think too much pressure can be very stressful for students
You're absolutely right, but if there isn't enough competition, students can get lazy.

Picking a career

Unit 4
Yes, me! I tried three completely different jobs until I found the right one for me.
Really? What did you do?
I can't throw away $40,000, drop out of college, forget about my business major and start over.
I'd love to get a scholarship to go to Harvard, but it's so hard I won't even try.
All my friends will major in business, so that's what I'll do.
My parents have always wanted me to get into medical school. I can't disappoint them, and they are desperate for me to succeed.

Phrase Bank

I'd love to get a degree in music, but what will I do when I graduate? How will I get a decent job?
I have all the education I need, I'm not illiterate! It's time for fun, fun, fun!

Should have

Unit 4

I should have studied English when I was a kid.
I should have thought about it more carefully.
I shouldn't have listened to him.
What should I have studied instead?
You should have studied harder for the test.
I shouldn't have missed so many classes.
Me, too. I should have participated more.
They should have stayed at home.
I shouldn't have told my sister I didn't like her new dress.

First and second conditional

Unit 4

If I have time, I'll come and visit you.
If you could travel anywhere in the world, where would you go?
If I get my driving license soon, I'll be able to get a better job.
What kind of job would you get if you passed your test?
If I'd had more confidence, I would have sung at the karaoke competition.
Do you think you'd have won?

Third conditional

Unit 5

If she hadn't gone to college, she might'nt have gotten into debt.
If I hadn't played so many video games, I'd have been better at sport!
Which sports would you have played?
I'd volunteer to help with reading at my local elementary school.
I think some parents would donate to V2Z.

Criticizing

Unit 4

Will you ever learn?
You should have known better.
How could you do such a thing?
What were you thinking?

Expressing sympathy

Unit 4

It could have been worse.
Don't let it get you down.
What's done is done.
It's not the end of the world.

Shopping

Unit 5

I expect good customer service.
Yes, and I like it to be well organized, so I can find things easily.
Well, they probably all shop online and don't go to real stores anymore.
I agree with a lot of it, but I still prefer to buy things online. It's so much easier.
No way, what for? Who would care about my shopping?
There's no need to stand in in that long line. They have self-checkout here.
My battery is running out. Are there charging stations in here?
Smart brands use customers' user-generated content, such as YouTube videos and blog posts, to advertise their products.
I would rather do in-store shopping than shop online. At least you can try things on.
I've got a discount for that store—you get 10% off everything today.
I can't get online to check the reviews. They don't even have free Wi-Fi in here!
These glasses looked good on me with virtual try-on, but they don't look good in real life.
I don't have much brand loyalty except for my cell phone— I'd never consider getting any other make.
I guess I'm 4 for most things except clothes. I like to try things on before buying.
It could be good for clothes hoarders.
Yeah, they could sell clothes they haven't worn.

Talking about products

Unit 5

I bought some really expensive sunglasses and left them in a taxi. I felt really guilty afterward – and stupid, too.
I bought it on impulse. It was pure madness!
It seemed like a wonderful product, but it was such a disappointment.
They go on and on in the infomercial about how it's natural.
I guess it's just so fashionable these days.
I like to wear dark colours, especially at night.
Not me. I'm into bright shirts or T-shirts.

Shopping problems

Unit 5

Do you have a size ten in stock?
I'm sorry ma'am, we're sold out.
Ah, that's a shame. It seems impossible to find larger sizes.
Can you email me when you have some in stock?
Ah. I'm afraid your card has been declined.
Declined! I don't understand! It's a new card, and I know I'm not over my limit. There must be a problem with your card machine.
I'd like to return this phone. I bought it here the other day and it's damaged.
Well, uh, unfortunately we can't give you a refund, but we'd be happy to exchange it for another one.
Sure, uh, I just need to see your receipt.

Other useful expressions

Unit 1

I guess one advantage is that you get to know a lot of different people.

Neither of us has a nickname.

Unit 3

My parents never used to pick up after their dog, but now they always do.

Word List

This is a reference list. ▶ The audio is on the ⏸ Richmond Learning Platform.

Unit 1

Relationships

to be attracted to someone
to break up
to drift apart
to fall for someone
to fall out with someone
to get along (well)
to get (back) together
to get to know someone (better)
to hang out
to move in

Personality adjectives

adventure-seeking
confident
easygoing
fun-loving
funny
honest
impolite
kind-hearted
knowledgeable
like-minded
open-minded
outgoing
self-centered
shy
sociable
thoughtful

Unit 2

Going green

appliances
bottled water
carbon footprint
disposable products
eco-friendly
energy-efficient light bulb
environment-friendly appliances
faucet
household waste
insecticides
nature-friendly
plastic bags
public transportation
recycled paper
refillable bottles
renewable energy
reusable cloth bag
solar heating
Styrofoam cup
vegan

The environment

climate change
deforestation
droughts
dumping
floods
fossil fuels

global warming
poaching
rising sea levels
threatened species

Threatened species

Giant panda
Golden lion tamarin
Ivory-billed woodpecker
Javanese rhino
Monk seal
Mountain gorilla
North Atlantic right whale

Unit 3

Cities

harbor
landmark
neighborhood
skyline
skyscraper
smog
square

Adjectives

chaotic
dangerous
exceptional
fashionable
flat
lively
magnificent
marvellous
rundown
ugly
upscale

Social conventions and manners

to blow your nose in public
to blow on your soup
to bow
to chew
to hug
to kiss on the cheek
to leave a tip
to push your way through the crowd
to shake hands

Urban problems

crime rate
debt lines
littering
loneliness
noise pollution
pickpocketing
parking spot
potholes
roadwork
security checks
theft / thieves
to go through red lights
to honk

traffic jams
trash
vandalism
work-life balance

Rules and regulations

fine
lifeguard
on duty
to fasten
to pick up after
to refrain from
to tow away
trespasser
under surveillance

Unit 4

School life

badly paid teachers
career counseling
discipline problems
extracurricular activities
one-on-one tutoring
overcrowded classrooms
pressure
report card
schedule
subjects
to behave badly
to cheat on exams
to do the homework
to do well (in school)
to fail a test
to get a low / high grade
to get kicked out of class
to make mistakes
to take a class / tests
tuition fees

College life

certificate
degree
graduate
major (in)
scholarship
to drop out of college
to enroll
to get into (medical) school
to start over

Other words

autism
deadline
gifted
illiterate
IQ (intelligence quotient)
jigsaw
learning disability
to learn by heart
to skip
trouble sleeping
volume

Unit 5

Money and shopping

brand loyalty
charging stations
discount code
self-checkout
shop online
shopping sprees
to do in-store shopping
to save money
user-generated content
virtual try-on

Word formation

actually
apparently
appearance
comfortable
convenience
currently
enjoyment
fitness
flatten
freaky
generalize
gorgeous
remarkable
seriously
shockingly
solution
tighten
useless

Other words

aisles
checkout
gadgets
lucrative
to donate
to get into debt

◪ Richmond

58 St Aldates
Oxford
OX1 1ST
United Kingdom

Third reprint: September 2020
ISBN: 978-84-668-3252-6
CP: 105621

Publishing Director: Deborah Tricker
Publisher: Luke Baxter
Media Publisher: Luke Baxter
Content Developers: Paul Seligson, Deborah Goldblatt, Damian Williams
Managing Editor: Laura Miranda
Editors: Shona Rodger, Helen Wendholt
Proofreaders: Lily Khambata, Diyan Leake, Rachael Williamson, Daniel Deacon
Design Manager: Lorna Heaslip
Cover Design: Lorna Heaslip
Design & Layout: emc Design Ltd
Photo Researcher: Magdalena Mayo, Helen Reilly
Audio Production: John Marshall Media Inc.
ID Café Production: Mannic Media

We would like to thank all those who have given their kind permission to reproduce material for this book:

SB Illustrators: Bill Brown, Alexandre Matos, Beach-o-matic, Laurent Cardon, Guillaume Gennet, Phil Hackett, Alvaro Nuñez, Leonardo Teixeira, Rico

WB Illustrators: Alexandre Matos, Rico

SB Photos:
123RF/mopic, Getty Images Sales Spain; A. G. E. FOTOSTOCK/ Lubitz + Dorner; ALAMY/Everett Collection Inc, David Cattanach, Jim Newberry, Maciej Bledowski, Eddie Gerald, TP, Marmaduke St. John, PJF Military Collection, age fotostock, Marek Poplawski, Jemastock, Andrea Raffin, Jim O Donnell, Ian Allenden, WENN UK, runsilent, Jochen Tack, Elnur Amikishiyev, aberystwyth, B Christopher, ABC/ Everett Collection Inc, Jess Kraft/Panther Media GmbH, Mim Friday, Astronaut Images, dbimages, dpa picture alliance, Cyberstock, Steve Sant, Terry Harris, ZUMA Press, Inc, Domiciano Pablo Romero Franco, Moviestore collection Ltd, Fernando Quevedo de Oliveira, Mpi04/Media Punch/Alamy Live News, Irina Fischer, Collection Christophel, Ink Drop, M4Os Photos, WENN Ltd, Panther Media GmbH; CARTOONSTOCK/Way, Roy Delgado, Ian Baker, Zuvela.O, Bucella, Mike Baldwin; GETTY IMAGES SALES SPAIN/Hero Images, Andriano_cz, Littlebloke, Soren Hald, Thinkstock, Kadmy, NikFromNis, BenLin, wwing, Bulgac, Gipi23, Jodiecoston, Champc, BartCo, Kike Calvo, Joe_Potato, Brosa, ASIFE, Vladimir Vladimirov, shootdiem, ZIG8, Fuse, ViewApart, BSIP, StockFood, Andreas Schlegel, Steve Hix, Tzogia Kappatou, Stephan Hoerold, Sirawit99, Purestock, Altrendo Images, Martin-dm, Dulezidar, comptine, Paul Zimmerman, Neustockimages, S-cphoto, RapidEye, Sally Anscombe, Jhorrocks, Daniel Schoenen, Moodboard, Lily Roadstones, ShutterOK, Kyle Lee/EyeEm, Catherine Ledner, TIMOTHY A. CLARY, Stockbyte, Monika Proc/EyeEm, Wavebreak, Weedezign, Westend61, Witthaya Pradongsin, Aiqingwang, Andy Sacks, Dave Reede, Portland Press Herald, Juanmonino, Alessandro De Carli/EyeEm, Fotog, NNehring, Peter Cade, Petrunjela, Tom Hoenig, Ktsimage, CaseyHillPhoto, Shironosov, AndreyPopov, AntonioGuillem, Austinadams, Imagno, Karwai Tang, Kondor83, Leungchopan, Hanohiki, Elena Pueyo, Phaelnogueira, Filmovic, Nick Clements, Barcroft, Monty Rakusen, Lisa Stirling, marcduf, Wrangel, Johner Images, TVP Inc, RoNeDya, Jason LaVeris, JGI/ Tom Grill, Rmnunes, MixMike, Alex Lapuerta, Llgorko, Tim Robberts, Steve Cicero, Jpa1999, South_agency, Alex Robinson, Ariel Skelley,

Doug McKinlay, SergeyNivens, Humonia, Jeffrey Mayer, Joel Carillet, PeopleImages, Jupiterimages, Keith Brofsky, Klaus Vedfelt, Mike Coppola, Beinder, Marcelo Horm, Paul Bradbury, Luis Alvarez, Stuart Pearce, Studio-Annika, Wundervisuals, Andresr, KateSmirnova, Cecilie_ Arcurs, GoodLifeStudio, Johnny Louis, Manuel ROMARIS, Martin Barraud, Mischa Keijser, da-kuk, Image Source, Paulprescott72, Philipp Nemenz, FreezingRain, Silverlining56, Zero Creatives, AleksandarNakic, Rayman, David Forman, Desiree Navarro, Igor Vershinsky, Alvis Upitis, Photos.com Plus, Priscilla Gragg, Simona Flamigni, Pumba1, Yuri_Arcurs, Yagi-Studio, PIKSEL, T3 Magazine, Alexander Spatari, Corbis Historical, Fancy/Veer/Corbis, Phil Walter, laszlo_szelenczey, Andrew Bret Wallis, Michael Heim/EyeEm, Hill Street Studios, Lee Whitehead/EyeEm, Pascal Le Segretain, Richard Theis/EyeEm, Mmac72, Nancy Honey, Andrey Vodilin/EyeEm, Ben Pipe Photography, GIUGLIO Gil/Hemis.Fr, Jose Luis Pelaez Inc, Monkeybusinessimages, Jean Baptiste Lacroix, Mint Images, Gareth Cattermole/TAS18, Narin Deniz Erkan/EyeEm, PhotoAlto/Odilon Dimier, Lowryn, Kittiyut Phomphibul/EyeEm, Mark Edward Atkinson/Tracey Lee, Manuel-F-O; ISTOCKPHOTO/Getty Images Sales Spain; SHUTTERSTOCK/ Lucasfilm/Bad Robot/Walt Disney Studios/Kobal, 20th Century Fox/ Paramount/Kobal, Red Umbrella and Donkey, Patrimonio designs Ltd, KA Photography/KEVM111, Ultimate Prods./Kobal, Lewis Tse Pui Lung, Gurgen Bakhshetyan, Moviestore Ltd, Netflix/Kobal, Moviestore collection Ltd, Intararit, Artazum, Ollyy; Tom Fishburne/Marketoonist. com; copyright Vixisystem; Penguin Random House; Arnos Design Ltd; www.govloop.com; copyright PLeIQ; www.italki.com; Faber & Faber; SPLASH NEWS; telfie.com; player.me; Starbucks; copyright Kengaru; geobeats; iTunes; IUCN; Gap; ARCHIVO SANTILLANA

WB Photos:
ALAMY/Zoonar GmbH, PictureLux / The Hollywood Archive, imageBROKER / Alamy Stock Photo, Jeffrey Blackler; GETTY IMAGES SALES SPAIN/Kati1313, Pidjoe, Bmcent1, Tim Hawley, Sam Edwards, LordRunar, Maskot, Ridofranz, Wavebreak, Westend61, RobHoglund, RugliG, Popperfoto, SensorSpot, Jacobs Stock Photography Ltd, Graiki, LittleBee80, 10'000 Hours, Giuilio Fornasar, Paul Quayle, Aldo Murillo, Ethan Miller, Luis Alvarez, Caspar Benson, Klaus Vedfelt, Siri Stafford, Wavebreakmedia, Yuricazac, William Perugini, Betsie Van der Meer, Jose Luiz Pelaez Inc, Monkey Business Images, High Street Studios LLC, Maria Taglienti-Molinari, Portra, Tetra Images - Jessica Peterson, JohnnyGreig; SHUTTERSTOCK/ Rovio/Columbia/Sony Animation/ Village Roadshow/Kobal/Shutterstock, ZQFotography, Preto Perola, Levent Konuk, A SDF_MEDIA, gorbelabda, iQuoncept, Poznyakov, Gravicapa, file404; ARCHIVO SANTILLANA

Podcast / Video: My Damn Channel; Geobeats